Coniectanea Biblica · New Testament Series 23

Olle Christoffersson

The Earnest Expectation of the Creature
The Flood-Tradition as Matrix of Romans 8:18–27

Almqvist & Wiksell International
Stockholm, Sweden

Doctoral dissertation at Uppsala University 1990.

Abstract

Christoffersson, O., 1990. The Earnest Expectation of the Creature. The Flood-Tradition as Matrix of Romans 8:18-27. Coniectanea Biblica. New Testament Series 32. 174 pp. Uppsala. ISBN 91-22-00988-4.

The present dissertation seeks to establish a coherent religio-historical background of Rom 8:18-27 in the light of which the text can be interpreted with greater certainty. After an exposition of vocabulary, motifs and structure which cause problems, the second part of chapter one offers a broad outline of the history of research on the text.

In agreement with most of today's scholars the author assumes that Rom 8:18-27 uses apocalyptic ideas which can be found in early Jewish and Christian texts. However, in this dissertation it is held that all the different motifs and thoughts, which are contained in the text, can be found in a single coherent tradition, vix. that of the Flood. This religio-historical background is discussed in the second chapter. An early version of this tradition is reconstructed from Gen 1-6 and 1En 6-11.

The second half of chapter two demonstrates how the tradition was used in Jewish, Christian and Gnostic texts.

In the third chapter Rom 8:18-27 is examined against the background of the Flood tradition. The chapter begins with a discussion of the train of thought of the text, which is divided into smaller units. In the second part of the chapter the possible connections between the Pauline text and the Flood tradition are treated. It is shown that all of the motifs, which usually cause the exegetes problems, can be explained from the background of the Flood tradition. Paul uses elements from the Flood tradition when he speaks of the new world.

Thus the Flood tradition supplies an universal and apocalyptic perspective to the exposition in Rom 8:18-27 and the text thus fits well into the general outline of Romans as Pauls's discussion of the relation between Jews and Gentiles in the Church.

Olle Christoffersson, Department of Theology, University of Uppsala, Box 1604, S-751 46 Uppsala, Sweden.

ISBN 91-22-00988-4

Printed in Sweden 1990
Textgruppen i Uppsala AB

To
Kerstin
Johan and Andreas
my mother Märta

Contents

Introduction

"Er [Paul] blickt also auf die κτίσις. Es ist nicht ganz sicher, was er darunter an unserer Stelle versteht. Schon Augustinus erklärt: Hoc capitulum obscurum est, quia non satis apparet, quam nunc Apostolus vocat creaturam."[1]

This quotation from Professor Schlier's commentary shows how two exegetes from different ages agree on the existence of a problem in Rom 8:19[2] which creates uncertainty for the understanding of the passage. One of these exegetes, Augustine, wrote his comment at the beginning of the fifth century, and the other, Schlier, recently. It is not by chance that both exegetes mention the word κτίσις, creation, as a central problem. In fact the meaning of the word κτίσις in this text has been the primary difficulty for exegetes through the ages, and several different solutions have been presented. Most of them are old, while some have been suggested only in modern times.

However, this is only one of diverse problems which face the interpreter of Rom 8:18–27. The text contains several other problems in regard to vocabulary. Furthermore, modern exegesis has uncovered difficulties inherent in both the structure of the text and the strange thought-world which dominates the passage. These difficulties are particularly annoying since this passage belongs to a central chapter of a letter, the importance of which for the Church goes without saying. In fact, according to some exegetes the passage under discussion constitutes the very centre of the entire letter[3]. Further advance in the study of the riddles of the text depends, in my opinion, on the solution of this latter problem, viz. that of the religio-historical background of Paul's thought therein.

It may be presumptuous to offer a new solution to a problem of the dimensions intimated. However, during my study of the text I have come to the conviction that new light can be thrown on the text if its religio-historical background is carefully re-examined. Thus, in the present study I shall suggest that the passage be read against a religio-historical background which I believe has not yet been taken into due consideration, viz. that constituted by what I shall term the Flood tradition.

---

[1] Schlier 1977, 259. Quotation from Augustine *De octog. trib. quaest.* 67, 1.

[2] Quotations from the English Bible will be done from the RSV.

[3] Schlier calls the eighth Chapter "der Höhepunkt" of the letter. (1965, 599). Similarly Griffith (1945, 153): "Is there a crowning passage in this Epistle also, from which the specific doctrines of the Epistle may be viewed in their true perspective? It is the assumption of this study that there is, and that we have it in the eight chapter—the passage in which 'the sufferings of this present time' are contrasted with 'the glory which shall be revealed' . . . ". Cf. 1.2 note 4.

The procedure will be as follows. As already mentioned, the problems are of different kinds, and therefore an overall view of the situation is necessary. Thus, the first chapter will begin with an exposition of the problems contained in the passage, and go on to a sketch of the history of research done on the text. Although I do not intend to write the complete history of exegesis of the passage, I have found it necessary to be somewhat extensive at this point. The exegesis of the passage has built on certain presuppositions in regard to the religio-historical background, which, I think, restrict the range of vision. In trying to establish a new theory I find it necessary to account for the major lines of this previous work on the passage.

After this review of research I shall present the traditional material which I consider to be the background of Paul's text. I shall first outline the tradition and then examine different ways in which this material is employed in literature outside Romans in order to be able to determine Paul's use of it in Rom 8:18–27.

In the last part of the study I shall try to read Rom 8:18–27 against this religio-historical background. Thus I hope to be able to make some contribution to the discussion of Rom 8:18-27.

Chapter 1
Survey of Research on Rom 8:18–27

1.1 Introduction

The intention of this chapter is to place the present investigation of Rom 8:18–27 into the history of research. As the literature has now become very extensive no more than a rather brief general map of the exegetical landscape can be drawn. An impressive *Forschungsbericht* has already been presented by Hans Gieraths as the first part of his dissertation in 1950,[1] and similarly Balz 1971, in the first chapter of his study of the subject, deals with earlier scholarly work on this passage.

Gieraths concentrates his study on the meaning of the word κτίσις, seeing this as the central problem, the solution of which would enlighten the entire text. This concentration in fact made Gieraths biased and selective when describing the history of research, and it is now evident that the riddle of the text cannot be solved by a study of this single problem. An introduction to the present state of research on the text has to take into account studies on its structure[2] and furthermore, as Paul clearly relies on traditional material which he shares with the recipients of the letter, a more explicit report is needed in regard to the religio-historical background. The limitations of Gieraths' survey of research thus makes it unsatisfactory for our present purpose, although it is both brilliant and learned.[3]

I shall begin this survey of the history of exegesis of the text with an exposition of the exegetical problems inherent therein. Thereafter I shall try to outline the research done on these problems. This exposition will be divided into two sections. In the first part I shall briefly recount Gieraths' presentation of the main lines of interpretation of the pre-modern period. In the second part, which must be more elaborate, I shall review the current research on the text.

---

[1] It has been the standard procedure for exegetes who study Rom 8:18ff. to refer to Gieraths for the history of research although Eareckson (1977, 12) mentions Balz (1971) as the major treatment thereof.

[2] The way the letter is treated in regard to the situation of the addressees and the author also affects the interpretation to some extent. To this Gieraths pays no attention in his survey.

[3] As several of the questions raised in the modern research were not relevant to the interpreters of the pre-modern era, Gieraths' report can be accepted as satisfactory for that period.

1.2 Exegetical Problems in Rom 8:18–27

In later exegesis the verses 8:18ff. have been regarded as the very peak of a large section of Romans.[4] Oddly enough, however, precisely these verses are among the most enigmatic of the letter.[5] The problems, which are to a high degree intertwined, are diverse. First: there are major pitfalls as regards vocabulary. Second: the line of thought is difficult to follow through the text. Third: there are considerable difficulties in defining the rôle of the text in the letter, as well as in the smaller section thereof to which it belongs. Fourth: the religio-historical background of the text is confused. This last point in fact may be the major hindrance for the interpretation of the text. To substantiate these points I shall exemplify each of them.

1.2.1 Vocabulary and Concepts

a) The text contains unusual words. In Rom 8:18–27 Paul uses the following words which are *hapax legomena* in the undisputed letters: ματαιότης[6] (v. 20), συστενάζειν, συνωδίνειν[7] (v. 22), συναντιλαμβάνεσθαι,[8] στεναγμός,[9] ἀλάλητος[10] and the expression καθὸ δεῖ[11] (v. 26). There are also ἀποκαραδοκία[12] and ὑπερενρυγχάνειν (v. 26),[13] for the use of which we

---

[4] Käsemann says that vv. 26-27 "den Höhepunkt der ganzen Argumentation des Apostels bilden" (1969 "Schrei", 219). Similarly Dunn: "vv.18-30 . . . is the climax to ch. 6-8, and indeed of 1.18-8.30" (1988, 2864).

[5] An exposition of the problems involved is presented by von der Osten-Sacken (1975, 80f.).

[6] In the rest of the New Testament only in Eph 4:17 and 2Pet 2:18 (Computer-Konkordanz 1980).

[7] These two verbs combined with the prefixed συν are *hap.leg.* in the NT and very rarely found in the Greek literature. Bauer-Aland (1988 *s. v.*) gives the following references for συνωδίνειν: " . . . das Wort bei Eur., *Hel*.727. Aelian, on.an 3,45 p.78,5 nach Aristot. Porphyr., abst. 3,10 . . . Rö 8.22 . . . zum στενάζειν u. den ὠδῖνες der κτίσις vgl. Heraklit Sto. c. 39 p. 58,9 ἐπειδὰν ἡ μεμυκυῖα γῆ τὰς κουφορουμένας ἔνδον ὠδῖνας ἐκφήνῃ = wenn—nach Ende der Winterstarre—die stöhnende Erde das in ihr Entstandene unter Wehen gebiert.—Diod. S. zietiert 5,5, 1 den Tragödiendichter Karkinos: ganz Sizilien, schwanger vom Feuer des Aetna, stöhnte [στενάξαι] über den Verlust der Kore". The words occur nowhere else in the entire literature cited by Bauer-Aland.

For συστενάζειν (*op. cit. s. v.*): "Eur., *Ion* 935 u. TestIss. 7:5 . . . Nicetas Eugen. 1, 342 H. . . . Rö 8.22". These are the only occurrences of the word in the entire literature accounted for by Bauer-Aland.

[8] In the LXX only in Gen 30:8, Ex 18:22, Nu 11:17, and Ps 88:22 (Hatch and Redpath 1975). In the NT only here and in Lk 10:40.

[9] Except our text only in Acts 7:34 in the NT.

[10] *Hap. leg.* in the NT. Found by Bauer-Aland (1988, 67 *s. v.*) only in "Philod. *Anth. Pal.* 5,4. Kyraniden p.19, 19" in the literature cited outside the NT.

[11] καθὸ δεῖ is *hap. leg.* in the NT. καθό elsewhere in the NT only in 2Cor 8:12 (καθὸ ἐάν twice) and in 1Pt 4:13.

[12] The noun, which is not found in Greek literature before Paul, is found in the NT only here and in Phil 1:20. The verb ἀποκαραδοκεῖν is found in "Poly. 16, 2, 8. 18, 48, 4 . . . 22, 19, 3. Sostratus: 23 fgm. 4 p. 187 Jac. Aesop, fab. 177 P. 194 P. Jos., bell. 3.264. Ps 36,7 Aq". (Bauer-Aland 1988, 185 *s. v.*).

[13] "The double compound verb ὑπερεντυγχάνειν occurs nowhere else in the Greek Bible, and

have no example before Paul. Likewise the expression οὐχ ἑκοῦσα is rare. ἑκών occurs only twice in the LXX (Ex 21:13, Job 36:19)[14] and twice in the NT (Rom 8: 20, 1Cor 9:17).[15] In v. 20 Paul writes ἐφ’ ἐλπίδι instead of the usual ἐπ’ ἐλπίδι (cf. Rom 4:18; 5:2; 1Cor 9:10 (twice); thus also the pseudopauline Tit 1:2).

b) Paul also uses some common words in an unusual way. Thus Paul speaks of an ἀποκάλυψις of the sons of God, who are identified by all exegetes as the Christians. In the NT the word is never used together with an object of this kind. Schläger comments: "Mit ἀποκάλυψις ist sonst immer der Gedanke eines Herabstiegens aus einer tranzendenten Welt in die Welt der Wirklichkeit verknüpft, während sie hier ein Aufstieg, eine Verwandlung aus der Zeitlichkeit in Himmelshöhen wäre".[16]

The word κτίσις is used in a way which makes its significance very uncertain. In fact, the uncertainty of what is encompassed by this word is seen as a major hindrance to a clear understanding of the text. The interpretation of the meaning of the word κτίσις influences the interpretation of several other words. ὁ ὑποτάξας (v. 20) is particularly unclear. Who subdued Creation to meaninglessness (ματαιότης)?

Finally, the use of the word δόξα as a contrast to φθορά[17] is unique. Usually this word is contrasted to ἀφθαρσία (e. g. 1Cor 15:42) or ζωὴ αἰώνιος (e. g. Gal 6:8).

One should not draw too hasty conclusions from the fact that some words in a text are unusual. Paul, like most other writers, sometimes uses uncommon expressions. However, the fact that the text contains so many words, which Paul otherwise does not use, is already a sign that the conceptual world of the passage is peculiar and deserves special attention from the exegete.

1.2.2 Context and Line of Thought / Structure

The reader of Rom 8:18ff. very soon finds the line of thought difficult to follow. This partly depends on the uncertainty of the world of ideas (see above), but to a great extent also on the syntactical structure of the text. Here I shall only indicate some problems which are direct obstacles to a full comprehension of the text. A more specific discussion of the line of thought will be given in chapter 3.1.

---

is not known to occur in any Greek writer before the Christian era" (Cranfield 1980, 423 note 1). In all the literature listed besides the NT Bauer-Aland (1988, 1675, *s. v.*) find the word only in Clem. Alex. *Paed.* 1, 6, 47, 4.

[14] Hatch and Redpath 1975.

[15] Bauer-Aland (1988, 499 *s. v.*). The adjective ἑκούσιος is found in the NT only in Philemon v. 14 and the adverb ἑκοσίως only in Heb 10:26 and 1Pet 5:2.

[16] 1930, 359.

[17] φθορά is also a rare word found in the undisputed Pauline letters only in 1Cor 15:42, 50; Gal 6:8. Besides these it occurs in the NT only in Col 2:22; 2Pet 1:4; 2:12 (twice); 2:19.

1.2.2.1 The Delimitation of the Text

The delimitation of the text is not immediately clear. In two subordinate clauses (εἴπερ συμπάσχομεν ἵνα καὶ συνδοξασθῶμεν) Paul in 8:17 twists the line of thought into new directions in such a way that the reader has difficulty in comprehending what really is the theme of the text that follows. Certainly our question whether a sentence "belongs" to a given pericope or a neighbouring one is often misplaced: texts written to be read aloud do not always have so distinct paragraphs. But the rôle of v. 17 is nonetheless uncertain. If it is a transition, how does it affect the contents? Even more complicated is the delimiting of the end of the text. Does the natural end of the text fall after v. 27, v. 30, or v. 39?

Closely related to the question of structure is that of the place of the text within its immediate context and within the whole of the Epistle. Romans is naturally divided into three major sections: 1–8, 9–11, 12–15.[18] In view of its place at the end of 1–8 the rôle of our text within the section has to be defined. In regard to the letter as a whole the question of the relation to the following chapters, 9–11, is important. This question touches the problematics connected with the circumstances and the aim of the letter which will be briefly mentioned below.

1.2.2.2 The Syntactical Structure

Certain problems are connected with the syntactical structure of the text. The expressions in v. 20 οὐχ ἑκοῦσα, διὰ τὸν ὑποτάξαντα, ἐφ᾽ ἐλπίδι all make the sentence confusing. In v. 23 the repetition of καὶ αὐτοί is strange.[19] In v. 26 it is unclear to what Paul refers by ὡσαύτως.

1.2.3 Religio-Historical Background

The research on the text has indicated that the world of ideas, i. e. the religio-historical background, of Rom 8:18–27 is problematic. Certain motifs shine through the text which cannot be found elsewhere in the NT, and which are very difficult to localize even outside our present Bible. These motifs can be listed as follows:

1.2.3.1 An Expected Revelation of Sons of God

Paul speaks of an ἀποκάλυψις τῶν υἱῶν τοῦ θεοῦ (v. 19). On the basis of the statements in vv. 12–17 οἱ υἱοὶ τοῦ θεοῦ has normally been interpreted as

---

[18] On the debate concerning the unity of the epistle see below "The Roman Church and the aim of the epistle" (1.3.2.2).

[19] The difficulty was apparently perceived by the scribe of P[46] who omitted the first καὶ αὐτοί.

a designation for the Christians. The NT speaks of the revelation of many things, such as for instance the wrath of God (Rom 1:18), the day of judgment (Rom 2:5), or the Lord at His return (1Cor 1:7; 2Thes 1:7; Rev 1:1, cf. also 2Cor 12:1). However, the words ἀποκάλυψις and ἀποκαλύπτειν seem never to be applied to objects of such character as the Christians themselves. In my discussion below I shall also contend that the concept has other references than those otherwise assumed in the exegetical literature.

1.2.3.2 The Concept of Creation

Paul has several strange things to say about Creation: ἡ ἀποκαραδοκία τῆς κτίσεως ... ἀπεκδέχεται (v. 19).[20] We may ask how Paul conceives of a Creation which has the capacity of feeling. Even more surprising is the thought of v. 21: καὶ αὐτὴ ἡ κτίσις ἐλευθερωθήσεται ἀπὸ τῆς φθορᾶς εἰς τὴν ἐλευθερίαν τῆς δόξης τῶν τέκνων τοῦ θεοῦ. Creation will a) be freed from the slavery under destruction, and b) obtain the freedom which belongs to the children of God. The significance of both the "slavery under destruction" and this freedom are unclear. Furthermore there is still greater doubt concerning what is meant by Creation's obtaining this freedom.

Paul hints at an answer to the question of how the present situation came about, but this information is just as incomprehensible: τῇ γὰρ ματαιότητι ἡ κτίσις ὑπετάγη, οὐχ ἑκοῦσα ἀλλὰ διὰ τὸν ὑποτάξαντα (v. 20). Paul refers to an event at which Creation was subjected (ὑπετάγη, aorist) to meaninglessness (ματαιότης). He does not define the event which he has in mind nor who was the one subjecting (ὁ ὑποτάξας) Creation.

According to v. 22 "we" know that πᾶσα ἡ κτίσις συστενάζει καὶ συνωδίνει, but such a knowledge has left no traces: nowhere else in the Scriptures, which we call our Bible, do we find the thought that Creation is groaning and in travail.[21]

1.2.3.3 The Groaning and Praying Spirit

At the end of the text Paul speaks of the Spirit: τὸ πνεῦμα συναντιλαμβάνεται τῇ ἀσθενείᾳ ἡμῶν (v. 26). The expression is unusual but the thought that the Spirit supports the believers recurs elsewhere, e. g. in John 16:7ff.[22] But in the same verse two other strange ideas are presented:

[20] ἀπεκδέχεσθαι is a rare word, never used in the LXX and very rarely in Greek literature (Balz 1971, 36 note 1). In the NT only in Rom 8:19, 23, 25, 1Cor 1:7; Gal 5:5; Phil 3:20; Heb 9:28 and 1Pet 3:20.

[21] It should, however, be remembered that we find rather similar ideas in e. g. Is 24:4, 7 and Joel 1:18. In the apocalyptic texts Balz finds "nur gewisse Anklänge" thereof (1971, 52f.).

[22] "Nur an dieser Stelle in den echten Paulusbriefen ist Pneuma nach Art des engelhaften Führsprechers gesehen, wie er z.B. in der apokalyptischen Literatur des antiken Judentums, aber mit bestimmten Differenzen auch unter dem Namen 'Paraklet' im Johannesevangelium erscheint" (von der Osten-Sacken 1975, 85f.).

τὸ πνεῦμα ὑπερεντυγχάνει στεναγμοῖς ἀλαλήτοις. Nowhere else do we find the picture of the Spirit as groaning wordlessly and "this is the only passage in biblical writings where the Holy Spirit is described explicitly as an intercessor".[23]

1.2.3.4 The Picture of the Believers

In connection with the Spirit Paul says something about the believers which sounds somewhat unusual: τί προσευξώμεθα καθὸ δεῖ οὐκ οἴδαμεν. This is the only place in the New Testament where it is stated that Christians do not know what, or how, they should pray.

1.2.3.5 God's Relation to the Spirit

In v. 27 we read: ὁ δὲ ἐραυνῶν τὰς καρδίας οἶδεν τί τὸ φρόνημα τοῦ πνεύματος. Obviously that "the One who knows the hearts" is God, but then it is strange that God should be described as the One who knows what is in the Spirit's mind, especially in His capacity of knowing the hearts. As a rule the Spirit is understood as one expression of the deity, but here Paul seems to assume an unusually wide distinction between God and the Spirit. The expression is the more strange as Paul in v. 14 refers to the Spirit as "God's Spirit", saying that "all who are led by the Spirit of God are sons of God" and in v. 15f. that as Christians we have received the Spirit of adoption and "when we cry 'Abba Father!' it is the Spirit himself bearing witness with our spirit that we are children of God".

1.2.4 Some Conclusions

Some conclusions may be drawn from these observations. It is evident that vv. 18–27 separate themselves from the preceding and the following text. They are marked by a strange set of words and thoughts. All these strange thoughts can, taken together with the peculiarities of the vocabulary, strengthen the suspicion that Paul alludes to some background which is so particular that we do not immediately recognize it.[24] The difficulties in comprehending the rôle

---

[23] Obeng 1986 "reconciliation", 165. MacRae remarks that the expression τὸ φρόνημα τοῦ πνεύματος, "what is in the mind of the Spirit", in the NT is found only in Rom 8:6 and 8:26, and further that the phrase κατὰ θεόν "at first sight suggests a clear distinction between πνεῦμα and θεός" (1980, 229).

[24] As support for the opinion that Paul is using traditional material, von der Osten-Sacken submits that some words, which appear in the text, are otherwise used by Paul only when he quotes traditional material. Thus ἀπολύθρωσις (v. 23) is used in Rom 3:24 and 1Cor 1:30, ἐντυγχάνειν in connection with ὑπέρ (v. 26) in Rom 8:34, and ὡσαύτως (v. 26) in the undisputed letters only in 1Cor 11:25. von der Osten-Sacken finds further support in ἀπεκδέχεσθαι which

18

of this text in the rest of the letter, and thus also its specific message and purpose in regard to the addressees, can be supposed to be dependent on these problems.

1.3 History of Research

1.3.1 The Interpretation of Rom 8:18–27 in the Pre-Modern Era

In the pre-modern era[25] the interpretation of the text was bound to the understanding of the word κτίσις. The word was translated in five different ways, which were modified according to whether the words ματαιότης and φθορά were interpreted morally or physically. Gieraths concentrates especially on ματαιότης, which he finds to be an exceedingly important concept in the text. For the following outline of the research in the pre-modern era I am dependent on Gieraths' survey.

1.3.1.1 Universal Interpretation

Origen, who is the primary advocate of the universal interpretation of Rom 8:18ff., includes the human and subhuman Creation as well as angels and stars in the connotation of the word κτίσις. Man is said to be enslaved because his soul is bound to the body and thus not free. The stars are enslaved as well, because they are bound to bring forth fruit by their movements which affect the plants. The angels, finally, are bound to serve men and thereby bound to men's fate. Origen was followed by Ambrose (339–397) and Hilary of Poitiers (d. 367). Origen's concept of an ἀποκατάστασις πάντων is also to be seen in relation to this view of "Creation's" situation.

1.3.1.2 Cosmic-Angelological Interpretation

In the cosmic-angelological interpretation κτίσις means the sub-human world and the angels. Thus men are not included. This line of interpretation was advocated by the so-called Antiochene theologians, especially Diodorus of Tarsus (d. before 394). To punish man because of the Fall God gave the power over the subhuman Creation to Satan who thus through the environment causes man toil, trouble and all manner of wickedness. Thus man is punished

---

is otherwise used in 1Cor 1:7; Gal 5:5 and Phil 3:20, and in the expression ἐλπὶς ἀπεκδέχεσθαι which belongs to apocalyptic language of the disputed letters but is not characteristic of Paul's language (von der Osten-Sacken 1975, 80–82).

[25] With the term "pre-modern era" I refer to the period from the Early Church until c. 1700. In the following exposition of the interpretation of Rom 8:18ff. during this period I follow Gieraths.

through famine, diseases and other kinds of evil. Satan torments the sub-human Creation through man's abuse thereof (Rom 1:25). This is Creation's subjection to ματαιότης and φθορά. However, as the sub-human Creation is inanimate it cannot groan. When Paul speaks of the groaning of Creation, he thinks of the angels, who are the guardians of Creation and groan on its behalf. At the Resurrection men, and thereby the entire Creation, will be freed from this evil situation. This line of interpretation with modifications was advocated also by Theodore of Mopsuestia (d. 428), Gennadius of Constantinople (d. 471) and Theodoret of Cyrrhus (d. 460).

1.3.1.3 Cosmic Interpretation

According to the cosmic interpretation κτίσις only denotes the sub-human Creation. This approach has been advocated by most interpreters.[26] Some exegetes, especially the Roman Catholics, use the cosmic interpretation besides some other.[27]

The main argument for the cosmic interpretation is found in vv. 19, 21 and 23 in which Creation seems to be separated from the Christians. The expressions υἱοὶ τοῦ θεοῦ (v. 19), τέκνα τοῦ θεοῦ (v. 21) and τὴν ἀπαρχὴν τοῦ πνεύματος ἔχοντες (v. 23) can only be applied to the believers. In v. 21 the word κτίσις cannot denote non-believers, who are hardly to be "liberated", and therefore κτίσις cannot include men. Nor can angels be meant because this would not fit what is written in v. 20: they are not subdued under ματαιότης.

There are two answers to the question of how the present situation came about: a) these conditions belong to the created order from the beginning, everything was created perishable from the beginning and thus independent of the Fall,[28] and b) the present situation is a result of the Fall.[29]

[26] The best known of the Greek fathers are Irenaeus (d. 202), Gregory of Nazianzus (d. 390), John Chrysostom (d. 407), Cyril of Alexandria (d. 444), Oecumenius of Tricca (the 10th cent. Confused by Gieraths with the Oekumenius who lived in the 5th cent.). Of the Latin fathers Tertullian (d. 220), Ambrosiaster (the second half of the 4th century). After the Reformation it has been accepted by *inter alios* Martin Luther in his commentary on Romans 1515, 16, Desiderius Erasmus (d. 1536), Melanchthon (d. 1560), Beza (d. 1605), and Calvin (d. 1564).

[27] So for instance Hugh of Saint-Cher (d. 1263), Thomas Aquinas (d. 1274), Nicolas of Lyra (d. 1349), Dionysius the Carthusian (d. 1471), Cajetan (d. 1534) and Salmerón (d. 1585).

[28] Ambrosiaster, Thomas Aquinas, Nicolas of Lyra, Dionysius the Carthusian, Luther.

[29] Chrysostom, Oekumenius of Trikka, Calvin, Sedulius Scottus (d. c. 858), Rabanus Maurus (d. 856), Thomas Aquinas, Nicolas of Lyra, Dionysius the Carthusian, Peter Lombard (d. c. 1160) (some of these interpreters have already been mentioned because they did not always use the same interpretation), and finally, Cajetan and Salmerón. The cosmic interpretation has sometimes been used by exegetes who on other occasions advocated the anthropological interpretation.

1.3.1.4 Anthropological Interpretation

Since very early times exegetes have maintained that by κτίσις Paul meant humanity. Only men would have the feelings and intellectual capacity accordant with the text. Having held to cosmic interpretation from the beginning Augustine (d. 430) turned to the anthropological in his fight against the Gnostics, who wanted to contrast body and soul. Thus he was able to maintain that the text does not speak of the material world but of mankind as subject to destruction. He claims that by the expression κτίσις Paul designated the Christians who thus are longing for the future glory to be revealed.[30]

Gregory the Great (d. 604) followed Augustine's interpretation. Augustine also had a strong impact on the interpretation of the text during the Middle Ages.[31] In later times the anthropological interpretation was advocated by Lightfoot (d. 1675), Knatschbull,[32] Limborch,[33] and Aletaeus.[34]

1.3.1.5 Angelological Interpretation

In angelological interpretation κτίσις stands only for the angels. Only Pelagius (d. c.420) can be shown to have advocated this interpretation. The angels, who were set to serve men, through their service have been enslaved to destruction. The reason is that men distorted the image of God which they carry within themselves. Finally the angels will be delivered from their enslavement and therefore they rejoice over everybody who repents of his sin and they groan because of those who are not contrite.

---

[30] Augustine notices that in vv. 19, 21 and 23 there is a difference between the Christians and κτίσις which he explains as follows: In v. 19 Paul differentiates the present from the future state of the Christian; thus both expressions, Creation and sons of God, designate Christians. In v. 21 the word αὐτή seems to indicate a difference between the Christians and another subject, with which the Christians are united. According to Augustine Paul thinks of the non-believers who are on their way to faith and salvation. In v. 23 Paul speaks of αὐτοί . . . τὴν ἀπαρχὴν τοῦ πνεύματος ἔχοντες as contrasted to Creation. This problem Augustine solves by interpreting the verse as an expression of the Christians' inner longing for deliverance (Gieraths 1950, 70-72).

[31] The anthropological interpretation was advocated by *inter alios* Pseudo-Hieronymus (end of the fifth cent., independent of Augustine), Gregory the Great (d. 604), Lanfranc (d. 1089), Abélard (d. 1142), Peter Lombard, Hugh of Saint-Cher, Thomas Aquinas, Nikolas of Lyra, Dionysius the Carthusian (in some places), Cajetan and Salmerón (besides their uses of the cosmic interpretation), Sedulius Scottus, Rabanus Maurus (already mentioned because they used different explanations).

[32] 1701, 82.

[33] 1711, 375f. Limborch found the major reason for this interpretation to be that there could be no existence of a future world after the present world had been destroyed. Gieraths summarizes this opinion in the following words: "sie [the exegetes of Limborchs' time] setzen die Leugnung der Existenz einer künftigen materiellen Welt voraus, die bei der kosmischen Deutung ausgesprochen wäre. Eine materielle Welt sei im kommenden Äon überflüssig, sie habe keinen Sinn mehr, weil sie nicht mehr benötigt werde" (1950, 66).

[34] 1714, 166-172.

1.3.2 The Interpretation of Rom 8:18–27 in the Modern Era

As already mentioned[35] Balz devotes the first chapter of his book to the history of research on Rom 8:18–39.[36] His survey concentrates on the differences in Roman Catholic, Anglican, and Protestant[37] exegesis of the text. Balz finds a conspicuous display of essential theological interests in the treatment of the text. Thus Reformed theologians concentrate on vv. 28ff., because these verses are essential for the dogma of predestination. Roman Catholic and older Lutheran exegesis concentrates on vv. 19–22, wrestling with the questions of the meaning of the word κτίσις for the issue of the relation between man and world, and for a natural theology. Newer Lutheran exegesis tends to pass by the statements on the present situation of Creation and concentrate on the meaning of hope and the prayer of the Spirit. Anglicans concentrate on the question of Paul's theology of history, 8:28ff., while the Lutherans have devoted more attention to the eschatological perspectives of the text.

In addition to the information on how different denominations have influenced the research, Balz's survey indicates certain central points of the text which have attracted the interest of the exegetes. These points are Creation's rôle in the text, the rôle of hope, and finally the rôle of the Spirit. Other important concepts depend on these key terms. The following survey of the modern exegesis of the text will be related to the different problems defined under 1.2. However I shall not follow the outline of 1.2 in detail.[38]

1.3.2.1 The Beginning of Modern Research

It may be illusory to fix a certain occasion for the shift from premodern to modern exegesis. But for our purpose it is enough to take as a starting point F. C. Baur's radical application of historico-critical techniques in NT studies. In his struggle to establish a historical method for the study of the beginning of Christianity Baur turned to the oldest evidence of that history, the Pauline letters. In 1835 he published an article discussing the circumstances of Romans.[39] The letter, in his opinion, should be explained from a) the background of the prevailing situation of the adressees and b) the intention of the

---

[35] 1.1.1. Balz does not comment on the pre-modern exegesis of the text but only on modern research.

[36] 1971, 9-26. I have not had the opportunity to read the recent dissertations by Mary Carolyn Thomas, *Rom 8:18-30 and its Relation to the Current Romans Debate.* New York 1985, and F. Menezes, *Life in the Spirit; a Life of Hope; a Study of Rom 8,18-30.* Roma 1986.

[37] I use the word "protestant exegesis" as a translation of Balz's term "evangelische Auslegung".

[38] I shall pay no attention to the confessional aspects of the exegesis.

[39] Baur presupposes that Chapters 15f. are not by the hand of Paul. For the discussion of the authenticity and integrity of the letter see Kümmel [6]1987, 314-320.

22

author.[40] Both of these matters Baur reconstructs from the letter, finding Rom 1–8 to be the theological centre and 9–11 an application thereof to topical questions in Rome. Thus he concludes that the section 9–11 contains the author's purpose and consequently constitutes the hermeneutical centre of the epistle. Chapters 12–15 explicitly state the topical questions at stake and consequently can be used for a more precise definition of the addressees. Baur concluded that the Church in Rome mainly consisted of Jewish Christians, more explicitly Ebionites, who claimed priority. Paul reacted against their claim,[41] and the letter constitutes his major effort to defend his universalistic view of the Church.[42]

Baur's new line of interpretation was further developed by, *inter alios*, Köster (1862) and Frommann (1863). Frommann in particular provoked the reaction of the conservative Zahn (1865). The modern research on the text has its roots in this debate.

The old type of interpretation was, however, not ended by Baur's attack,[43] and there is no clear-cut break between the pre-modern and the modern exegesis of Romans. Most modern interpreters agree that the letter is marked by a tension between different groups of Christians, but from this insight they do not draw congruent conclusions for the interpretation of the letter. Sanday and Headlam well describe the two different ways of exegesis:

When the different views which have been held come to be examined, they will be found to be reducible to two main types, which differ not on a single point but on a number of co-ordinated points. One might be described as primarily historical, the other primarily dogmatic; one directs attention mainly to the Church addressed, the other mainly to the writer; one adopts the view of a predominance of Jewish-Christian readers, the other presupposes readers who are predominantly Gentile Christians.[44]

The tension between Jew and Gentile is certainly mentioned in most dogmatic expositions of the letter, but mainly as compelling Paul to formulate a general doctrinal statement.[45] As an extreme example of the dogmatic exegesis Ny-

---

[40] Zahn comments that, by the presupposition that Chapter 16 was not originally part of the letter, and by not paying due attention to the information available in 1:1-15, Baur deprived himself of the possibility of precisely defining the situation in Rome (1910, 6f.).

[41] However, Zahn rightly remarks: "In der Tat war der Rm für Baur doch nicht ein Sendschreiben, welches Pl als Apostel d. h. als Missionar im Interesse seines Berufs an eine einzelne Gemeinde von besonderen Bedürfnissen und eigenartigen Beziehungen zu seinem Lebenswerk gerichtet hat, sondern eine letzte, förmlich systematische Darlegung seines Standpunktes innerhalb der Gegensätze jener Zeit" (Zahn 1910, 7).

[42] Baur 1836, XX.

[43] Melanchthon's description of Romans as a *"doctrinae Christianae compendium"* was generally accepted until the time of Baur. This old type of exegesis can be exemplified by the following works: Toluck (1856) followed by Reiche (1834), Köllner (1834), de Wette (1847), Olshausen (1835, most extreme of them all), Beck (1884), Bernard Weiss (1899), Barth (1962), Knopf (1930), Nygren (1947), Dodd (1963), Kertelge (1971), J. A. T. Robinson (1979), Kieffer (1979, 138).

[44] Sanday and Headlam 1962, xxxix. This was written no later than 1905. I have not had access to older editions.

[45] Despite the lines quoted above, Sanday and Headlam can stand as an example of this

23

gren could be cited. As Paul did not know the Roman Church, Nygren says, he did not have the possibility to discuss topical problems in Rome. He was therefore free to write a treatise which penetrates his own inner theological thoughts.[46] The letter is thus pure Pauline theology without any disturbing relation to situational problems. Although it would be unfair to describe all modern exegetes, who take the letter as an exposition of the Christian faith, as equal to the interpreters of the pre-modern era, it has to be said that to many exegetes, if not to the majority, the letter is still a piece of dogmatic writing.[47]

1.3.2.2 The Roman Church and the Aim of the Letter

Baur succeeded in breaking new ground in the study of Romans by centering his interest on a part thereof, Chapters 9–11, which had hitherto been regarded as secondary in importance. By judging the entire letter from this position Baur was able to reconstruct a concrete picture of the writer and the addressees. The majority of modern exegetes regard the text as a solid unity.[48] However, to scholars who interpret the letter as a doctrinal treatise, Chapters 9–11 cause problems, since they seem to differ in character from Chapters 1–8.[49]

dogmatic exegesis. They suppose a) that the tension between Gentiles and Jews was resolved, and b) that Paul had worked on the question of how Israel could be excluded now when the promises to the people had been fulfilled. "This more advanced stage has now been reached; the Apostle has made up his mind on the whole series of questions at issue; and he takes the opportunity of writing to the Romans at the very centre of the empire, to lay down calmly and deliberately the conclusions to which he has come . . . it is a letter which contains here and there side-glances at particular local circumstances" (op.cit. xliii). Similarly for instance Kümmel: "Romans is the theological selfconfession of Paul, which arose out of a concrete necessity of his missionary work" (1966, 22); Michel:" . . . ausgesprochenen *Lehrbrief*" (1978, 31–35).

[46] "I stället för en uppgörelse med motståndare möter oss Pauli uppgörelse med sig själv, med sitt förflutna, ty också han hade en gång vandrat på lagens frälsningsväg" (1940, 16). Nygren's understanding of the letter could be seen as a perfect example of the following words by Sanday and Headlam: "According to this [the dogmatic] theory the main object of the Epistle is doctrinal; it is rather a theological treatise than a letter; its purpose is to instruct the Roman Church in central principles of the faith, and has but little reference to the circumstances of the moment" (1962, xl).

[47] Cf. Donfried: "Up until the very recent past, the above mentioned advances and contributions of contemporary biblical scholarship [the historical-critical method] have hardly been applied to Romans; for many it just continued to be a *christinae religionis compendium*. Slowly scholars became restless with this state of affairs and increasingly they began to raise the matter of Paul's intention in writing Romans" (1977 "Debate", xi).

[48] Schmithals thinks that Romans is composed from three separate documents: a) "Letter A", 1:1–4:25; 5:12–11:36; 15:8–13, Paul's first letter to the Romans; b) "Letter B", 12:1–21; 13:8–10; 14:1–15:4a, 7, 5f; 15:14–32; 16:21–23; 15:33, a second letter to the Romans; c) a letter of recommendation for Phoebe 16:1–20 (1980, 10ff.).

[49] According to Dodd the line of thought is broken off in 8:30 to be resumed in 12:1. Thus Chapters 9–11 constitute a "separate treatise" (1963, 161f.). Thus also Kertelge (1971, 159), J. A. T. Robinson (1979, 8).

An increasing number of theologians have come nearer to Baur's perspective on the letter. Among them Munck (1959) and Stendahl (1976) have maintained most radically that the letter primarily discusses the salvation of the Jews because the question of the rôle of the people of the old Covenant was the great problem of the Christians in Rome. Consequently Chapters 9–11 contain Paul's central statement of the letter, for which the way is prepared by the theological discussion of Chapters 1–8. As Stuhlmacher too states the wrestling with the question of Jews and Gentiles in the local Church in Rome is the crux of the letter. Although there were no Judaizers in Rome at the time when the letter was written, Judaizers had heckled Paul wherever he preached. " ... Paul is confronted with the problem that the critique of the Jewish Christians, which up until this point had only followed after him, has now preceded him. He is aware of it through the friends and acquaintances listed in Rom 16:3ff."[50] Paul therefore writes a letter to prevent their influence on the Church.[51] Lietzmann had gone even further in this direction, suggesting that Peter already had arrived in Rome, when the letter was written.[52] Thus the confrontation in fact was with the Apostles in Jerusalem, who tried to turn the Romans against Paul.[53]

A new phase in the debate on the reason for Romans[54] was introduced by Manson 1948, who argued that the letter was sent in two copies, one to Rome, the other to the Church in Ephesus.[55] The idea that Romans was a circular letter was later further developed by Fuchs who maintains that it was sent to Rome but with a "secret address" to Jerusalem, i. e. Paul thought of the problems in Jerusalem. Some sort of a Jerusalem perspective is assumed by several commentators. Thus, according to Bornkamm and Wilckens the letter was written as a draft for the defence which Paul would deliver in Jerusalem.[56] In his article "The Letter to Jerusalem" Jervell made the idea

[50] 1985, 92. The position is further argued in Stuhlmacher 1986.

[51] An extreme position is taken by Bindemann according to whom there was a rapidly increasing group of Jewish Christians in Rome since the Edict had been abrogated. This group was closely associated with the Synagogue and threatened Christian unity not only in Rome but throughout the Empire. "Dann aber ist der oft betonte 'Doppelcharakter' des Römerbriefs ein Scheinproblem: Zwar bestand die römische Gemeinde zur Abfassungszeit des Briefes wohl vorwiegend aus Heidenchristen, die auch nebenbei angesprochen werden; *der Römerbrief aber ist nicht an Heidenchristen, auch nicht an die Gemeinde als ganze, sondern an eine judenchristliche Gruppe in der Gemeinde gerichtet*" (1983, 62).

[52] 1933 (1st ed 1906).

[53] Cf. Jervell, "The Letter to Jerusalem" (1977). According to Schmithals letter A was directed to the synagogue in Rome, and the letter B to the Roman Church (1980, 12-17) (see note 48).

[54] For the later debate see Donfried's collection of essays (1977), Kettunen (1980), Campbell (1981), and Wedderburn (1988).

[55] Thus also Karris (1977) and Koester (1982 I, 138f.). In opposition to the idea of a circular letter Jervell, Wiefil, Minear and Donfried.

[56] " Wie alle anderen Breife ist auch er [the letter to the Romans] gebunden an eine bestimmte Geschichte, . . . in Ausrichtung jedoch auf die vor dem Apostel liegende bedeutsame Begegnung mit der Jerusalemer Urgemeinde und die Vollendung seines apostolischen Auftrags" (Bornkamm

of a letter to Jerusalem still more explicit. Paul writes to the Church in Rome. But he expects this Church to recognize him as the Apostle to the Gentiles and take his side together with the other Gentile Churches in the confrontation with the Apostles in Jerusalem. Thus the letter is really addressed to Jerusalem.[57]

According to Klein Peter does not seem to have appeared yet in Rome, nor any other Apostle, and thus the Church in Rome was not founded by any Apostle. Therefore Paul writes in order to introduce himself as the Apostle who will come to lay the necessary Apostolic foundation which the Church in Rome still lacks.[58]

Older exegesis usually regarded Romans as Paul's introduction of his Gospel to the Roman Church in view of his planned mission to Spain for which he asks the Romans to support (15:22–24).[59] This perspective has been retained by most modern scholars although they recognize Paul's preparation for the journey to Jerusalem as an essential aspect of the letter.[60] Wedderburn recently tried to unite all these different views.[61] Paul wrote the letter to the Roman Church, which had originally been strongly Judaizing in character. In that situation a Christian message, which dispensed with obedience to the Jewish Law, had been proclaimed and the small group of Gentile Christians rapidly increased in number. By the time Paul wrote his letter Jews, who had been forced to leave Rome because of Claudius' edict, had returned and

---

1969, 110). To Bornkamm Paul's aim is to win the Roman church for his side in the conflict and thus the letter really is a letter to the Romans (similarly Kettunen 1980). Wilckens (1978, 46) writes: "So gestaltet sich ihm wie von selbst *der Römerbrief* zugleich als Vorbereitung seiner Verteidigungsrede in *Jerusalem*". Similarly Jewett 1987, 220. Both Bornkamm (1969, 103ff.; 1971; 1977) and Wilckens (1980, 47f.) maintain that Romans should be read as Paul's "testament".

[57] In the debate Karris prefers the idea of a circular letter (1977 "Occasion"). Achtemeier (1987) concludes from his study of the information, gained from a comparison of Acts and the Pauline letters, that Paul's collection was rejected by the Church in Jerusalem. If this is right the conflict was deeper than we are wont to think, and the suspicion that the Church in Jerusalem was in Paul's mind when he wrote the letter to the Romans may gain new support. The situation is very differently estimated by Fitzmyer, according to whom the Judaizing crisis was already past history when the letter was written (1989, 830). According to Fitzmyer Romans is an "essay-letter" presenting Paul's " . . . missionary reflections on the historical possibility of salvation, rooted in God's uprightness and love, now offered to all human beings" (*loc. cit.*).

[58] Klein 1977, 32–49. By Jewett it is called an "ambassadorial letter" (1982), and by Koester "a letter of recommendation" written by Paul himself on his own behalf (1982, II,140).

[59] This explanation is found in most of the commentaries, e. g. Gaugler (1945, 4ff.), Nygren (1947, 13), Althaus (1954, 1f.), Dodd (1963, 18f.), Sanday and Headlam (1962, xliii), Schmidt (1962, 2f.), Kertelge (1971, 10), Bruce (1971, 12), J. A. T. Robinson (1979, 8). Similarly Russell III: "In an exhortative letter confronting their Jewish/Gentile relationships, Paul challenged the Roman churches to participate fully in God's present harvest of all peoples by showing that their ethnocentrism opposed God's eternal plan of justifying people by faith, of giving them new life in the Spirit, and of mercifully placing them in His redemptive plan" (1988, 180). Lietzmann says Rom 1:17 to be "Thema und Text der folgenden Predigt" (1933).

[60] Thus Beker (1984, 71–74), Koester (1982 II, 142), Jewett (1982, 9f.; 1987, 219).

[61] 1988, 140–142.

the Jewish Christian group was reinforced. Paul wrote to admonish the Judaizers to recognize his Law-free Gospel and to inform the Gentiles that they could not relinquish their Jewish inheritance.[62] All this was necessary in order to obtain the support of the Roman Christians for the journey to Jerusalem and a planned further mission.

This debate affects the view of the letter considerably. If it was written as a circular letter the dogmatic aspects are made stronger and the relation to topical problems in the Roman Church is diminished. Thus dogmatic interpretation gains new support. It is clear that the letter voices Paul's opinion on the awkward question of Jews and Gentiles in the Early Church. Romans thus is not an exposition of Paul's dogmatics in general. But was it despatched to more than one Church? It is difficult to prove conclusively that the letter was sent only to Rome. The most specific Chapters, 12–15, in fact speak in rather general words. However, this may depend on the fact that Paul did not have the same detailed knowledge of the Church in Rome, as he had of the Churches to which he wrote his other letters. Besides, he may have been careful not to appear offensive to a Church, which had not seen him and to which he planned a visit. Not to speak of his plans for support for further mission.

However, it is still more difficult to prove that the letter was intended for more than one Church, be it Ephesus or Jerusalem. Paul may have written in order to obtain support for his visit to Jerusalem, but it is difficult to prove that the content of the letter was intended somehow to be delivered as a message to the Apostles or the Church there. In conclusion I think that there are no compelling arguments for the idea that the letter should be addressed to other than the Roman Church. Rather it can be satisfactorily explained as a letter to this particular Church discussing its problems.

For my further work with Rom 8:18–27 I shall basically keep to the following view of the letter. We have no information about the beginning of Christianity in Rome. Probably Jewish Christians formed the first Church there. Claudius' Edict[63] forced these Jewish Christians to leave Rome and to stay

---

[62] Minear (1971, 8ff.) sees five groups (or at least "distinct factions" or "positions") among the recipients of the letter.

[63] The Edict of Claudius is ususally dated to the year 49 C.E., the main arguments being built on Acts 18:2. Orosius quotes Suetonius *Caes. Claudius* 25, and says that the Edict was issued in the ninth year of Claudius' reign. However, Dio Cassius 60.6.6 also reports from an order of Claudius that the Jews should not hold meetings. This order is dated to the year 41, the first year of Claudius' reign. Luedemann maintains that the early dating is the correct one (Luedemann 1984,164–175). He redates the chronology of Paul so that Paul's visit to Corinth (Acts 18:1f.) happens in the year 41. Romans according to Luedemann was written in 51/52, or possibly 54/55. If the Edict was abrogated only on the death of Claudius, the expelled Jews were not allowed to return to Rome before 54. Thus if Luedemann is right in regard to the dating of Claudius' Edict, the Roman Church, which had started as a predominantly Jewish Church, had developed as a Gentile Church for at least 10 years before Paul wrote his letter. If the usual dating is accepted (represented for instance by Kümmel 1987, 308) the Edict was imposed in 49 and the letter written in 54 or 55. The section in Dio Cassius' work discussing the year 49 has been preserved

away until the Edict was canceled, at which time they probably returned. In the meantime the number of Gentile Christians increased and the Jewish Christians lost their former predominance. The letter shows that there are both Jewish and Gentile Christians present in Rome. However, it is uncertain whether there was only one Church in Rome. The fact that Paul never mentions the Church in the singular in the letter may indicate that there were two or more groups of Christians among the addressees.

This situation was unacceptable to Paul. Although he defended the freedom of Gentile Christians from circumcision and obedience to the Jewish Law he sought the unity of the Church. To him Christ was the Saviour of the entire world, not just the Jews. As the tension between at least two groups of Christians is evident in the letter we need not infer that any other situation caused it. However, these local problems may have strengthened Paul's wish to unite the Christians in Rome. A split between them would hurt the debate in Jerusalem as well as Paul's further plans as he wanted support from the Roman Christians for a mission to Spain.

Paul speaks to both groups of Christians in Rome. This principal situation had caused a serious discussion of two questions: of righteousness through faith and the rôle of the Law. The theological foundation is laid in the first part of the letter which ends in an eschatological perspective (8:18–39). I shall discuss this section in the following pages.

1.3.2.3 The Structure of Romans 8:18–27s

The line of thought in Rom 8:18–27 is not easy to follow. Many interpreters have held the text to be "poetic" in character and therefore not to be pressed in regard to line of thought.[64] This is an old recourse to explain the pecularities of the text. Frommann, being of the opinion that Paul wrote these lines not as a poetic vision but as a well considered theological statement, opposes this explanation.[65] Thus Frommann concludes that if in Rom 8:18ff.

---

only in late Byšantine texts (Luedemann, *op. cit.* 166), and we do not know whether he spoke of an expulsion in 49. Dio Cassius explicitly states that the Jews were not expelled in 41 but forbidden to assemble. This may have been Claudius' first attempt to master the problems which forced him to issue the Edict in 49.

[64] Thus Kühl (1913). Jülicher: "Die Mischung von Phantasie und Gemüt, aus der heraus das Bild 8,19-22 geboren ist, gehört zu dem Kostbarsten, was die alte Welt an Dichtung uns hinterlassen hat" (quote from Schläger 1930, 354). Similarly Dodd (1963, 148), Cranfield (1980, 404f.). Zyro tried to clarify the text by making v. 20 a parenthesis which explains the expression ἡ ἀποκαραδοκία τῆς κτίσεως. Within v. 20 he saw a second parenthesis: "Der Satz οὐχ ἑκοῦσα, ἀλλὰ διὰ τὸν ὑποτάξαντα, ist offenbar ein parenthetischer, so daß wir also eine Parenthese in der Parenthese haben" (1845, 410).

[65] Frommann 1863, 39ff. The two different understandings of the character of the text still compete with each other. Thus Balz writes: "Manche Exegeten haben Röm 8,18-39 als eine wenig gegliederte und durchwegs 'poetisch' gehaltene Perikope beurteilt. Dieser Eindruck trügt aber. Nur selten läßt sich im Römerbrief der Gedankengang so deutlich verfolgen wie hier, selbst wenn die Momente doxologischer Sprache wesentlichen Anteil an der Gestaltung haben" (1971, 32f.).

Paul refers to the subhuman Creation by the word κτίσις, he then expresses ideas, which cannot be found elsewhere in our present Bible nor even supported by Biblical texts.[66] Frommann determines the groaning and longing of Creation as an "in dem Bewußtsein des Menschen liegende Sehnsucht nach einer Fortdauer in einem vollkommenen, von der Endlichkeit dieser Welt befreiten Zustande, welche er als Thatsache einer natürlichen Offenbarung Gottes an dem Menschen nachweiset".[67] Thus the result is rather strange: Paul proves a theological statement by a reference to a natural revelation, adducing something which belongs to the very nature of man.[68]

The modern work on the question of the structure of the text was introduced by Zahn in his objection to Frommann.[69] Like Frommann Zahn is of the opinion that Paul has well considered the text, but after an analysis of its structure comes to wholly different conclusions as to the Biblical status of the passage. As Zahn's structuring lies at the root of most subsequent work on this text it deserves to be discussed in more detail.

According to Zahn Paul writes Rom 8:18ff. in order to comfort the believers who are distressed by their shortcomings in regard to the demands described in 8:12–17. To strengthen them Paul describes the greatness of the coming glory, first presenting a thesis in v. 18, which is then developed. The aim is not to demonstrate the hope, or the certainty of salvation but rather the greatness of the expected glory: "Dann aber wird eben nicht die Nähe oder Gewißheit, sondern die Größe und Bedeutung der Herrlichkeit begründet; denn der Apostel hatte nicht gesagt: Wir haben eine überaus große Herrlichkeit zu **erwarten**, sondern: Die Herrlichkeit, die uns erwartet, **überwiegt** weit alle Leiden der Gegenwart".[70] The greatness of the glory is demonstrated through threefold evidence arranged as it were in concentric circles: "1) das auf eine Befriedigung hinweisende Harren der κτίσις, 2) die in den Christen wohnende Sehnsucht und Hoffnung auf des Leibes Erlösung und 3) das für uns eintretende, Gott wohl verständliche Seufzen des heiligen Geistes in uns".[71] Thus the theme of this section is "groaning". The δέ in v. 28 leads to the next section, which speaks of the assurance of the coming glory. Zahn thus arrives at the following division of the text: a thesis (v. 18), followed by threefold evidence: a) vv. 19–22, b) vv. 23–25, and c) vv. 26–27.

Many exegetes, although they may see the central proposition of the text

---

[66] "Demnach steht es mit den **Lehrgedanken**, welche sich aus der Erklärung der κτίσις von der Natur an unserer Stelle ergeben, so, **daß sie entweder in der anderweitigen Schriftlehre keine Bestätigung finden, oder daß, was die Schrift sonst wirklich lehrt, sich mit dem Ausdruck in der paulinischen Stelle nicht vereinigen läßt**" (Frommann 1863, 39).

[67] 1863, 49.

[68] Frommann adduces Acts 14:17; 17:23; Rom 1:19f.; 2:14f. in support of his view that Paul also in other places used this kind of evidence for theological statements (1863, 50).

[69] Zahn 1865.

[70] Zahn 1865, 515.

[71] *Loc. cit.*

differently,[72] have accepted this threefold structure.[73] Some exegetes who delimit the text differently still retain Zahn's structure for the vv. 18–27. Thus Nygren holds vv. 18–30 together but follows Zahn in structuring vv. 18–27 as a threefold groaning.[74] The last section in his organization of the text, vv. 28–30, acquires a headline somewhat different from the vv. 18–27, "Fulfilment of God's eternal plan of salvation".[75]

Some interpreters do not emphasize the groaning as a structuring theme. Thus Sanday and Headlam do not find this section to befit the line of thought in the Chapter: "At the end of the last paragraph St. Paul has been led to speak of the exalted privileges of Christians involved in the facts that they are sons of God. The thought of these privileges *suddenly recalls to him* the contrast of the sufferings through which they are passing. And after his manner he does not let go of this idea of 'suffering' but works it into his main argument" (my italics).[76]

An alternative to this kind of structure is presented by Schwantes, although he only discusses vv. 18–23:[77]

V.18 anthropologische Aussage
V.19 kosmologische Aussage
   V. 20f. kosmologische Aussage (Glosse)
V.22 kosmologische Aussage
V.23 anthropologische Aussage

Schwantes' exegesis of the text tries to prove that Paul uses apocalyptic material to make kerygmatic statements, although he has no interest in the apocalyptic cosmology *per se*.[78] The message which Paul would proclaim is that the believers should place their present sufferings under the light of the cosmic act of God.[79] This understanding is strengthened if vv. 20f. are regarded as a later insertion.

[72] E.g.: Paul's aim is to comfort the readers in their sufferings: Nygren (1947, 335ff.), Kuss (1959, 621); to infuse certainty of salvation: Schlatter (1935), Kertelge (1971).

[73] Godet (1893), Schlatter (1935, 278), Schniewind (1952, 82), Althaus (1954, 83), J. Schneider (1964, 600-603), Käsemann (1973), Michel (1978), Schields (1981, 126), Schmithals (1980, 138f.), Bindemann (1983, 67), Fitzmyer (1989).

[74] 1947, 335ff. Similarly Cranfield, who delimits vv. 17-30, (1980, 404), Kuss (1959), Schlier (1977, 258), Wilckens (1980), and even Althaus, who keeps vv. 18-39 together (1954). Thus also Schmithals who thinks that Paul in his first letter (see note 48) inserted a "kleine Dogmatik", 7:17-8:39, which he had written earlier (1980, 18). Within this "Dogmatik" 8:18-30 treats eschatology.

[75] "Guds eviga rådsluts fullbordan" (1947, 343).

[76] 1962, 205. The headlines may show the structure by Sanday and Headlam: Sonship and heirship (12-17), Suffering the path to glory (18-25), The assistance of the Spirit (26-27), The ascending process of salvation (28-30).

[77] 1963, 47. Schwantes' interest in the study of Rom 8:18ff. is expressed in the subtitle of his book, "Ein Beitrag zum Verständnis der Auferweckung bei Paulus".

[78] "Den Sätzen über die Gegenwart und Zukunft des Kosmos (V. 19-22) kommt keine *Aussage*-, sondern nur eine *deutende Funktion* zu" (1963, 51).

[79] Paul does not seek to teach cosmology but speaks of cosmos as awaiting its fulfilment

Käsemann uses Zahn's outline in an unexpected way. He accepts Zahn's structure with a thesis in v. 18 and three following arguments. However, instead of seeing the three "circles" as evidence for the thesis in v. 18, Käsemann understands them as a "Gegenbewegung zu diesem Obersatz".[80] Thus in v. 18 Paul says that the present sufferings are not worth comparing with the coming glory. In order to prevent a concentration on this coming glory Paul gives three tokens of the present sufferings. Paul, according to Käsemann, turns against the enthusiasts who concentrate on ecstatic glossolalia in the service which has gone wild and disturbs the ordinary worship. In his fight against the irregularity Paul reinterprets the meaning of glossolalia not as a proof of a freedom of the Spirit, but rather as a cry for freedom. "Gründlicher kann man nicht theologia gloriae in die theologia viatorum hinein entmythologisieren", Käsemann concludes.[81] In this way Paul, still according to Käsemann, in fact opposes the belief in a realised eschatology.[82]

Zahn's structuring is also taken up by Balz who describes the structure still more precisely:[83]

vv. 19–22 ● introductory conjunction γάρ
● main proposition (v. 19) ἀποκαραδοκία τῆς κτίσεως . . .
● demonstrative clause introduced by γάρ
● conclusive reference to a concrete object (κτίσις)

vv. 23–25 ● introductory conjunction ἀλλὰ καί
● main proposition (v. 23) ἡμεῖς τὴν ἀπαρχὴν ἔχοντες . . . στενάζομεν
● demonstrative clause introduced by γάρ
● conclusive reference to a concrete object (ἡμεῖς)

vv. 26–27 ● introductory conjunction ὡσαύτως καί
● main proposition (v. 26bc) τὸ πνεῦμα συναντιλαμβάνεται τῇ ἀσθενείᾳ
● demonstrative clause introduced by γάρ
● conclusive reference to a concret object (τὸ πνεῦμα)

". . . in der Absicht, der Gemeinde in Rom am Bild kosmischer Lage die eigene Situation, die noch unter Leiden sich vorfindet, in eindringlicher Weise verständlich zu machen" (Schwantes 1963, 49). Thus also Vögtle (1970, 189f.).
[80] 1969 "Schrei", 233.
[81] Op.cit., 234.
[82] Käsemann has not won support in this matter.
[83] 1971, 33f. Balz, like Zahn, takes the δέ and the οἴδαμεν of v. 28 as introducing a new section of the text.

However impressive this structuring of the text appears, it has been shown not to be true to the character of the text. Thus Luz observes that there is a certain refractoriness in the thought material constituting the three "circles". Since the groaning of Creation and of men is not equal to the groaning of the Spirit, the groaning does not have the same meaning in all the three circles. "Während hier das Seufzen [v. 22f] Ausdruck der Unerlöstheit ist, wird es dort [v. 26] als Ausdruck des Für-uns-Eintretens des Geistes interpretiert. Die drei Arten des Zeufzens dürfen nicht einfach formal mit einander parallellisiert werden, sondern V. 26f. muss für sich interpretiert werden".[84]

To Luz's observation Paulsen adds a second: all of the motifs are not kept throughout the text.[85] Thus he finds that the hope is the predominant motif and outlines it as follows:

V. 19 ἀποκαραδοκία—ἀπεκδέχεσθαι
V. 20 ἐφ' ἐλπίδι
V. 23 ἀπεκδέχεσθαι
V. 24 ἐλπίς
V. 25 ἐλπίζειν—ἀπεκδέχεσθαι

Even though the motif is present already in v. 19 Paulsen also observes that it does not play any central rôle until v. 23, and in vv. 26–27 it is missing.

Luz finds a rather complicated "Denk- und Zeitstruktur" under the surface of the text, which complicates its structure. Not only is present time opposed to future, but there is also an opposition between different aspects of present time, namely "die Gegenwart des unerlösten Menschen und die Gegenwart Gottes".[86] Over against such considerations Luz suggests that the text is structured in another way: v. 18 functions as the theme of vv. 19–27: the sufferings of the present time cannot be compared to the coming glory. He thus outlines the theme and the structure in the following words: "Es geht darum, daß die Leiden der Gegenwart nicht zählen im Vergleich zur zukünftigen Herrlichkeit. Dies zeigt Paulus in zwei parallelen Gedankengängen, nämlich für die Schöpfung in V. 19–21, für die Christen, die durch Gott den Geist als Erstling besitzen, in V. 22–30".[87] There is a discrepancy between the designation of v. 18 as a theme for vv. 19–27 and the actual construction in two parallel chains of thought. Luz does not, however, explain this difference. Consequently the text must be delimited not after v. 27 but after v. 30.[88]

---

[84] 1968, 377.

[85] Paulsen 1974, 107ff.

[86] Luz 1968, 370. Thus to Luz the structure seems confusing: "Überhaupt scheint in der zweiten Hälfte unseres achten Kapitels des Römerbriefs ein gewisses Durcheinander in der zeitlichen Fixierung der Heilsaussagen zu herrschen" (op. cit. 374).

[87] Luz 1968, 377.

[88] Loc. cit.

Although critical voices such as those mentioned have been heard, Zahn's structuring is still accepted by many exegetes today. Thus Zeller, who sees v. 17 as the thematic verse, pays no attention to the observations made by Luz and Paulsen but writes: "Die VV. 19–27 werden zusammengehalten durch Ausdrücke wie Sehnsucht, Erwartung, Hoffnung, Seufzen".[89]

Structural analysis of our text has not confirmed Zahn's structure. Rolland finds a rhythmic rhetorical pattern throughout the letter. According to Rolland certain thoughts and words create corresponding patterns between different parts of the letter. Chapter 8 forms a long antithesis to Chapters 5–7.[90] Thus Rom 5:5–19 corresponds to 8:24–39; 6:4–23 to 8:13–21; and 7:8–25 to 8:2–11.[91] This pattern thereby assumes a division right in the middle of our text. This analysis is not very instructive concerning the problems of the text.

A structural analysis concentrated to 8:18–25 was also performed by May (1980) who delimits the text to vv. 18–25 because it is determined by the theme of Creation. The theme of hope which is introduced in v. 20 is regarded as part of the text. However, May pays no attention to vv. 26f., as those verses do not fit the pattern and consequently are omitted from the diagram.[92]

It is evident that Rom 8:18ff. cannot easily be organized in a clear structural pattern. It is difficult to determine the rôle within the text of the different subjects, glory, Creation, hope and Spirit. It would instead be reasonable to assume that the relation between these subjects is determined by their collocation in the background material on which Paul draws. Thus the structure of the text cannot be made clear unless the underlying thought pattern is decerned. In what follows I shall try to prove that I have found this pattern.

1.3.2.4 Concepts and Ideas in Rom 8:18–27

As has already been mentioned, an essential part of the interpretation of this text is occupied by discussion of the meaning of several words and ideas therein. The problems are rather complicated and involve philology, judgment on unusual syntactical constructions, and not least religio-historical considerations.

1.3.2.4.1 What does Paul Mean by Creation (κτίσις) ?
V. 19 contains a series of controversial issues. The interest has been primarily directed towards the problem of what Paul means by the word κτίσις as he

---

[89] 1985, 150f. In spite of keeping vv. 19–27 together Zeller delimits the section 17–30, saying "Der Gedanke des 'Zusammen mit Christus' (V. 17.29) umschließt den ganzen Abschnitt" (*op. cit.*, 151).

[90] The parallel of Chapter 5 often has been observed and studied. Thus already Frommann (1863, 25).

[91] Rolland 1980, 6. The parallels are worked out in more detail in Rolland's article in 1988.

[92] May 1980, 46.

speaks of it as knowing and feeling (ἀποκαραδοκία[93] τῆς κτίσεως τὴν ἀποκάλυψιν τῶν υἱῶν τοῦ θεοῦ ἀπεκδέχεται). Most modern interpreters have made their choice from among the lines of interpretation used already in the pre-modern era. However, only four of the five possible approaches have been advocated.[94] One further interpretation has been upheld (below marked d).

a) The angelological interpretation is taken up only by Fuchs[95] but assessed merely as "nicht ausgeschlossen" by Schmidt.[96]

b) The anthropological interpretation is favoured by several scolars. Broadly speaking, the old arguments are repeated. Interpreters have felt that the text demands an understanding of the word κτίσις which grants "Creation" consciousness and feelings. To several interpreters κτίσις thus denotes the human world. But this would mean that all men will be saved (v. 21), a thought which cannot be accepted by some exegetes and is certainly difficult to support from Pauline texts. Schlatter answers that only those who reject the grace of God will not be saved. By κτίσις Paul means all men who do not explicitly repudiate the grace of God, thus also those who do not know Him.[97] Thus a conscious faith is not absolutely necessary for salvation.

However, several interpreters have found κτίσις to denote the manifestly non-believing mankind, the reason being the difference between the Christians and the κτίσις expressed by the construction in vv. 19–22, 23. κτίσις therefore is understood as the human world.[98] Because Christians are called

---

[93] According to Delling the word ἀποκαραδοκία is derived from a combination of the ancient κάρα (head) and δέκομαι (Ionic form of δέχομαι) meaning "stretch out for". From these words is prompted the conjecture καραδόκος, which has never been found in Greek literature, and which would mean "stretching forth the head". ἀποκαραδοκία thus should be translated "abwarten (in Ruhe oder in Spannung)" (Delling 1933a, 392. This interpretation of the word is given by Godet 1893). Balz objected to this explanation without presenting another translation (1971, 37 note 2) "mit vorgestrecktem Kopf warten befriedigt sachlich wie formal nicht . . . Wenigstens bei Jos Bell 3, 264 ist sie unvorstellbar, denn wer wird mit vorgestrecktem Kopf den Anflug von feindlichen Pfeilen erwarten? Sicher hat nicht Paulus solche Untertöne in das Wort hineinlegen wollen, sondern erst die reflektierenden Paulusexegeten haben sie darin gefunden". This objection Balz repeats in 1980. A particular interpretation of the word is given by Kuss who makes ἀποκαραδοκία, and not κτίσις, the direct subject of the verb. Paul thus indirectly mentions the groaning of Creation, thus showing that he wants to speak of the Creation as unconscious. Bertram (1958) explains the prefixed ἀπό not as an intensifying but a negative element giving to the word a meaning of anxiety (a possibility intemated by Delling 1933). Thus also Vögtle (1970, 193). Against this Denton (1982).

[94] A concise survey of the arguments of modern scholars along these lines is given by Vögtle 1970, 184–186.

[95] 1949, 109.

[96] 1962, 146. Similarly Gerber (1966, 65): "Man mag hier im Sinne des Paulus auch Dämonen und Engelmächte hinzuzählen (vgl. Kol.i 23)".

[97] "Paulus spricht von der doppelten Offenbarung des Lebens, von einer ersten, die den Kindern Gottes zuteilwerden und ihnen die herrliche Freiheit bringen wird, und einer darauffolgenden, die den Tod von der Menchheit wegnehmen wird" (Schlatter 1935, 273).

[98] Schlatter (1935, 270), Schläger (1930), Dulau (1934), Schmidt (1962, 145f.). To this is added the argument that the word κτίσις denotes the non-Christian world in Mk 16:15 (Wettstein in Ἡ καινὴ Διαθήκη, 1752).

καινὴ κτίσις in 2Cor 5:17; Gal 6:15, the expression must mean the non-Christians.[99] Building on the contrast between those who are "subjected to futility" (v. 20f.) and those who "have the first fruit of the Spirit" they therefore limit κτίσις to the non-Christian humanity.[100] To most exegetes it seems impossible that the non-believers should obtain the glorious liberty which belongs to the sons of God (v. 21).

c) The cosmic interpretation is upheld by most modern scholars.[101] Moreover the cosmic interpretation is generally advocated by arguments presented in the pre-modern exegesis. Beside these arguments reference is made to the use of the word κτίσις in the LXX (Jdt 16:14; WisSol 2:6; 5:17, 20ff.; 16:24f.; 19:6f.; Eccl 49:16).[102] The question of the strange consciousness and capacity of feelings, which are expressed in regard to Creation, is differently answered. Fritzsche thinks that Paul uses a "dichterische Sprache".[103] Other exegetes have thought of a "personalizing" of Creation. According to Althaus Creation does not understand the groaning but it is heard and interpreted by the believers.[104] This idea is also maintained by Vögtle,[105] who interprets the expression ἀποκαραδοκία τῆς κτίσεως as indirect speech.[106] In regard to the

[99] Dulau 1934.

[100] Manson, (1963, 946), Schweizer (1969a, 394, note 418). Cf. on the other hand, Schlatter: "Offenkündig ist, daß damit den Kreaturen völlig in derselben Weise wie den Glaubenden das persönliche Leben zugeschrieben ist" (1935, 273). "Die Einrede, die die Verheißung des Paulus von der Menschheit weg in die Natur oder das Weltall hinausschob, stammt aus der Ablehnung des Chiliasmus und aus dem Entschluß der Kirche, keine Verheißung zuzulassen, die über ihren eigenen Kreis hinausging" (*op. cit.* 374) .

[101] In modern times this line of explanation has been followed by *inter alios* Baur (1836), Zyro (1845 and 1851), Maier (1847), de Wette (1847), Köster (1862), Frommann (1863), Zahn (1865 and 1910), Bisping (1870), Weiß (1888), Lipsius (1892), Cornley (1896), Kühl (1913), Jülicher (1917), Gutjahr (1923), Hoppe (1926), Holtzmann (1926), Haering (1926), Bardenhewer (1926), Schläger (1930), Sickenberger (1932), Lietzmann (1933), Goguel (1935), Biedermann (1940), Huby (1940, 294), Gaugler (1945), Gieraths (1950, 97, 128), Althaus (1954), Kuss (1959), Sanday and Headlam (1962), J Murray (1959), Phildius (1958, 79,86), Cranfield (1980); Zeller (1985),

[102] Thus Fritzsche (1839, 151), Godet (1893, 102), Zahn (1910, 400f), Meyer (1872, 374). Zahn also refers to Col 1:23.

[103] 1839, 154. Thus also Dodd (1963, 148f.), Cranfield (1980, 412). Cranfield also mentions the possibility of a personification of Creation.

[104] "Nach diesem Tage sehnt sich unbewußt alle Kreatur. Paulus hört durch den ganzen Kosmos eine Klage und eine Sehnsucht gehen, die sich selber nicht versteht, deren Grund und Sinn und Recht aber der Glaubende kennt" (1954, 82).

[105] Paul is already thinking of v. 23 where he will use the Jewish apocalyptic topos of the increasing sufferings before the advent of the Messianic Age. He therefore introduces this topos as a sign of the present Creation, personifying Creation. However, he uses the word ἀποκαραδοκία in order not to make Creation the direct subject. "Unter Berücksichtigung des wahrscheinlich auch bei ἀποκαραδοκία in der Vorsilbe anzunehmenden negativen Gehalts könnte Paulus mit der Wahl dieses Substantivs als Subjekt des ἀπεκδέχεται auch andeuten, daß es sich bei dem Warten der Schöpfung auf die eschatologische Offenbarung nicht um einen bewußten Vorgang handelt, sondern um eine aufgrund des Offenbarungswissens erfolgte Deutung" (Vögtle 1970, 193, following Bertram 1958, 269).

[106] 1970, 193.

words ματαιότης and φθορά opinions differ concerning how Creation was subjected to these powers.[107]

d) The cosmo-anthropological interpretation understands κτίσις as the sub-human Creation together with non-believing men. This approach ensues from a combination of the cosmic and the anthropological interpretation mentioned in the discussion of the pre-modern exegesis.[108] Gieraths mentions no scholar from pre-modern times who has held to the cosmic-anthropological line of interpretation but shows that it has been followed by "neuere Erklärer".[109] Nowadays it is advocated by several exegetes.[110]

According to the cosmo-anthropological interpretation Creation's enslavement under φθορά means that it is subjected to meaninglessness,[111] that it is characterized by its struggle for survival,[112] or that it is characterized by disturbance due to men.[113] Destruction belongs to the created order and thus Paul can say that Creation was subdued οὐχ ἑκοῦσα. According to Gieraths the advocates of this interpretation of κτίσις do not explain what will be the fate of the sub-human Creation.[114] Paul was only interested in the non-believer's longing, and his explanation is directed towards the future of the believers.

To conclude this survey of the interpretations of the word κτίσις an observation may be made in regard to method. It has become evident that exegetes usually try to determine the meaning of the word exclusively from what is said within the pericope itself. Bindemann has pointed to the weakness of this method.[115] The religio-historical background has not sufficiently been taken into account. Actually only a few scholars have directed their attention to this problem. It will be a method of some concern in my discussion.

1.3.2.4.2 What does Paul Mean by a Revelation of the Sons of God (ἀποκάλυψις τῶν υἱῶν τοῦ θεοῦ)?

Among the rare expressions in Rom 8 we find "revelation of the sons of God". Usually the expression οἱ υἱοὶ τοῦ θεοῦ is interpreted from the

---

[107] Several different answers have been given to the question of when Creation was subjected to meaninglessness and destruction. Most exegetes hold that this happened through Adam's Fall. Others maintain that death belongs to Creation from the beginning and has not its origin in Adam's Fall (e. g. de Wette, Hoppe, Holzmann). See further Gierahts 1950, 33–50.

[108] See 1.3.1.3 and 1.3.1.4.

[109] Köllner (1834, 296), Olshausen (1835, 296), Otto (1886, 57), Foerster (1938, 1030), Brunner (1938).

[110] *Inter alios* Nygren (1947, 337), Viard (1952), Gerber (1966), Luz (1968), Bornkamm (1969, 140), Balz (1971), Bruce (1971), Käsemann (1973).

[111] Olshausen, Foerster.

[112] Brunner.

[113] Foerster.

[114] Olshausen excludes from the future glory only the people who reject the grace of God.

[115] "Es ist, methodisch gesehen, verkehrt, Sinn und Bedeutungsumfang von κτίσις allein aus dem Text der V. 19–22 zu entnehmen" (1983, 73).

preceding vv. 14–17 as denoting the believers. However, as already said, no-where else in the New Testament are the believers said to be revealed. Different solutions to this problem are suggested: The object of revelation is said to be some hidden quality of being sons of God,[116] the hidden glory which belongs to God's children,[117] or a hidden sonship of which the unbelieving world is at present unaware.[118] Schläger has remarked that these interpretations in fact change the usual meaning of the word ἀποκάλυψις.[119] As this solution seems very doubtful Schläger suggests that the text is corrupt, and surmises that Paul did not write τῶν υἱῶν τοῦ θεοῦ but τοῦ υἱοῦ τοῦ θεοῦ. Schläger thus makes Christ the object of revelation, which accords with the rest of the NT.[120]

1.3.2.4.3 Who is the ὑποτάξας in διὰ τὸν ὑποτάξαντα?

Several suggestions have been submitted as to whom Paul means by ὑποτάξας. Zahn believes that the background of the thought is Gen 3:17: "cursed is the ground because of you". He consequently interprets ὑποτάξας as man (i. e. Adam).[121] Now the construction of the Greek text of Gen 3:17 is different: ἐπικατάρατος ἡ γῆ ἐν τοῖς ἔργοις σου. Seeking an equivalent linguistic construction Zahn turns to Gen 8:21 where God says that He "will never again curse the ground because of man". This is expressed, just as in Paul's text, by διά with acc., διὰ τὰ ἔργα τῶν ἀνθρώπων. Zahn thus considers this verse to be a reflexion of Gen 3:17 constructed as Gen 8:21.

The expression διά with acc. should, according to the usual rules in Greek, be understood as "by someone's merit (as in Classical)".[122] According to Bauer "instead of dia w. gen. to denote the efficient cause we may have διά ... w. acc. of the person ... διὰ τὸν ὑποτάξαντα *by the one who subjected it*".[123] But who is meant by this "efficient cause"? The expression is extremely obscure and has provoked several suggestions. Sometimes it is adjusted so as to fit the presupposed idea of the origin of sin. According to Lietzmann: "ὁ ὑποτάξας kann, wenn die Beziehung auf Gen 3:17 richtig ist, nur Gott sein. διά c. acc. vom Urheber (= durch) s. zu 3:25".[124] This inter-

---

[116] E. g. Nygren (1947, 338), Sanday and Headlam (1962),

[117] E. g. Lietzmann (1933), Gaugler (1945),

[118] E. g. Zahn (1910), Schlatter (1935, 268f.), Althaus (1954), Balz: "die vollgültige Verifizierung ihrer jetzigen pneumatischen Heilswirklichkeit" (1971, 39), Cranfield (1980), J. A. T. Robinson: The transformation at the parousia of Christ (1979,101f.), Michel (1978), Schlier (1977), Riesenfeld (1977, 186).

[119] See 1.2.1.b.

[120] 1930, 359.

[121] 1910, 402.

[122] BDF § 222.

[123] Bauer–Aland 1988, *s v.* διά, B II 4b.

[124] 1933. Cf. Schlatter: Paul thinks of God, "denn es gibt bei Paulus keinen anderen, der über die κτίσις verfügt, als Gott" (1935, 272). Similarly Biedermann: "Auf die Authorität (Gottes) hin..." (1940, 75). Thus also Dodd (1963); Gaugler (1945, 303); Sanday and Headlam

pretation is rejected by Balz for two reasons: "διά mit Akk. kann aber nicht den Verursacher, sondern nur einen Beweggrund bezeichnen. Gott kann nicht Beweggrund seines eigenen Handels sein".[125] He therefore suggests that Paul refers to Adam.[126] Other exegetes have suggested that Paul is thinking of man,[127] or Satan,[128] or even Christ.[129] Hill by a different punctuation of the text tries to make the two the same person: ἡ κτίσις ὑπετάγη, οὐχ ἑκοῦσα ἀλλὰ—διὰ τὸν ὑποτάξαντα—ἐφ' ἐλπίδι.[130]

1.3.2.4.4 How is the Expression οὐχ ἑκοῦσα (v. 20) to be Interpreted?

The rather strange use of the expression οὐχ ἑκοῦσα has troubled the interpreters. It originally means "not willingly".[131] The supposed background of the Fall of Adam, however, impels the interpreters to change this meaning. Adam could not be said to have come under the curse without his own will, which, however, can be said of the rest of Creation. The word is therefore interpreted by some scholars in this case as "without its own action" meaning that Creation is without guilt.[132]

1.3.2.4.5 How should the Thought of an Intercession by the Spirit be Understood?

Paul writes: τὸ πνεῦμα συναντιλαμβάνεται τῇ ἀσθενείᾳ ἡμῶν· τὸ γὰρ τί προσευξώμεθα καθὸ δεῖ οὐκ οἴδαμεν, ἀλλὰ αὐτὸ τὸ πνεῦμα ὑπερεντυγχάνει στεναγμοῖς ἀλαλήτοις (v. 26). Three major lines of interpretation have been proposed. a) Lietzmann speaks of ecstatic utterances: "in dem wortlosen Stammeln des Verzückten redet der Geist eine Sprache, die Gott versteht".[133] The thought that Paul speaks of ecstatic utterances in the service as being expressions of the work of the Spirit was also put forward by Käsemann.[134] b) Delling thinks of an inner prayer coming from the heart of the believer.[135] c) Schneider suggests that the Spirit interceding in heaven is

---

(1962); Fahy (1956 "St. Paul", 179); Hill (1961, 297), Gerber (1966, 69), Jervell (1978, 151); Käsemann (1973); Paulsen (1974, 114); Cranfield (1980); Michel (1978); Black (1984); Hommel (1984 132), Forde (1984, 285), Heil (1987, 52 note 45), Morris (1988), Fitzmyer (1989).

[125] 1971, 41.

[126] *Loc. cit.* Thus also Foerster (1938, 1030), Delling (1969, 42), J. A. T. Robinson (1979, 102), Schlier (1965).

[127] Zahn (1865, 521), Nygren (1947), Gieraths (1950, 117), Kehnscherper (1979, 413),

[128] Pallis (1920), Schläger (1930, 357).

[129] Barth, 1985.

[130] 1961, 297. Cf. e.g. Kühl: "ὑπετάγη, sc. von Gott. Auch der ὑποτάξας im folgenden ist Gott" (1913, 293).

[131] See ch.1 at note 14, 15.

[132] "If ἡ κτίσις is taken to mean mankind or to include mankind, it would seem to bee necessary to explain οὐχ ἑκοῦσα along the lines of Augustine's interpretation as referring to the involuntariness of the Creation's submission to the penalty imposed on it" (Cranfield 1975, 414).

[133] 1933,86. Lietzmann sees Hellenistic mysticism as the background of vv. 26f.

[134] 1969 "Schrei", 211ff.; 1973.

[135] " . . . von dem pneumatischen Gebet des Christen, das dem noëtischen zur Seite tritt oder

fulfilling "den Dienst eines Parakleten an unserer Stelle".[136] Similarly also Balz,[137] and Michel.[138] Luz cannot accept Schneider's interpretation:" . . . es währe aber nicht einzusehen, wieso die Interzession des Geistes noch im Himmel die Form von Seufzern haben sollte. Außerdem fehlen für diese konkrete Ausmalung der Parakletvorstellung Parallelen".[139]

Most commentators do not mention the question of the strange relation between the Spirit and God. Sanday and Headlam, however, say that vv. 26f. "show that Paul regarded the action of the Holy Spirit as personal, and as distinct from the action of the Father".[140] Cranfield interprets the statement as an argument for God's knowing the heart of the believer, "He must *a fortiori* be supposed to know the unspoken desires of His own Spirit . . . ".[141] MacRae comments on this common understanding: "But one must pause over the picture of God's 'inner life' which this interpretation suggests: it supposes a form of communication between the divine persons which is much more at home in later Trinitarian theology than in Paul. In fact, it supposes a kind of duality in God which is unknown to the NT".[142] Macrae's own suggestion is that "the one who searches the heart" is the Spirit and renders v. 27: "That is to say, the one who searches hearts [the Spirit] knows what the (human) spirit has (i. e., should have) its mind set on because it is according to (the mind of) God that he intercedes for the saints".[143]

1.3.2.5 The Religio-Historical Background of Rom 8:18–27

In his study of Rom 8 Frommann finds that Rom 8:18–27 speaks of a natural revelation of God. Creation can be observed groaning and longing for the sons of God to be revealed thus proclaiming the existence, and a coming act,

---

es ersetzt. Das Pneuma ist offenbar nicht als tertia persona gedacht, sondern als das mit dem Menschen eins gewordene; es geht sogar mit der menschlichen καρδία eine Verbindung ein und formt dort Gebete, die dem Menschen nicht verstandesgemäß faßbar und Gott nicht unmittelbar adäquat sind, . . . Dieses pneumatische Gebet ist charismatisches Handeln mit Gott, ebenso wie die Glossolalie . . . " (1933, 376). Similarly Behm: "Paulus weiß, der Geist nimmt sich des um Gewißheit der Heilsvollendung ringenden Beters in seinem Unvermögen an und tritt durch das Stammeln von Glossolalen vor Gott für ihn ein" (1954, 811f.). Boyd says: "He [the Spirit] stirs up proper desires within us and teaches us to pray as John was not able to teach his disciples" (1954, 42). Dodd speaks of a "profound conception of prayer as the divine in us appealing to the God above us" (1963, 150). Similarly Schmidt (1962),

[136] " Er [Paul] behauptet vielmehr, daß der Geist an unserer Stelle handelt und für uns eintritt, so daß er den Dienst eines Parakleten tut, der unserer Gebetsnot zu Hilfe kommt. Paulus denkt also an einen Vorgang im himmlisch-göttlichen Bereich" (1964, 602). Thus also Balz (1971, 87ff.), Bindemann (1983, 79), Zeller (1985,163).

[137] 1971, 83ff. Thus also Sanday and Headlam (1962).

[138] "Es geht vielmehr um einen *himmlischen, apokalyptischen Vorgang*" (1978).

[139] 1968, 380.

[140] 1962.

[141] 1975. Similarly Michel 1978.

[142] MacRae 1980, 228.

[143] *Op. cit.* 230.

of God. This results in a particular exegesis: the revelation through nature seems to be taken by Paul as evidence of the Christian faith.[144] Frommann maintains that not only do these thoughts diverge from Christian thinking as presented in the NT, but nor can there be found a text from Jewish and Christian sources of that time which supports them.[145] He concludes that Paul must have used some source which is unknown to us. Frommann thus put his finger on a sore point in the text: What is its proper religio-historical background?

As has already been said, Fromman's article provoked opposition from Zahn. Zahn flatly denies both that Paul presents any unusual thought and that it cannot be paralleled in the Scriptures. Having devoted the first half of his article to an exegesis of the text in question he tries in the second half to prove that there are parallels to Paul's thoughts. Zahn's article made as strong an impact on the understanding of the religio-historical background as it did on the manner of finding the structure of the text. Thus for a long time no exegete dared to suggest any other background.

However, the observations made by Frommann could not be wholly rejected. Once introduced, the question of the sources of Paul's thought was here to stay. Exegetes have endeavoured to explain the unusual ideas of the text in different ways. A major contribution was delivered by Billerbeck, who found a series of parallels in Jewish literature.[146] He believes that in Rom 8:19ff. Paul builds on the cluster of ideas which were spun from the story of Adam's Fall according to Gen 3. References to Gen 3 have of course been made since the Early Fathers. Billerbeck, however, introduced something new: the Rabbinic literature and especially a series of apocalyptic texts.[147] Commenting on Rom 8:20f. Billerbeck says: "Die alte Synagoge hat ähnlichen Gedanken Raum gegeben: die Welt ist um des Menschen willen, d. h. für ihn oder zu seinem Dienst erschaffen worden; deshalb wurde, als der

---

[144] In the summary of his article Frommann writes: "Ziehen wir nun das Endergebniß unserer bisherigen Erörterungen, so würde Folgendes der Gedankengang des Apostels sein. Er beruft sich auf die erfahrungsmäßig in dem Bewußtsein des Menschen liegende Sehnsucht nach einer Fortdauer in einem vollkommenen, von der Endlichkeit dieser Welt befreiten Zustande, welche er als Thatsache einer natürlichen Offenbarung Gottes an dem Menschen nachweiset (V. 19-21.). . . . Insofern also diese Hoffnung der angestammten, von Gott verliehnen und in der ganzen Menschheit (πᾶσα ἡ κτίσις V. 22) vorhandenen Sehnsucht nach einem künftigen vollkommenen Zustande entspricht, derselben ihr Ziel weiset und sie befriedigt, empfängt sie selbst die Bestätigung ihrer Sicherheit und Gewissheit" (1863, 49).

[145] 1863, 31.

[146] First presented in 1922.

[147] The word ἀποκάλυψις has been connected to the certain genre which characterizes e.g. Rev and Dan (at least in parts). I shall use the word apocalypse to describe literary entities characterized by this genre. Further I shall use the word apocalypticism to describe the socio-religious phenomenon characterized by the specific eschatological perspective which was generated by the apocalyptic genre. Apocalyptic thus will be used to describe any text or phenomenon characterized by this perspective (see further Hanson 1976 "Apocalypticism").

Mensch, der Herr der Schöpfung, sündigte, auch diese in sein Verderben mit hingerissen".[148] Furthermore, he quotes 4Ezra 7:11ff.:[149]

... and when Adam transgressed my statutes, what had been made was judged. And so the entrances of this world were made narrow and sorrowful and toilsome; they are few and evil, full of dangers and involved in great hardships. But entrances of the greater world are broad and safe, and really yield the fruit of immortality. Therefore unless the living pass through the difficult and vain experiences, they never receive those things that have been reserved for them.

In 1940 Biedermann published a study on redemption which caused him to cope with our text.[150] He sets out to answer the following questions: "Kennt Paulus eine Erlösung der Schöpfung? Wenn ja, was weiß er darüber auszusagen? Weiter noch: Welches sind die Voraussetzungen und Quellen für die Lehre des Apostels? Endlich: Wie steht der Apostel mit seinen Anschauung in der Umwelt?"[151] The two last questions in particular coincide with those raised by Frommann in 1863. Whereas Frommann's answer had been that the thoughts found in our passage cannot be matched in any known text within or outside the Bible, Biedermann finds several close, although not uniform, parallels in the OT prophets.[152] "Der Kerngedanke aber, um den sie alle kreisen, ist ebenso klar: Die Welt wird einmal, und zwar zugleich mit dem Menschen, dem Gerichte Gottes unterstellt werden und also auch das gleiche Geschick mit ihm teilen".[153] Still more important, Creation will share the redemption of man.[154] In the Apocrypha Biedermann finds passages in 1 Enoch and 2 Baruch which are reminiscent of Paul's ideas.[155] However,

---

[148] Str-B iii, 1926, 247.

[149] *Op. cit.* 250.

[150] Biedermann writes: "Eine eigentliche Spezialarbeit über unsere Frage ist mir nicht bekannt geworden". Thus his work marks a new approach in the study of the text.

[151] 1940, 12.

[152] Biedermann (*op. cit.* 29ff.) indicates especially Isa 24 and Isa 11:6–9 but mentions also Isa 2:6–9; 13:9–11; Jer 4:24ff.; Joel 2:10; 4:15; Am 5:18ff.; 8:9; 9:5; Hab 3:6–11; Ez 2:10; Nah 1:5; Os 2:20 (page 30ff.).

[153] Biedermann 1940, 32.

[154] "Zusammenfassend können wir sagen: In der Eschatologie der Propheten findet sich zum erstenmal ein Ahnen wenigstens, das uns erlaubt, über den Gedanken einer Welterneuerung hinaus von einer Erlösung der Schöpfung zu sprechen. Wir begegnen hier der Vorstellung von einer Schuldverhaftung der Erde und des Himmels, von einem Gericht über sie und schließlich von einer Neugestaltung derselben, die zuweilen in unmittelbarem Zusammenhang mit dem Heilswirken des **Messias** gesehen wird. Dabei herrscht in all diesen Punkten zugleich eine weitgehende Parallelität zwichen der Schöpfung und der Menschheit bzw. dem Volke Israel" (Biedermann 1940, 36).

[155] 1 En 71; 80; 91:14,16. Biedermann finds 4Ezra 7 and 2Bar especially close parallels. From these two books Biedermann reconstructs the following background to Rom 8:18ff.: "Dieser gegenwärtigen Welt steht die zukünftige als ihr vollkommenes Gegenbild gegenüber: 'Die Wege in der größeren Welt sind breit und sicher und tragen Früchte der Unsterblichkeit' [4 Ezra 7:13]. Längst ist sie den Auserwählten versprochen [2Bar 14:13; 51:3; 44:13], ja die Hoffnung auf Erneuerung der Welt ward schon zur Zeit des Abraham grundgelegt [2Bar 57:2, cf. 4Ezra 3:14; 6:7f.; 2Bar 4:4]. Die Erde zittert und erbebt, sie weiß, sie muß am Ende eine Wandlung erfahren [4Ezra 6:16]. Die Welt eilt mit Macht dem Ende entgegen, damit das Ackerfeld erscheinen kann,

Biedermann denies the existence of a connection between Rom 8:18ff. and these texts.[156] And as to the Philonian material Philo is found to be "abseits vom Denken seines eigenen Volkes in diesem Punkte ... ".[157] Thus the study results in the conclusion that Paul drew on the story of Adam's Fall in Gen 3 and prophetic texts when he wrote Rom 8:18-27.[158]

To Bultmann it is clear that Paul uses material from Gnostic mythology.[159] Although Paul does not really share the dualistic world view of the Gnostics[160] he used Gnostic language to express his message.[161] Thomassen maintains that Paul's use of the word ἀποκαλύπτειν in Rom 8:18 (... τὴν μέλλουσαν δόξαν ἀποκαλυφθῆναι εἰς ἡμᾶς), paralleled in *Evangelium Veritatis*, is dependent on a Gnostic background.[162]

The significance of Billerbeck's parallels for the understanding of the background of Rom 8:18-27 was not realized until Schwantes' study in 1963. Schwantes defines the concept Creation in a new way: "Wir selbst sind der Auffassung: Paulus meint an dieser Stelle mit 'Schöpfung' den Kosmos der spätjüdischen Apokalyptik".[163] The suggestion that the text has an apocalyptic background opens new aspects on the interpretation.[164] However, it

worin das Gute gesät ist [4Esra 4:26-29]. Das wird geschehen am Ende der messianischen Zeit [4Esra 7:29f.; 2Bar 30:10; 40:3]. Da wird sich die Welt in das Schweigen der Urzeit wandeln, sieben Tage lang [4 Esra 7:30; cf. 6:39; 2Bar 3:7], d.h. sie wird zurückkehren in ein Chaos gleich dem am Uranfang der Schöpfung. Nach sieben Tagen aber erwacht die Welt, die noch nicht wacht, und die Vergänglichkeit vergeht [4Esra 7:31 cf. Rom 8:20f.]. Eingeleitet wird diese Umwandlung durch die Auferstehung der Toten und die Verklärung der Gerechten [4Esra 7:32; 2Bar 30:1-3; 50:2-4; 51:3]. Ihnen wird die neue Welt, die erneuerte Schöpfung zuteil, um die das ganze Interesse der beiden Bücher kreist [4Esra 5:45; 7:13, 31, 47, 75, 113; 8:1, 5; 2Bar 14:13; 15:7f.; 32:6; 48:50; 51:3, 8-11; 57:2; 74:2]". (Biedermann 1940, 40f. I have extracted the quotations from Biedermann's footnotes and put them into square brackets).

[156] Biedermann's article is marked by a rather repudiative attitude to apocalyptic. The chapter discussing the apocalyptic texts says already at its start:"Wohl enthalten die Apokryphen, die hier in Betracht kommen, manchen tiefen Gedanken in würdiger Form. Aber sie gehen unter in einem Schwall voll dunklen Phantastereien" (1940, 36). By the term "Apokryphen des A.T." Biedermann meant the Pseudepigrapha.

[157] Biedermann 1940, 49.

[158] Biedermann 1940, 88ff. Similarly the apocalyptic background (mentioning 1En 9:10) is dismissed by J Schneider: "In der **hermetischen Literatur** und in der **spätjüdischen Apokalyptik** gibt es gewisse Parallelen zu den Aussagen des Paulus in 2 K 5,2-4 und R 8,22-27; aber man wird nicht sagen können, daß hier ein direkter Einfluß auf Paulus vorliegt" (1964, 602).

[159] "Gnostic mythology lies behind the allusion to the *fall of Creation* in Rom 8:29ff., which, because of its allusiveness, is difficult to explain in detail" (1968, 174).

[160] Speaking of the spirits and powers Bultmann can say: "Like the character of the 'kosmos,' *the character of the spirit powers has a peculiar ambiguity*, for it is clear, in the first place, that Paul does not think in the dualistic manner of Gnosticism ... " (1968, 258)

[161] "Thus through these mythological conceptions the insight is indirectly expressed that man does not have his life in his hand as if he were his own lord but that he is constantly confronted with the decision of choosing his lord" (1968, 259). Bultmann has found no support in this matter.

[162] 1976, 26-29.

[163] 1963, 44.

[164] 1983, 74.

should be noted that Schwantes carefully makes clear that he does not suppose Paul to have been an apocalyptic himself: "Paulus denkt demnach gar nicht daran, *sich mit dem hier beigebrachten apokalyptischen Material zu identifizieren*. Ebensowenig will er es seiner Verkündigung einverleiben, geschweige denn selbst 'verkündigen'!"[165] Schwantes' dissertation is a crossroads in the exegesis of the text and 4Ezra 7:11 has become commonplace as a point of reference in treatment of Rom 8:18ff. in the commentaries.

However, although Billerbeck's parallels have been generally accepted, the problem of the background is not yet solved. It has not been possible to find any apocalyptic text which contains all the motifs involved in Rom 8:18–27. Balz writes: "Eine direkte Abhängigkeit von bestimmten apokalyptischen Aussagen läßt sich allerdings nicht erkennen. Paulus spricht vielmehr eine völlig eigenständige Sprache ,er formuliert thetisch . . . und er bleibt mit seiner Rede von den Gottessöhnen streng im Zusammenhang von Röm 8 . . . Dennoch scheint die apokalyptische Theologie unausweichlich ins Spiel zu kommen . . . ".[166] An attempt to reconstruct a more coherent pre-Pauline tradition is made by von der Osten-Sacken who finds no Jewish apocalypticism in the text. Instead he reconstructs a pre-Pauline text which is assumed to fit into an Hellenistic Christian environment.[167]

This has resulted in a situation where many exegetes find background material for the various motifs in very different contexts. Two examples may illustrate this.

According to Balz Rom 8 answers a question concerning the certainty of salvation, which has been present since 5:1 as a "geheimes Thema".[168] The longing of Creation, of Christians and of the Spirit is proof that salvation will be a reality. Creation's groaning, because of a presupposed solidarity with the Christians, becomes a sign of hope. Thus also the Spirit shows God's presence at the time of oppression. From this aspect Balz seeks a background. He finds a series of Rabbinic texts which show a "Verflechtung des menschlichen Geschicks mit dem der Schöpfung" similar to Rom 8,[169] as well as a series of OT passages. Balz also adduces a series of examples from 4Ezra saying: "Dieser Solidaritätsgedanke spielt in *4 Ezra* eine große Rolle".[170] However, turning to the Enochic literature Balz says: "In *äth Hen* fehlen entsprechende Aussagen, denn hier ist die Sünde durchgehend nicht mit der Schuld des

---

[165] 1963, 50. Thus also Luz (1968, 379), Vögtle (1970, 208).

[166] 1971, 38.

[167] "So scheint die Annahme näherliegend, daß die Überlieferung von Röm. 8,19–27 eine christliche Schöpfung ist, die am ehesten hervorgerufen ist durch enthusiastische Strömungen, wie sie sich nach dem Zeugnis der paulinischen Briefe im griechischsprachigen Christentum gebildet haben" (1974, 101). This proposal has found no support among exegetes.

[168] 1971, 31.

[169] *Op. cit.*, 41.

[170] *Op. cit.*, 42.

Menschen, sondern mit dem Fall der Engel in Verbindung gebracht'',[171] and thus this literature is dismissed.[172]

A similar sifting of the material in order to find the background occurs in Wilckens (1980). According to him Paul uses two motifs: a) suffering is necessary for the righteous before the advent of the Messianic kingdom, and b) not only men but also Creation will be encompassed in the final events of history. Having stated these two motifs Wilckens breaks down the text in its smallest parts, the background of which is sought.[173] Thus Wilckens does not find any coherent background of Paul's text. Rather Paul is assumed to make a series of allusions to diverse ideas.

Some few exegetes have hinted at another possible background. Thus Neary has seen that there are several parallels to the Biblical story of Noah and the Flood:[174]

The extension of redemption to incorporate the cosmos is not something new however. In the OT it is contained in embryonic form. Before the alliance established by God with man in the person of Noah when mankind was re-created after the Flood. This alliance incorporated the whole material universe with man as its centre. This covenant with Noah was designated in the broad heavens by means of the rainbow thus illustrating the point that it was not limited to any part of the created world but rather, embraced the totality of the universe. After the Flood, which was a punishment for man's sin, the material world regained its original harmony and rhythmic quality. At this point it is useful to recall Philo's interpretation of the call of Noah where Noah is presented as 'the beginning of a second race of men' (De Vit.Mos.ii XI,60). Consis-

---

[171] Loc.cit.

[172] A similar diversity is shown for instance in the work by Lietzmann. He finds Gen 3 to be the general background of the text. But as background of the different words and thoughts of the text he quotes disparate material from Isa, 1En, Jub, 4Ezra, Acts, Rev, WisSol, GenR and the Κόρη κόσμου by Stobaeus (Lietzmann 1933, 85).

[173] Suffering is necessary: Sinners fight against God and oppress the righteous (4Ezra 6:57f.; 7:79; 8:57; 1En 103:9-15). The suffering experienced by the righteous is a sign of their adherence to God (4Ezra 8:27). The time of suffering is limited. In the coming judgment the evil will be destroyed and the righteous will be freed from oppression (1En 95:7; 62:11; 53:7). They will experience the deliverance which belongs to the righteous (2Bar 15:8, cf. v. 7; 48:50). When the time for the judgment draws near it releases catastrophic signs on the earth (4Ezra 5:1-13; 6:12; 9:1f.; 2Bar 20:10; 25:2; 27:1-15; 48:30-41; 70:2-20; SibOr II:154-176; III:796-806; VIII:190-197; Rev 6:12-17). The signs of the end is described as "birthpangs" (Mk 13:8; Mt 24:8; Jn 16:21; 1En 62:4; 1QH III,7f.). In the time of the "birthpangs" the godless will be destroyed but at the same time the sufferings of the righteous will increase (Mk 13:14-20), but when the new era is introduced the sufferings will disappear for ever. From this perspective the sufferings should be seen as easy to bear (4Ezra 4:44-50). The righteous are exhorted to take the sufferings upon themselves to prove that they are worthy of their reward (1En 91:3f: 94:1-5) and they are comforted by the hope of what is prepared for them (1En 96:3) in order that they might patiently wait and hope (1En 96:1; 102:4f.; 104:1-4; 108:12). Therefore they are exhorted to rejoice (1En 105:2).

The second motif: Already the prophets said that the earth will take part in God's judgment on the unrighteous (Isa 13:9-13; 24:1-6.18-23; Jer 4:23-28; Ezek 32:6-8; Joel 2:10; 4:15f.; Am 8:9; Hab 3:6-7; 1En 96:1; 102:4f; 104:1-4; 108:12). Wilckens refers to Str-B III for evidence of the thought that Gen 3:17 has been interpreted in a similar way by the rabbis. Creation will at the end of time be glorified together with the righteous (1En 91:16; 106:1; Isa 65:17; 66:22). (Wilckens 1980, 148f.).

[174] Neary, 1981, 21.

tent with this approach of underscoring the God of history with the God of Creation the prophet Jeremiah had compared the Davidic covenant to the alliance with heaven and earth:

> "Thus says the Lord: If I have not established my covenant with day and night and the ordinances of heaven and earth, them [*sic.*] I will reject the descendants of Jacob and David my servant . . . For I will restore their fortunes and have mercy on them" (Jeremiah 33:25).

and again:

> "Thus says the Lord: If you can break my covenant with the day and my covenant with the night, so that day and night will not come at their appropriate time, then also my covenant with David my servant may be broken" (Jer. 31: 20–21).

Neary thus indicates some crucial parallels between Paul's text and the story of Noah and the Flood. At that point, however, Neary denies a connection with Rom 8:18ff. and returns to Gen 3:17 as the only possible background.[175] The similarities in the text to the Covenant with Noah are noted also by Fitzmyer who, however, believes that Paul was dependent on the story of the Fall of Adam.[176]

1.3.3 To Sum Up

This survey of research on Rom 8:18–27 can be summarized somewhat briefly. No consensus has been reached concerning the interpretation of this text. Their delimitation of the pericope may differ, but most scholars see vv. 18–27 as a natural entity, some treat vv. 18–30 and still others, but fewer, vv. 19–39. It is fairly clear that vv. 18–27 are held together because of a similar peculiar background, while vv. 28ff. return to more regular Pauline thought material.

---

[175] "Paul, as we have seen, declares that since man is no longer lord of Creation but is lorded over by it he must therefore battle against the elements for survival. Not only that but sinful man in many places worshipped the elements of the cosmos because of their apparent superiority: 'they exchanged the truth about God for a lie and worshipped and served the creature rather than the creator' (Rom 1:25). As he declares explicitly that Adam allowed sin an entry into the world, and that the havoc of distortion wrought on the sub-human cosmos is a direct consequence, so he implies that sinful men today are responsible for the continued groaning and suffering of Creation seeing that it cannot fulfil its purpose until sin is defeated (Rom 8:19-22). Since God's Creation was 'very good' and Adam distorted it, it is logical to expect that God, in His plan and purpose to renovate His Creation, would begin the process with the one who caused and perpetuated the distortion of His work, namely man himself. For that reason the cosmic dimension can be distinguished but not divorced from the anthropological implications of redemption. Paul believed that when God's process of the redemption of man is complete then the material universe also will participate in redemption (Rom 8:19-22)" (Neary, 1981, 22f.).

[176] Fitzmyer 1989.

The structure of the text which was outlined by Zahn in 1865 has set the pattern for most interpreters since then. Thus v. 18 is regarded by most scholars as a thesis which is supported by three following proofs. Still there are different ideas regarding the subject of the text. Some propose that it is "parenesis in suffering", others "the Christian hope", or "the universal scope of God's salvation", or even "the solidarity of man and Creation in God's plan".

It has become evident that not every scholar takes seriously the question of the rôle of the text within the letter as a whole. In a strange way our text seems to be regarded as an independent treatment of a subject more or less closely related to the rest of the letter.

Concerning the question of the religio-historical background of Rom 8:18–27 the following words by Bindemann can be taken as voicing the consensus among today's exegetes:[177]

Daß Paulus in Röm 8,19–22 konzentriert apokalyptisches Wort- und Vorstellungsmaterial verwendet, kann als gesichertes Ergebnis bisheriger Exegese dieses Abschnitts gelten . . . Unklar ist der literarische Charakter des von Paulus verarbeiteten Materials. . . . Nun finden sich alle apokalyptischen Motive des Abschnitts vereinzelt verstreut in der jüdisch-apokalyptischen Literatur, doch gibt es in keiner der uns bekannten apokalyptischen Schriften einen ähnlich geschlossenen Traditionsblock. Vor allem aber weist der Text von Röm 8,19–22 nicht genügend sprachliche Indizien auf, die den Schluß rechtfertigen könnten, daß Paulus auf ein vorgeformtes Traditionsstück zurückgreift. Röm 8,19–22 bietet also wohl *ein Referat apokalyptischer Gedanken, von Paulus ad hoc verfaßt*, das aber deutlich auf den Hintergrund jüdisch-apokalyptischen Denkens verweist.

From the research done up to now it is clear that the decisive question, which must be answered for further advance of the investigation of this text, pertains to the religio-historical background. Only when this problem is solved can we see what is the message in this specific part of the letter. It is my contention that the scholars who have seen a relation to the story of Noah and the Flood were on the right track to solve the questions of this enigmatic text. In the following chapter I shall study these parallels further.

[177] 1983, 29.

Chapter 2

The use of the Flood Tradition Prior to, During and After New Testament Times

2.1 The Flood Tradition

2.1.1 Ancient Flood Stories

Different myths of a flood and a surviving man were widespread in New Testament times.[1] The name of the survivor differs in different countries.[2] Thus many Greek texts recount the history of a surviving hero named Deucalion (also called Dardanos) and a flood.[3] However, only the Mesopotamian myths show striking resemblances to Gen 6–9 and 1En 6–11. The aforesaid Greek mythology was known to Jewish and Christian authors but the latter were apparently dependent on Jewish literature. The earliest evidence of the myth comes from the Babylonian cuneiform tablets recounting the Gilgamesh epos[4] from which the Genesis version of the myth most probably originated.[5]

---

[1] Cf. Josephus: "This flood and the ark are mentioned by all who have written histories of the barbarians. Among these is Berosus the Chaldaean . . . These matters are also mentioned by Hieronymus the Egyptian, author of the ancient history of Phoenica, by Mnaseas and by many others. Nicolas of Damascus in his ninety-sixth book relates the story as follows . . . this might well be the same man of whom Moses, the Jewish legislator, wrote" (*Ant* I, 93–95. Transl. Thackeray 1978). SibOr I, 217ff. clearly show affinity to the Greek myths.

[2] Flood myths are in fact known from ancient cultures in *Asia* (Babylonia, Palestine, Syria, Phrygia, ancient and modern India, Burma, the southern part of Vietnam (earlier Cochin China), the Malay Peninsula, Kamtchatka, but not, however, eastern, central and northern Asia), The Indian Archipelago (Sumatra, Borneo, Celbes, Nias, Engano, Ceram, Rotti, Flores), *Europe* (Ancient Greece, Wales, Transsylvania and Eastern Russia), *New Guinea and Australia* as well as *South, Central and North America*. *Africa* (including Egypt) does not seem to have any native flood-legends (Frazer 1988, 113–124, originally printed 1918). According to Peake (1930, 20ff.) the Flood is recounted also in Egyptian sources from the time of Seti I, i. e. around 1300 B.C.E. This story Peake thinks might have been handed down from a considerably older time.

[3] Caduff lists no fewer than 159 texts from classical literature containing a story of a flood (1986). Probably the same ancient sources lie behind both the Greek myths and Gen 6–9 and 1En 6–11 (Hanson 1977, 213).

[4] There are different myths from the Assyro-Babylonian and Sumerian areas in ancient times, the earliest records coming from around 1700 BCE. Evidently the Gilgamesh epos was known in pre-Israelitic Canaanitic Palestine since part of a copy of the epos was found at Megiddo in 1955 (Lambert 1980, 70). The copy is written in Babylonian language but Lambert points out that "solche Texte können auch in den einheimischen Sprachen Syriens und Palästinas in mündlicher Form vorhanden gewesen sein" (*ad. loc.*).

[5] Similar Flood stories with a survivor in a wooden ark are known from the Sanscrit literature: *Sathapatha Brahmana* 1.8.1-6, *Mahabharata* 3.188.80; 3.189.42; 3.190.2-56; *Bhagavata Purana* 8.24 (Rudhardt 1987, 353-357). For the ongoing discussion of the sources behind Gen 6: 1-4 see below 2.1.2.2.2.

The earliest evidence of knowledge of this myth in Jewish literature is to be found in Gen 6–9. According to W. D. Davies the myth, narrated in Gen 6–9, in earlier times represented the major answer to the question of the origin of evil, and only in later development was this function taken over by the story of the Fall of Adam and Eve.[6] However, there is ample evidence from intertestamental Jewish literature, as well as from Christian and Muslim sources,[7] that even in Paul's time and later the myth played an important rôle in the minds of people beside the myth of Adam and Eve. Outside of the OT the story of Noah and the Flood appears, or is mentioned, in the Apocryphal and Pseudepigraphal and Rabbinic writings as well as in Philo and Josephus. The NT writings testify that the Early Christian Church also knew and used different forms of the story of the Flood.[8]

Being of such long standing and so many applications the story underwent considerable changes. This development of the traditional story sometimes bewilders the interpreter as he cannot always recognize which version pertains to the text he is studying. The dilemma is not eased by the fact that authors often select a single element from the traditional material.[9] When working with the texts, in which only one motif from the traditional material of the Flood story is used, it often appears that the author actually draws on the whole story in one version or another. Thus in order to understand how the authors use the material it is necessary to have a reconstruction of the entire myth in the form which the author in question possibly knew. This is particularly important with texts where the use of the traditional material is more or less hidden, as is the case in Rom 8:18–27 in my opinion. Therefore in the first part of this chapter I shall try to outline an elementary form of the Flood story and also some of its more important developments. In the second and third parts of the chapter I shall make a short study of the way the tradition of the Flood was applied, i. e. the contexts in which it was actually used and how. In this way I hope to be able to show a) the general view of the story of the Flood in the minds of the people of Paul's time and b) how it was used for different purposes, i. e. how this tradition is given different functions in different concrete contexts and how different techniques are used in its application. Thereafter, in the next chapter, I shall move to a study of Rom 8:18–27.

[6] Davies 1965, 38.

[7] See Jung 1926, 66–72; 295–310; Bamberger 1952, 7–117.

[8] I shall deal with some relevant texts in part 2 of this chapter.

[9] I shall use the term "tradition" and "traditional" to denote material which is transmitted in either written or oral form and thus not invented by the author himself.

2.1.2 The Jewish Story of the Flood

A "Midrashic"[10] exposition[11] of the story of the Flood in Gen 6–9 is to be found in 1En 6–11.[12] Next to Gen 6–9 this seems to be the oldest version of the Flood story extant in Jewish writings.[13] The story in 1 Enoch differs considerably from that in Genesis. The author evidently used also another source when composing the text.[14] By combining the Book of the Watchers (1En 1–36)[15] with Gen 6–9 we shall have a more or less complete account of the story of the fallen angels, Noah, and the Flood, such as it is represented within the Jewish literature at a fairly early date. I shall call this material the

[10] I use the terms "midrashic" and "midrash" to denote the manner in which some author interprets or expounds a text not in the strict meaning of midrash but still using techniques and style borrowed from midrash. (Cf. Bloch 1957). I thus seek a freer mode of exposition of a biblical text.

[11] Alexander (1972, 60) calls 1En 6–11 "an elaborate midrash on Gen 6:1-4"; Hanson (1977, 197) calls it an "expository narrative" (similarly Kvanvig 1988, 275.) and says: "In this expository narrative, Gen 6:1-4 specifically (and in a broader sense, Gen 4-10) is interpreted from the perspective of apocalyptic eschatology"; Hartman (1983, 21f.) finds some of the interpretative techniques from the midrashim used in 1 En 10:16-11:2.

[12] According to Milik (1976, 31) Gen 6-9 is dependent on 1 En 6-11. Milik is supported by Matthew Black (1985, 125). That, on the contrary, 1En is dependent on Gen is held by Alexander (1972, 60), Hanson (1977, 197 note 111), Nickelsburg (1977, 404), Hartman (1983, 16), Kvanvig (1988, 95ff.; 275 note 209).

[13] The Apocalypse of Weeks (1 En 93:1-10; 91:12-17), fragments of a copy of which were found in the Qumran caves, seems to be older as text. But its short reference to the Flood can hardly be called a version of the Flood story. The dating of this apocalypse is uncertain, being determined by Eissfeldt to the time before the Maccabean revolt, i. e. c. 170 B.C.E. (1966, 619), but by Hengel, Schreiner, Russell, Kvanvig to the first half of the second century B.C.E. (Kvanvig 1988, 77 note 111). Milik thinks that it was composed by the author of the Epistle of Enoch himself towards the end of the second or the beginning of the first century B.C.E. (1976, 255f.).

[14] The questions regarding the sources of Gen 6-9 and 1En 6-11 are of minor interest to the present study as these texts had long been in use at Paul's time. Some remarks on the present state of research will be offered below. For the debate of the sources behind Gen 6-9 and 1En 6-11 see further Kraeling (1947), Westermann (1974,474-477), Hanson (1977), Nickelsburg (1977), Molenberg (1984), Frymer-Kensky (1988), Kvanvig (1988, 270-342).

[15] MSS. containing more or less complete versions of 1En have been preserved in the Ethiopic, Greek and Aramaic languages. The Ethiopic version has been translated by *inter alios* Charles (1913), Hammershaimb (1953-76), Knibb (1978), Isaac (in Charlesworth, 1983), and Black (1985). The Greek texts (*Codex Panopolitanus* and the *Syncellus* fragments), of which none contains a complete version of 1En, are published by Black 1976. The Aramaic fragments, which were found in the Qumran caves, are published by Milik (1976). Although fragments from several different manuscripts have been found a complete Aramaic text cannot be established. I shall therefore quote 1En from the Greek text where this is available, otherwise the Ethiopic as translated by Isaac in Charlesworth 1983. If nothing else is indicated I follow the CodPan in Black's edition. Isaac (in Charlesworth 1983, 6) holds that the Ethiopic version is a direct translation of the Aramaic or Hebrew original. Similarly Knibb: "Although I think that there is good evidence available for the view that the Ethiopic translators had access to an Aramaic text of Enoch, it seems to me very difficult, in the absence of more substantial Aramaic and Greek texts of Enoch than we at present posess, to determine the extent to which the translators made use of an Aramaic text" (1978 2, 46). Against this Black (1985, 3) maintains that the Ethiopic version is a translation of a Greek "Vorlage", which itself renders an Aramaic or Hebrew "Grundschrift".

"Primary Flood tradition". Versions of the Flood story which covers more material than that found in Gen 6–9 and 1En 6–11 I shall call Flood tradition.

The Book of Jubilees too renders the tradition fairly extensively. These three texts, Gen 6–9, 1En 6–11 and Jub 5–7, somehow lie at the very heart of the representations of the Flood stories found in later Jewish and Christian writings. Considering these three texts together we are in possession of a version of the story, which was probably known to Paul and to the Christians of his time.

My reconstruction of such a primary version of the Flood tradition will begin with a study of Gen 6–9 and 1En 6–11[16] to which I shall add some comments on the rest of the Book of the Watchers.[17]

After this outline of the Primary Flood tradition from these two texts, the third extensive version of the Flood tradition, that of the Book of Jubilees, will be considered. The addition of this version to the two already mentioned will show that already at this early date there was a combination of the motifs found in Genesis and the Book of the Watchers, something which really can be called "Flood tradition". In order to simplify the exposition of the motifs involved I shall not insert the material specific to The Book of Jubilees in the first outline of the Primary Flood tradition but rather present the motifs found there as an expansion of the tradition. This second exposition may also be used for examination of other texts, which I shall then consider.

The Primary Flood tradition as contained in Gen 6–9 and 1En 6–11 is graphically outlined as follows: I present the different motifs using different indentations so that the material on the left together with the material in the middle represent the Genesis story. The pieces with the middle indentation together with those of the right represent the story according to 1 En. This outline as a whole conveys a picture of the motifs involved in the complete representation of the myth at the time of 1En 6ff. Furthermore, I shall there mark the motifs found only in Genesis with an "A", the motifs found only in 1 Enoch with a "B", and the motifs found in both Genesis and 1 Enoch with a "C". I hope that it will hereby be possible easily to recognize both the similarities and dissimilarities between these two texts.

[16] The reason for limiting the text used for the outline to 1 En 6–11 is that this text apparently contains an old version of the Flood tradition which was inserted into 1En (see Milik 1976, 25f.; Nickelsburg 1981, 48–55; Kvanvig 1988, 85–104). This can be inferred from the following evidence: 1) 1En 12:1 makes a clear break in the text. It starts a new section by returning to a presentation of Enoch, although the story from the previous text is continued in some sense. 2) In this book of 1En the figure of Enoch, who is otherwise central in the text, is not present at all. 3) The material in 12–36 is of a different content. We certainly hear of the Flood and its result but what is told has a different centre of interest: We are informed of Enoch's petition for the fallen Watchers and their answer to them, and further of his journeys to the different parts of the universe.

[17] Chapters 12–36 are apparently built on the material in chapters 6–11 but have a different character.

2.1.3 The Flood Tradition in Gen 6–9 and 1 Enoch 6–11

C	Men multiply and fair daughters are born to them
B	The sons of God (angels) see the women and desire them
B	The angels swear an oath to descend
C	The angels marry the women
B	The names of the rebellious angels are listed
B	The angels teach the women heavenly secrets
B	The angels consume the produce of men, then they consume animals, men and finally each other
B	The earth cries and complains
A	God limits the life of men to 120 years
C	The giants are born
B	The giants destroy creation
B	Earth (or the murdered men's souls) complains
B	The good angels discover the bloodshed on earth
B	The angels petition the Lord on behalf of the earth
A	God sees the wickedness of men on earth
C	Noah, being righteous, finds favor in the sight of God
A	God regrets the creation of mankind
C	A message is delivered to Noah how to save himself
B	The good angels are sent to bind the fallen angels
B	The evil angels are cast into prison
B	The fallen angels will be judged
B	The children of the angels are made to kill each other
B	Earth is promised a new life
C	Noah is told to build the Ark
A	God instructs Noah about the building of the Ark
A	God orders Noah to take into the Ark all kinds of animals on earth
A	Noah enters the Ark
A	God sends the Deluge
A	The rising of the waters is described
A	God remembers those in the Ark
A	God stops the water
A	Noah sends a raven and a dove to see if the earth is accessible
A	Noah leaves the Ark
A	Noah builds an altar and makes an offering to God
A	Noah is ordered to multiply and fill the earth
A	Noah [= man] is made to rule over everything on earth
A	Noah [= man] is forbidden to consume blood
A	God makes a Covenant with Noah
A	The sign of the Covenant, the rainbow, is introduced
C	The blessing of Creation is described
B	Injustice, oppression, pollution, plague, suffering are destroyed
B	The "plant of righteousness" will appear
B	The earth will be cultivated in righteousness
B	The earth will produce in abundance
B	All nations will prostrate themselves and worship the Lord

2.1.3.1 Some Comments on the Flood Tradition according to Genesis and 1 Enoch

The opening verses of Genesis and 1 Enoch demonstrate the differences between the books. The opening words of Genesis make the aim of the book clear: "In the beginning God created ... ". Genesis explains the beginning of all things and thus concentrates on laying the foundation for Jewish religious beliefs.[18] This relates especially to the first eleven chapters of the book. 1 Enoch, on the other hand, opens: "The blessing of Enoch, by which he blessed the elect righteous who will have to be present on the day when all the enemies are cursed and the righteous are saved".[19] The book is addressed to "the elect", thus to a distinct group of people. As it is designated a "blessing" it is comforting rather than dogmatic in outline. These observations on the different perspectives will help us understand the different characters of the two versions of the Flood story.

Regarding the above outline of the motifs contained in the Flood tradition, several differences immediately leap to the eye: Thus the two texts assign different weight to the different parts of the story. Genesis shows very little interest in the sons of God and the giants, who on the other hand are crucial for 1 Enoch. In fact, in Genesis we only hear that the sons of God went to the daughters of men who bore them children. The giants are just mentioned as being on earth at that time and as the mighty men of renown. The interest is on the righteous Noah and the salvation of Creation. Thus a long sequence of the story tells how the waters rise and stand still, Noah sends out the birds and the ground dries and finally how Noah with his family and all the animals disembark from the Ark. As his first action Noah makes an offering on the new earth. In the following context the story of the three sons, who are the origin of mankind, is told.

The author of 1En 6–11, on the other hand, does not seem at all interested in the Ark nor in the development and cessation of the Flood. In fact the Ark is never mentioned. The text only says: "Tell him in my name. 'Hide yourself!' ... And now instruct him in order that he may flee, and his seed will be preserved for all generations" (10:2–3). Nor does the text state that the animals were saved with Noah in the Ark. In contrast 1 Enoch puts much weight on the story of the angels. In the later part the text dwells on the promised new earth.

---

[18] The Genesis text is in itself characterized by different sources (J and P) each of which has its own centre of interest. However, as the text of Genesis was established as a coherent unity at the time of the composition of 1En I take it here as one coherent version of the Flood tradition. (On the question of the sources of Gen 6–9 see further 2.1.3.2.)

[19] Λόγος εὐλογίας Ἑνώχ, καθὼς εὐλόγησεν ἐκλεκτοὺς δικαίους οἵτινες ἔσονται εἰς ἡμέραν ἀνάγκης ἐξᾶραι πάντας τοὺς ἐχθρούς, καὶ σωθήσονται δίκαιοι. The badly damaged Aramaic fragment 4QEn, reconstructed by Milik (1976, 141f.) seems to be very close to the Greek text.

So much for the general differences between the Genesis and the 1 Enoch versions of the Flood story. Now, let us concentrate on each of the versions separately.

2.1.3.2 The Flood Tradition According to Gen 6–9

In the introduction to the Genesis version of the story of Noah and the Flood the author has some problematic verses:

When men began to multiply on the face of the ground, and daughters were born to them, the sons of God saw that the daughters of men were fair; and they took to wife such of them as they choose. Then the Lord said, "My spirit shall not abide in man for ever, for he is flesh, but his days shall be a hundred and twenty years". The Nephilim were on the earth in those days, and also afterward, when the sons of God came in to the daughters of men, and they bore children to them. These were the mighty men that were of old, the men of renown (Gen 6:1-4).

This text is widely debated both in regard to its background[20] and concerning syntax, structure[21], and rôle in the context.[22] These first four verses in Gen 6, which in fact are developed into the centre of interest in the version of 1 Enoch, give the impression of belonging to a background different from their present context.[23] What is said of the sons of God sounds like pieces of old mythology which somehow or other happened to be included in the story. That the sons of God take daughters of men as wives seems not to be regarded as sin nor are they connected to corruption and evil on earth. After v. 4 these sons of God disappear for good from the story of the Flood in Genesis. Two further groups are mentioned in the text, the "Nephilim who were on the earth in those days", and the children of the sons of God and the daughters of men, "the mighty men that were of old, the men of renown", the giants.[24] Neither the Nephilim nor the giants appear again in Gen 6-9.[25]

---

[20] It is generally believed that the text was built on some Babylonian myth or myths, but such dependence is denied by Dexinger (1966, 29) and Westermann (1974, 474-477). For a discussion of the sources of Gen 6:1-4 see Kvanvig (1988, 260-295).

[21] See Closen (1937), Dexinger (1966,44-46), Westermann (1974).

[22] Wellhausen (1885, 317) called the text an "erratic cracked boulder" referring to what he found to be misplacements in the text, and the broken structure of the section. It has been seen as misplaced also by many other scholars, e. g. Gunkel (1901, 59), Budde (1883), Smend (1912), von Rad (1961), whereas others have tried to explain its meaning in the Gen context, e. g. Kraeling (1947), Dexinger (1966), Hendel (1987).

[23] The questions about the sources of the Genesis text of the Flood story are complicated. Usually two sources, J and P, have been presupposed, but the problem may be even more intricate. For the discussion of the sources see Gunkel (1964) Lambert (1955), Dalton (1988), Speiser (1964, lxi-lciii), Dexinger (1966), Noth (1972), Petersen (1976), Anderson (1978), Hooke (1963, 184), Hamilton (1982), Habel (1988, 13-28). Kvanvig (1988, 280-286).

[24] The LXX translates בני-האלהים as υἱοὶ τοῦ θεοῦ. In Gen 6:4 both the נפלים and the גברים are translated γίγαντες. (In Deut 2:10f., 20f. the word ענקים is transcribed Ενακιμ and the word רפאים as Ραφαϊμ.)

[25] The Nephilim are mentioned in Num 13:33, the Anakim in Deut 2:10, 21, and the Repha'im in Deut 2:20. For a discussion of Gibborim, Anakim and Nephilim see Kraeling (1947).

These points imply that behind the text of Genesis lies a more comprehensive story from which the author (or redactor) of Genesis selected those parts which were in agreement with his aim.[26]

There are two main suggestions concerning the background of Gen 6:1–4.[27] From different texts a myth has been reconstructed which is usually called a myth of "rebellion in heaven". Several passages in the OT picture Yahweh as the highest god, or even judge, seated in an assembly of gods in heaven (Deut 32:8, 43; Job 1:6; 2:1; 38:7; Ps 29:1; 82:1; 89:6ff.; Isa 14:5–21; Ezek 28:1–10, 11–19; 32:2–8). Sometimes these heavenly beings are called sons of God (Deut 32:8; Job 1:6; 2:1; 38:7).[28] In some texts we hear of a rebellious angel who was thrown out of heaven and came down to earth (Isa 14:5–21; Ezek 28:1–10, 11–19; 32:2–8). The myth behind these texts thus seems to speak of divine beings, gods or angels, who are subordinated to Yahweh in heaven. One of these demi-gods was rebellious and was cast out. This god, or angel, went down to earth in order to attack God's Creation. According to this hypothesis of the background of Gen 6–9 the sons of God are identified as these demi-gods who being cast out of heaven went down to earth for revenge.[29]

The other theory of the background of Gen 6:1–4 and 1En 6–11 refers to the Mesopotamian myths of the Flood.[30] The lists of antediluvian kings which are found in these myths according to some scholars are the origin of the expression "sons of God".[31]

In the Genesis account of the Flood the evil on earth is the starting-point for the story proper. The evil is caused by mankind. Noah is said to be the only righteous man and therefore God cares for him and through him saves all living beings for the new world after the Flood. As we have seen this motif is highly developed. God instructs Noah in detail about the Ark and the coming Flood. He orders him to save the animals. The offering of Noah and

[26] Hendel recently maintained that Gen 6:1–4 is not a foreign element inserted into the Flood story. "In Gen 6:1–4 the Yahwist has transformed the old myth according to his plan for the Genesis Primeval Cycle. The myth has been detached from the flood narrative, though it still precedes it, and a new motive for the flood has been supplied. The motive for the flood in Gen 6:5–8 is the increase of mankind's evil on the earth, not the increase of population, nor the mixing of gods and mortals" (1987, 23).

[27] For the discussion see especially Dexinger (1966), Hanson (1977), Nickelsburg (1977), Hendel (1987), Kvanvig (1988, 280–295).

[28] The meaning of the expression sons of God has been differently explained but according to most scholars they were heavenly beings, gods or angels (e.g. Herrmann 1960; von Rad 1961, 110; Hendel 1987).

[29] For a discussion of this outline of the myth see Herrmann 1960.

[30] E. g. Eissfeldt (1966, 36), Hanson (1977), Frymer-Kensky (1988), Kvanvig (1988, 286–294), Clifford and Murphy (1989).

[31] Kvanvig 1988, 159–213. Dexinger thinks that the source of Gen 6:1–4 is not a Rebellion in heaven myth nor Babylonian myth but sagas of heros who in the development of Jewish apocalypticism became angels (1966, 87). According to him the "sons of God", the "Gibborim" and the "Nephilim" are the same persons and they were not deities but heroes (*op. cit.*, 44–54).

God's response are reported at some length, and the Covenant with Noah is described in detail.

The picture of God is strongly anthropomorphic. He is directly involved with His Creation, seeing to it, and directly talking to Noah. God has feelings: He regrets that He created the living beings on the earth and smells the pleasing odour from Noah's burnt offering (8:21).

In the exposition of the Covenant after the Flood, it is to be noted that the Covenant is not only with Noah, or with mankind, but with the entire world. First, Noah is ordered to multiply and fill the earth with a new population (9:1). Second, new relations between man and animals are enjoined: a) all animals are to fear man, b) all animals are given as food for man, c) both man and animals must have reverence for the blood because life is located therein. Third, God promises not to extinguish either man or animal from the earth again. This promise is accentuated in 9:8–17 where the different kinds of animal are explicitly mentioned, "every living creature that is with you, the birds, the cattle, and every beast of the earth" (v. 10), "all flesh" (vv. 11, 15 twice, 17), every living creature (vv. 12, 15, 16) and "the earth" (v. 13). Fourth, the Covenant with Creation is marked by a special sign, visible whenever rain falls on the earth, i. e. the rainbow.

The story continues by describing the beginning of life in the new world. Noah discovers and grows the vine (a story which ends in the curse of Canaan), and divides the earth between his three sons. To the author of Genesis the rôle of Noah's sons is important as explaining the geographical distribution of the races of mankind upon the earth. Thus the whole of Chapter 10 is devoted to the description of the Semitic, Hamitic and Japhetitic races and their regions on the earth. However, I did not include this part of the account in the above outline because it does not belong to the Flood story proper.

Thus the function of the Genesis version of the Primary Flood tradition is to explain the origin of a series of phenomena and laws. It thereby also introduces a series of fundamental theological insights. These interests and theological insights can be listed as follows:

- how the rainbow came into being,[32]
- why it is forbidden to drink blood,[33]
- why there are different peoples on earth, and in particular why Canaan is accursed,

---

[32] Westermann (1974, 634) writes "Hier dient die Fluterzählung dazu, das Phänomen der Regenbogen zu erklären . . . Bevor P ihn als 'Zeichen des Bundes' erklärte, hatte der Regenbogen, wo er am Ende einer Fluterzählung vorkam, den einfachen und sich von selbst ergebenden Sinn einer Natur-erscheinung am Ende eines Urwetters oder Gewitters". Wellhausen's idea, that the rainbow was understood as the bow of the warrier Jahweh, Westermann rejects as a "völlig abwegige Erklärung" (loc. cit.).

[33] Life is understood to be contained in the blood (Gen 9:4).

- how God is directly involved in and leads history,[34]
- how God cares for the righteous, and
- how punishment was imposed on the sinners when sin increased on earth.

2.1.3.3 The Flood Tradition According to 1En 6–11

As mentioned above, the Enochic version of the Flood tradition mainly expands the picture of the angels, the "sons of Heaven" and the archangels who do not fall. What in Genesis more or less resembled a piece of foreign mythology (6:1–4) holds the central position in the story in 1 Enoch. In 1 Enoch too there is uncertainty concerning the sources of the present text.[35] Nickelsburg sees in 1En 6–11 a conflation of two traditions[36] the more important of which is connected to Semihazah and the other to 'Asa'el. The text is strongly influenced by Greek mythology.[37] Particularly the Semihazah source was greatly affected by the Prometheus myth.[38]

---

[34] According to von Rad (1968, 161f.) the idea that all people have the same origin in Noah is important to the author of Gen: "Both the Jahwist and the Priestly Document derive all the nations from the three sons of Noah: Shem, Ham, and Japheth. In so doing they follow an idea which had already taken definite shape by their time. This idea expresses, with a clarity unparalleled in the whole of the ancient world, the thought of the unity of mankind given in creation". It is remarkable, von Rad writes, that the nation of Israel is not mentioned in the list of nations. "This omission may of course be explained away by saying that, in the time of the sons of Noah, Israel was not as yet in existence. But in its picture of the spread of the nations, the Table far anticipates historical development, and does not hesitate to put into the list nations which only very much later—in fact, in the seventh century—came within the range of Israel's political field of vision. . . . . This is an end, for in the nations one of God's plans in creation was realised. Because of this Gen. x has been described as the real end of the creation stories, for the created world in which Israel found herself is here presented in its historical aspect". That the Flood story marks the shift of two epochs is confirmed by Westermann who also remarks that this is in agreement with the function of the Flood story in the Babylonian lists of kings (1974, 609).

[35] There might have existed a Book of Noah which is referred to in Jub 10:13 and 21:10 but which is now lost. Charles maintains that the following sections from 1En possibly belonged to this work: 1En 6-11; 31:1, 2a; 54:7-55:2; 60; 65:1-69:25; 106-107 plus possibly Jub 7:20-39 and 10:1-15 (Charles I, 1913, 168. For a discussion of the Book of Noah see Charles 1912 and Lewis 1968, 10-15) The existence of a Noah book is accepted by Hammershaimb (1953, 71), Hartman (1966, 51), Milik (1976, 56) and Kvanvig (1988, 88 without exact definition of which passages belonged to it). It is denied by Frost (1952, 166). As in Gen 6-9 Hanson sees a myth of rebellion in heaven behind the story of the Flood in 1En (1977). Nickelsburg speaks of a myth of angelic revolt (1977, 404). For the recent debate see Kvanvig (1988, 270-275, 280-283).

[36] 1977, 384-386, 399-404. Cf. Dimant (1978, 323ff.), Hanson (1977), Collins (1978, 315f.).

[37] The Semihazah Tradition Nickelsburg believes has been developed out of the old tradition of a revolt in heaven (e. g. Isa 14). "However, in the present case, the nature of the revolt was deduced from the text of Gen 6, which was read in the light of non-Jewish ideas of divine descent circulating in the Hellenistic world" (1977, 404). According to Nickelsburg the Greek myths have influenced the Semihazah story in 1En 6-11 (op cit, 395ff.). The 'Asa'el story was probably developed from Gen 4:22-24 (*op. cit.*, 399).

[38] Indeed the questions of the sources of Gen 6-9 and 1En 6-11 only affect the present study to a slight extent since I am here primarily interested in the version of Gen which was read by Paul and the Early Church. They probably had access to a version of Genesis which was very close to what we have to day.

The Enochic version of the Flood tradition starts in heaven where the angels, οἱ ἄγγελοι υἱοὶ οὐρανοῦ, (the name in 1En 6:2 for those who in Gen 6:2 are called "sons of God"[39]) see the daughters of men and desire them. The angels are aware that this is a sin and fearing that not all will participate therein they bind themselves with an oath to fulfil the deed. They descend and take earthly women as wives. The angels begin to tell the people forbidden heavenly secrets: "and they taught (ἐδίδαξαν) them about poison and charms and cutting of roots and [the use of] plants they made known (ἐδήλωσαν) to them" (7:1b).[40] And still more explicitly 8:1–3:[41]

Azael taught men how to make swords, weapons, shields, and breastplates, which is knowledge belonging to angels. And he showed them the metals and how they are worked, and further armlets, decorations, the shadowing of the eyelids, and all kinds of selected stones, and dyeing. And a great impiety came into existence and they fornicated and erred and they vere corrupt in all their ways. Semihazah taught enchantments and cutting of roots, Armaros releasing of charms, Baraquial astrology, Chochial knowledge of signs, Sathial seeing of stars, and Serial the course of the moon.

The women gave birth to the giants "whose heights were three thousand ells" (πηχῶν τρισχιλίων, 1En 7:2).[42] In their insatiable appetite they devoured all that men produced and thereafter "turned against the people in order to eat them. And they began to sin against birds, wild beasts, reptiles, and fish. And their flesh was devoured the one by the other, and they drank blood" (7:5). Being violated in this way the earth cried out to heaven. The cry of the earth is described twice: "Then the earth accused the lawless" (7:6); "when the people were killed the cry rose to heaven" (8:4).[43] It is reiterated in the comments by the angels: "the voice of those crying on the earth reaches to the gates of heaven" (9:2), and finally in their prayer: "and now see the souls of those who are dying cry out and complain unto to the gates of heaven and their groaning has ascended" (9:10).[44]

---

[39] The expression υἱοὶ οὐρανοῦ paraphrases the OT בני-האלהים. In Jewish intertestamental and later literature אלהים is often paraphrased שמים (Kuhn 1935, 570). The double designation seems to express the author's interpretation of the sons of God as angels.

[40] Sync. 7:2: καὶ ἐδίδαξαν ἑαυτοὺς καὶ τὰς γυναῖκας ἑαυτῶν φαρμακείας καὶ ἐπαοιδίας.

[41] Ἐδίδαξεν τοὺς ἀνθρώπους Ἀζαὴλ μαχαίρας ποιεῖν καὶ ὅπλα καὶ ἀσπίδας καὶ θώρακας, διδάγματα ἀγγέλων, καὶ ὑπέδειξεν αὐτοῖς τὰ μέταλλα καὶ τὴν ἐργασίαν αὐτῶν, καὶ ψέλια καὶ κόσμους καὶ στίβεις καὶ καλλιβλέφαρον καὶ παντοίους λίθους ἐκλεκτοὺς καὶ τὰ βαφικά. καὶ ἐγένετο ἀσέβεια πολλή, καὶ ἐπόρνευσαν καὶ ἀπεπλανήθησαν καὶ ἠφανίσθησαν ἐν πάσαις ταῖς ὁδοῖς αὐτῶν. Σεμιαζᾶς ἐδίδαξεν ἐπα[ο]ιδὰς καὶ ῥιζοτομίας· Ἀρμαρὼς ἐπαοιδῶν λυτήριον· Βαρακιὴλ ἀστρολογίας· Χωχιὴλ τὰ σημειωτικά· Σαθιὴλ ἀστεροσκοπίαν· Σεριὴλ σεληναγωγίαν. τῶν οὖν ἀνθρώπων ἀπολλυμένων ἡ βο[ὴ] εἰς οὐρανοὺς ἀνέβη. (1En 8:1–3).

[42] The Ethiopic reads: "the women became pregnant and gave birth to great giants whose heights were three hundred cubits".

[43] τότε ἡ γῆ ἐνέτυχεν κατὰ τῶν ἀνόμων (7:6); τῶν οὖν ἀνθρώπων ἀπολλυμένων ἡ βοὴ εἰς οὐρανοὺς ἀνέβη (8:4). The first sentence is missing in Sync. 8:4 can partly be read in the Qumran fragments (4QEnᵃ): ‎ולקבל מבד ק[צת אנשא] מן ארעא וק[לה] סלק ק[דם שמיה.

[44] καὶ νῦν ἰδοὺ βοῶσιν αἱ ψυχαὶ τῶν τετελευτηκότων καὶ ἐντυγχάνουσιν μέχρι τῶν πυλῶν τοῦ οὐρανοῦ, καὶ ἀνέβη ὁ στεναγμὸς αὐτῶν.

57

The archangels heard the cry and saw what was happening. They were dismayed and petitioned God on behalf of the earth and its inhabitants (see below). At the prayer of the angels God acted. The punishment for the crimes was decided and the archangels were sent to execute judgment. The text ends with a description of the unbelievable blessings and the righteousness of the coming age, which will appear after the cleansing of the earth (i. e. the Flood).

The version of the Flood tradition contained in 1 Enoch differs on some decisive points from that in Genesis.

1) There is a difference in regard to the question of the origin of evil: The evil on earth is introduced by the angels who left heaven to marry the daughters of men. The "sons of heaven" are presented as highly ranked angels. The sins of the angels are explicitly mentioned: they were heavenly beings and the original crime happened already in heaven. This crime is committed consciously and intentionally. The sins of the angels are the following: a) they desired the daughters of men, knowing that this desire was sinful (6:2f.), b) they polluted themselves by the sexual contact with the women (9:8), c) they taught the women heavenly secrets which provoked sinful behavior on earth (8:1–4; 9:8; 10:7f.), and d) the offspring of the angels and the women, the giants, were evil and started bloodshed on earth (7:3–6; 9:10). Thus evil was forced on helpless Creation, both human and subhuman. The evil is thereby described as twofold: a) the violence of the giants and b) the teaching of the angels which penetrated and perverted the entire world. The main interest falls on the teaching of the angels.

2) The picture of God in 1En 6–11 differs considerably from that of Gen 6–9. 1 Enoch shows a God Who is transcendent and Who does not act except through the angels, whereas in Genesis He acts directly with His Creation. Thus it is the archangels who observe what happens on the earth (9:1ff.), petition God on behalf of the earth (9:4–11), and are sent to execute His will in regard to the evil (Chapter 10). But although God seems to be aware of what happens on earth only through the action of the angels, He is not conceived as ignorant. The angels pray:[45]

You are the Lord of lords, and the God of gods, and the King of the ages. Your glorious throne stands throughout all the generations of the world, and your holy and great and blessed name lasts throughout all ages. For you have made everything and possess all power, and everything is open and revealed (ἀκάλυπτα) in front of you. You see all that Azael has done, who taught all forms of unrighteousness on earth and who made known (ἐδήλωσεν) the eternal secrets (μυστήρια) which are in heaven which men perform and learned, and (so did) Semiazas, to whom you have given power to rule over his companions. They went to the daughters of men of earth, and they slept with them and defiled themselves and made known (ἐδήλωσαν) to them all sins. And the women gave birth to giants by whom the whole earth has been filled with blood and injustice. And now see, the souls of those who have died cry and complain

[45] 1En 9:4–11.

unto the gates of heaven and their groaning (ὁ στεναγμὸς αὐτῶν) ascended, but it cannot escape from the face of the unlawfulness that is being done on earth. And you know everything even before it comes to existence, and you see these things and you allow them but you do not tell us what they should do about it.

God is thus pictured as knowing everything but remaining silent until the time when the groaning of oppressed Creation rises high. He will act at the proper time through His intermediaries, the angels.

3) Noah as a person plays no prominent roll in 1 Enoch. However, the Covenant which is made after the Flood sets the stage for the new era to come. The importance of this part of the story is evident from the wide range of the material. There are two very prominent features of this motif. First, in the new promised era the earth will blossom as in Paradise. All plants will bear abundantly and life will be easy. Secondly, much space is devoted to the thought of the righteousness of this era: "And the earth will be worked in righteousness" (1En 10:18). Hartman drew attention to the unusual width of the eschatological perspective of this text.[46] God says: "And all nations shall serve and give thanks and worship me" (10:21).[47]

4) 1En 6–11 applies a perspective of history very different from that of Genesis, and this is an important feature of the book. Genesis considers the story as part of past history. At first 1 Enoch likewise describes the situation before the Flood as an historical event. However, when God's order of punishment for the sinners has been recounted, the story moves over into a future perspective.[48] God orders the binding of the evil angels, their imprisonment, the warning of Noah together with his family and the new era after the Flood. But all this is reported as not yet established.[49] Furthermore, the water of the Flood acquires new significance in the Book of the Watchers in that it means both punishment and cleansing and thus makes the new world possible. Thus the text performs a prophetic function. The judgment pronounced by God is expressed in the future from the perspective of the assumed author, Enoch. Of course the readers of 1 Enoch know the story of Noah and the Flood which has already happened. This is evident already in the fact that the text is written as a "midrash"[50] on Gen 6–9. However, by applying the

[46] 1983, 19f.

[47] καὶ ἔσονται πάντες λατρεύοντες οἱ λαοὶ καὶ εὐλογοῦντες πάντες ἐμοὶ καὶ προσκυνοῦντες. The Ethiopic version: "And all the children of the people will become righteous, and all nations shall worship me; and they will all prostrate themselves to me" (10:21).

[48] Hartman 1983, 22.

[49] The Ethiopic version of 1En 10:4b-6 is rendered by Isaac (in Charlesworth 1983) in English in the past tense: "And he made a hole in the desert which was in Duda'el and cast him there; he threw on top of him rugged and sharp rocks. And he covered his face in order that he may not see light; and in order that he may be sent into the fire on the great day of judgment." Knibb (1978), however, translates these verses as part of God's order and thus renders the events as not yet fulfilled. Thus also Hammershaimb (1953). Similarly the cod. Pan. and Sync. The text is missing in the Qumran fragments.

[50] See notes 10 and 11.

future perspective the author makes the story a type of the coming final judgment. Thus the Flood story is offered to the readers as an assurance that justice will finally be established, and that rest and blessing will come for the righteous and oppressed at the end of time.

The "midrash" in 1En 6–11 thus seems to present a set of ideas which are different from those of Gen 6–9. The main problem treated in the text pertains to evil. The perspective of this text could even be rephrased as a series of questions and answers:

- Question: Whence did evil come? Answer: It did not come from man but from spiritual powers, from the heavenly sphere, actually from powers originally subject to God.
- Question: Why is God silent in regard to evil on earth? Answer: He knows everything and He will extinguish evil.
- Question: Why does evil rule the world? Answer: The rule of evil is only illusory. God has the real power and He will put an end to evil.
- Question: What will become of the earth, so ruined by evil? Answer: God will recreate paradise on a new, righteous earth. The whole world will return to its original conditions and all mankind will fear God.

In 1En 6–11 we easily recognize the story of Noah and the Flood although the author in fact develops his text mainly from the first four verses of that text. He did not only use Genesis but also some other source when composing his text. His main interest was to discuss the question of the origin and end of evil. In the text the story of Noah and the Flood is turned into an eschatological vision. The author thus places his readers in the time before the Flood and tells the story in the form of God's command to destroy the earth, save Noah and recreate the world. Thus what the author of Genesis tells as past history in 1 Enoch is told as still to happen. This way of using the Flood tradition follows the device *"Urzeit wird Endzeit"*.[51] The story thus becomes an apocalypse speaking of the current fight between good and evil. Like so many other "apocalyptic" writers the author of 1 Enoch thus used the traditional material in order to speak to his own time.[52]

---

[51] Thus Nickelsburg 1977, 388. Cf. Hanson (1977, 201): "The primordial drama is used to account for the sum total of evil in this world, since that evil is derived from the gigantic offspring generated by heavenly rebels. . . . This is not exactly the pattern *Endzeit wird Urzeit*, in the classical sense of *repetition* of the primordial drama, but rather represents the extension of that drama to encompass all time from the original rebellion of divine beings to the eschaton. What it amounts to is nothing short of a radical mythologization of Israel's earlier perception of history".

[52] Discussing the apocalyptic genre exemplified in Dan7-12, 1En, 4Ezra and 2Bar. Hanson says: "Most of the apocalypses mentioned above seem to stem from settings of persecution within which they reveal to the faithful a vision of reversal and glorification" (1976 "Genre", 28).

2.1.4 Some Further Motifs from the Book of the Watchers

The Book of the Watchers (1En 1–36) has gone through a redaction history. The tradition contained in the Watcher story (1En 6–11) was expanded by a series of new motifs. The introduction (1–5) belongs to the younger elements, and still later other parts were added so as to create the present version of the Book of the Watchers.[53]

Enoch appears as a petitioner on behalf of the fallen angels. This motif seems to have been important to the author as it is discussed in great detail (12:4–16:3).[54] The book further explains the origin of the evil spirits in 15:8–12.

But now the giants who were born from the (union of) the spirits and the flesh are mighty spirits upon the earth, and their dwelling place shall be in the earth. Evil spirits went out from their bodies because they were of the higher world, and from the holy Watchers was their beginning and creation and original foundation. They will be called evil spirits. Heavenly spirits shall have their residence in heaven but the spirits who were born on earth shall have their residence on earth (15:8–10).

The Giants were born of women, and consequently were flesh and blood. However, as their fathers were angels, when their bodies died in the Flood their spirits survived, being of heavenly origin, and continue to lead people astray.[55] The angels are imprisoned since the Flood and are waiting for their judgment: the evil spirits, however, will not be punished until the last day (16:1).[56]

A large part of the *Book of the Watchers* recounts how Enoch, who is the protagonist, travels to the utmost ends of the universe (1En 17–19, 20–36). During these travels he sees the places of final punishment of the Watchers (18:10–19:3; 21:1–10; 27:1–5) as well as those where the righteous will dwell (24:1–26:6). There are places for the fallen angels where they wait for the judgement (21:1–10) and also for the righteous where they await their reward (25:1–26:6). The place where the righteous dwell is one of rest and peace but the place of the fallen angels and the sinners is one of torment.

[53] I do not intend here to go into the question of the sources behind the Book of the Watchers. For the history of redaction see Nickelsburg 1981, 47-54, 90-93, 145-149.

[54] A whole story is built on this idea: The angels send him to proclaim destruction to the fallen angels (12:4–13:2); The fallen angels ask him to petition God for them (13:3-5); Enoch writes the supplication down, and reads it (13:6-7); Enoch has a dream and returns to the angels (13:8–14:7); Enoch is taken to the throne of God (14:8-25); Enoch is sent by God to the Watchers (15:1–16:3). The motif of Enoch's intercession is taken up and further developed in 2En 7:1-5; 18:1-9.

[55] The story of the unclean spirits is further developed in Jub 10. Noah, seeing that the evil spirits lead his descendants astray, prays to God that the power may be taken from the spirits. The leader of the evil spirits, Masthema, however, protests. God then allows one tenth of the spirits to remain and the rest of them are imprisoned in hell.

[56] This thought is known also in Jub 10:5-11 and in the New Testament, Mt 8:29 (Charles II, 1913, 198 note 1), and Mt 25:41.

The author has thus further developed the theological implications of the sins of the angels. Fundamentally their offence consists in disobeying divine commands. As immortal beings, the angels belong to heaven and do not need procreation. But they abandon their place in heaven and go down to earth where they act "like the children of the earth" (15:3). The significance of their actions is that the divine order of difference between heaven and earth is broken. The sin is accurately defined by a description of what the angels were and what they have done. They were a) holy, b) spiritual, c) eternal and d) living in the high heaven (15:4), but defiled themselves with the earthly women and produced blood and flesh. In contrast to angels men and women need reproduction because flesh is mortal which angels are not. The angels also defiled people and led them astray so that they offered sacrifices to demons as to gods (19:1).

This picture does not accord with Gen 6–9. In Genesis the sin was not introduced by angels but by the serpent. The author of 1 Enoch thus faces a conflict between Genesis and the "midrash" he built on it (1En 9–11). He avoids a radical dualism by saying that because of the lust of the angels God gave them the women as wives (15:5–7). God made their thoughts real, and allowed the Fall, which had already happened in their minds, to become a reality. Guilt is also attached to the women who attracted the angels. The women will be punished for this sin—they will be transformed into sirens (19:2).[57]

The heavenly secrets which the angels revealed to the women are said to be rejected secrets (16:2f.). This statement explains how heavenly secrets could be evil and how it was possible for fallen angels to know secrets in heaven.

The author of 1En 1–36 only mentions Noah in passing (10:1–3) and concentrates his story on the angels, the giants, and the evil spirits. Above all he dwells on the description of the place of punishment of rebellious angels and humans and the corresponding place of blessing for the righteous. The author thus moves further in developing and applying the tradition.

2.1.5 The Flood Tradition in the Book of Jubilees

A third major representation of the Flood tradition is to be found in the Book of Jubilees which is dated to the middle of the second century BCE.[58] Nickelsburg describes the historical setting for the book as that of the oppres-

---

[57] Cod. Pan.: καὶ αἱ γυναῖκες αὐτῶν τῶν παραβάντων ἀγγέλων εἰς σειρῆνας γενήσονται. The Ethiopic text is uncertain. Hammershaimb, Knibb and Isaac translate "peaceful". (Hammershaimb points to the possibility of a dittography of the ς in εἰς). The Ethiopic is differently translated. Knibb translates: "And their wives, having led astray the angels of heaven . . .", Isaac: "And their women whom the angels have led astray . . ." (in Charlesworth 1983).

[58] Nickelsburg 1981, 79; according to Wintermute 161–140 B.C.E. (in Charlesworth 1985, 44); Eissfeldt dates the book to around the end of the second century B.C.E. (1966, 607f.).

sion in the reign of Antiochus Epiphanes.[59] All Jewish customs such as circumcision, celebration of the Sabbath and the feasts, avoidance of certain foods, reading the Jewish scriptures were forbidden, and Gentile customs were enforced. The Book of Jubilees was written as a protest and as encouragement to the people not to abandon the customs of their forefathers but, if so was necessary, even to die for the Jewish religion. As in Genesis and 1 Enoch the introductory verses of the book reveal the aim of the author:

This is the Account of the division of Days of the Law and the Testimony for Annual Observance according to their Weeks (of years) and their Jubilees throughout all the years of the World, as the LORD told it to Moses on mount Sinai when he went up to receive the tablets of the Law and of the commandment, by the word of the LORD, as he said unto him, "Come up to the top of the Mountain".[60]

The reader is informed that an essential aspect of the following account pertains to chronology or, rather, to calendar problems, which are to be assessed according to the Law given to Moses on Sinai.

The author of The Book of Jubilees used both Genesis and 1En, although, as we have seen, at certain points these differ from each other.[61] Here, however, the author follows Genesis more than 1 Enoch. God sent the Watchers to the earth (5:6) "in order to teach the sons of men, and perform judgement and uprightness upon the earth" (4:15). Thus they arrived on earth for a good purpose. However, seeing the earthly women they desired them and took wives from them. This was a sin, and Enoch "bore witness to the Watchers, the ones who sinned with the daughters of men because they began to mingle themselves with the daughters of men so that they might be polluted" (4:22). Still, the Flood did not come on account of the sin of the watchers but because of "all of the evils of the children of men" (4:24). Sin has been present on the earth since Adam.

The Flood story proper is presented in Chapters 5–7, starting with a slightly changed quotation from Gen 6:1–2, 5 to which is added a passage compiled from Genesis and 1 Enoch:

And injustice increased upon the earth, and all flesh corrupted its way; men and cattle and beasts and birds and everything which walks on the earth.[62] And they all cor-

---

[59] 1981, 78-80.

[60] Jub is quoted from the translation by Wintermute (in Charlesworth, 1985).

[61] Concerning the relations between Gen, Jub and 1En see VanderKam 1978.

[62] Sin is associated only with Creation, just as in Gen and the guilt is on all the created earth (cf. 4:23). Cf. 1En 7:5: "They began to sin against birds, wild beasts, reptiles and fish. And their flesh was devoured the one by the other"; Gen 6:5: "The Lord saw that the wickedness of man was great in the earth, and that every imagination of the thoughts of his heart was only evil continually"; Gen 6:12: "And God saw the earth, and behold, it was corrupt; for all the flesh had corrupted their way upon the earth". In Gen 6:3 we find the statement that the lifetime of men will be limited to 120 years. This notice is not to be found in 1En 6-11 but is taken up in Jub 5:8 in a quotation from Gen. But being placed in the middle of an exposition of the giants the time limit here becomes applied to antediluvian people.

rupted their way and their ordinances, and they began to eat one another. And injustice grew upon the earth and every imagination of the thoughts of all mankind was thus continually evil (Jub 5:2).

The continuation of Jubilees, however, is close to 1 Enoch. The fallen Watchers are bound and kept beneath the surface of the earth, while the giants are destroyed. A new situation is created. In 1En 10:7 we read: "And he will proclaim life to the earth: that he is giving life to her", and further "and in those days the whole earth will be worked in righteousness" (10:18). These items are recast in Jub 5:12: "And he made for all his works a new and righteous nature so that they might not sin in all their nature for ever, and so that they might all be righteous, each in his kind always". According to The Book of Jubilees the Lord thus created a new nature in the righteous people after the Flood, a nature which would prohibit evil from again entering the world. The final judgment is also proclaimed. Noah is bidden to build the Ark and save himself and his family. The Flood comes. Noah's offering after the Flood is given a new character by the words: "And he made atonement for the land, and he took a kid of a goat, and he made atonement by its blood for all the sins of the land" (6:2). This is followed by the Genesis story of God's Covenant with Noah. The sacrifice of Noah thereby in The Book of Jubilees[63] constitutes an etiology of the Feast of Weeks (6:20bf:).[64]

The author assigns great significance to chronology. Throughout the story he is careful to point out the days, weeks and years in which the different events happen.[65] Similarly he frequently uses the expression "it is written and ordained on the heavenly tablets",[66] which enforces the idea of a divine plan according to which everything must occur. The day of Noah's landing and sacrifice is particularly important: "And on the first of the third month, he went out of the Ark, and he built an altar on that mountain" (Jub 6:1f.). The commandment to keep exactly that day as the Feast of Weeks is repeated over and over again.[67] To strengthen this still further it is told that Noah and his sons, Abraham, Isaac and Jacob and their children celebrated the Feast and kept the Covenant (6:18f.). In order that the Feast be held on the correct day the solar year is commanded. This idea is voiced by Noah admonishing

---

[63] According to Charles (II, 1913, 22 notes 17f.) the Feast of Weeks is connected to the Covenant with Noah only in Jub 6:17f.

[64] This recasting of the motif opened up new possibilities for its use. Noah was seen as acting on behalf of the earth. When the 120 years mentioned in Gen 6:3 later became a time of repentance before the Flood Noah was regarded as a preacher of repentance (SibOr I, 127-129, 147-198; Josephus *Ant* I, 74; GenR 30, 7; EcclR.9, 15 §1; TBSanh 108a—b; Yashar Noah 14a—b; Sifre N, 43; Midrash Tannaim 39; Mekilta Shirah 5, 38b; Mekilta RS 32).

[65] 5:1 (even the angels arrived in "a certain year of this jubilee"); 5:22, 23, 27, 29 (twice), 30 (twice), 31, 32; 6:1, 10 ("in this month"), 17 ("in this month"), 21 ("in this month"), 23, 25, 26, 27; 7:1, 2.

[66] 5:13, 14, 17, 18, 6:29, 31.

[67] 6:11f., 13f., 17, 20f., 22, 24, 28, 31f.

his children (6:32–38) and thus made part of the Flood story. Thus already prior to the Covenants with Abraham and Moses there was a divine Law which should not be broken.

In Chapter 7 the author, following the text of Genesis, recounts the story of Noah's plantation of the vine. Noah admonishes his children in a farewell discourse. In this speech the author uses traditional material earlier found in the Book of the Watchers: the Watchers sinned against their nature and went "fornicated with the daughters of men" (7:21). It was the giants who killed and devoured one another. The author even quotes 1En 7:5: "And afterward, they sinned against beasts, and birds and everything which moves or walks upon the earth".[68] Noah also warns his sons against the demons which mislead people (7:27).

The author thus makes use of the story of the Watchers in 1En 6–11. However, coming in conflict at certain points with Genesis version he twists the motifs from the Enochic version to fit the former text.

Finally a word about the temporal perspective. The apocalyptic coloring so prominent in 1 Enoch is not central to the interpretation in Jubilees which rather follows the view of Genesis. Thus the material is considered to refer to the past. Nevertheless the author wants to say something about his own time. He does so out from the narrated "history". Everything is told as a "midrash". The homiletic elements become the more frequent the more the story develops and the author finally preaches. The major interest is clear: By denoting the precise time at which the different episodes happen the author creates a calendar for the necessary festivals in the liturgical year. This interest also obliges him to be careful in preserving the notices of sacrificial character in Genesis.[69] Noah's sacrifice therefore is made in order to bring atonement for the world.

To sum up: in The Book of Jubilees we recognize material concerning Noah and the Flood which is common to several different texts, primarily Genesis and 1 Enoch. The author has reshaped the tradition. He tries to enforce certain cultic usages. In regard to the Flood tradition the following characteristics can be observed:

- The chronological notices are of primary interest to the author of The Book of Jubilees since they enabled him to stress the importance of the liturgical year.
- The main purpose of the story is to explain the origin and the importance of the Feast of Weeks.
- The commandment to keep to the solar year is made part of the Flood tradition.

---

[68] The text is a sophisticated compilation of Gen and 1En which I do not analyse.
[69] Jub 6:1-4 (cf. Gen 8:20-22).

- The angels were sent by God and came to teach men righteousness.
- The angels fell while they were on earth. Sin thus was already present on earth when the angels arrived, i. e. it was introduced through Adam.
- Noah's sacrifice was a sacrifice of atonement for the earth.

The three versions of the Flood tradition (in Genesis, 1 Enoch, Jubilees) now discussed were available in Paul's time. That the tradition was used by the Earliest Church is evident from the quotations in the NT[70] and in the writings of the earliest Fathers.[71] The traditional material was considerably larger in Paul's time. The development had not ceased as will be shown. What has been said up till now illustrates the kernel of the traditional material which authors used as they saw fit. Some aspects of this use will now be studied.

2.2 The Use of the Flood Tradition

The Flood tradition contains such rich material that it naturally attracted the interest of many authors and was used as a source of ideas in many different fields of work. As we have seen c. 100 B.C.E. comprehensive versions of the Flood tradition were in use among Jewish authors, and, in fact, it has never been neglected.[72] It was used extensively in Jewish[73] and Christian literature.[74] Thus it is no surprise to find it also in Muslim writings.[75] The Flood tradition was important also to the Gnostics, and with them underwent interesting metamorphoses.

I have outlined the elements of the older tradition above.[76] However, in the literature it has assumed different shapes. Sometimes many, sometimes few of the motifs are used. Or the motifs are augmented and changed to such a degree that they are hardly recognizable. I shall now, for my purpose, try to indicate a) different uses of the Flood tradition in terms of content, and b) different ways or methods of application.

[70] Gen and 1En are represented in the NT writings but Jub is poorly, if at all, represented.

[71] Bamberger (1952, 73-86), Lewis (1968, 101-120).

[72] See for instance Allen, 1949.

[73] Material from the Flood tradition is in fact used in all the different layers of the Jewish literature, Old Testament, Apocrypha, Pseudepigrapha, Qumran, Wisdom literature and the Rabbinic literature. See further Bamberger (1952, 3-54, 89-194), Lewis (1968), Jung (1924-26).

[74] Some evidence of the early Christian use will be presented in the following pages. For an exposition of the overwhelming mass of references made by the Church Fathers see Lewis (1968, 100-120, 156-180), Jung (1924-26).

[75] Jung (1924-26).

[76] See 2.1.3-5.

2.2.1 The Flood Tradition as Expression of Religious Beliefs and as Argument for Religious Institutions

In the texts, which served to outline the early content of the Flood tradition, we have already seen several examples of the use which will be discussed here. In the Jewish faith the story of the Flood was comprehended as part of God's revelation of Himself in history. In the mythological understanding of history the tradition was yielded for etiological explanations of different religious doctrines as well as of natural phenomena.

2.2.1.1 Etiological Uses

From the texts already discussed the etiological use of the Flood tradition may be summed up as follows:

● The natural phenomenon of the rainbow is explained (Gen 9:8–17). At the same time the tradition gives a religious interpretation of this phenomenon: it is a sign of God's Covenant with Creation that He will never again destroy it by a flood.

● The Law's prohibition on eating blood is given an etiological explanation. In the new world after the Flood people were allowed to eat meat from animals but not to drink the blood as the giants did. The religious interpretation of this Law is that the principle of life is contained in the blood (Gen 9:4).

● The Flood tradition explains the distribution of the races on earth. The story of the drunkenness of Noah enables a religious interpretation (of some kind) of the hostility between the Jews and the Canaanites. Noah said: "Cursed be Canaan; a slave of slaves shall he be to his brothers . . . Blessed by the Lord my God be Shem; and let Canaan be his slave. God enlarge Japheth, and let him dwell in the tents of Shem; and let Canaan be his slave" (Gen 9:25–27).

● The Book of Jubilees uses the Flood tradition as an etiological explanation of the Feast of Weeks. According to Jubilees the Feast originated in Noah's sacrifice on Ararat. In order to be able to celebrate the feast on the right day the solar calendar is instituted. Thus the holy chronology is explained and at the same time religiously promoted.

2.2.1.2 Dogmatic Uses

2.2.1.2.1 The Question of the Origin of Evil
There are two areas of ancient religious thought in which the Flood tradition played a particularly important part, i. e. the beginning of evil and its end.

According to Gen 3 evil is introduced in the world through the Fall of Adam and Eve. The Book of the Watchers on the other hand assigns the origin of evil to the descent of the Watchers, who taught secret knowledge on earth and who through their offspring, the giants, caused violence and bloodshed. When recounting the story of the Flood Genesis avoids giving the impression that the sons of God had anything to do with the origin of evil. On the contrary the author presupposes that evil is already present on earth (Gen 6:5).

Jubilees combines the two stories but allows the Genesis version to dominate. The Flood is said to have come because of the perversion of Creation and not because of sin, the beginning of which lies outside the world. The main idea is that the divine order has been disturbed, and it is expressed in such sentences as: "all flesh corrupted its way; man and cattle and beasts and birds and everything which walks on the earth. And they all corrupted their way and their ordinances" (Jub 5:2). This description fits both the story of the Fall of Adam and the story of the Fall of the angels and is an important theme in 1 Enoch (e. g. 1En 2–5). In a similar way the author of 1En 65:1 (in a fragment of the assumed Book of Noah) finds the earth to have been changed: " . . . Noah saw the earth, that she had become deformed, and that her destruction was at hand". The texts use the expression "changed its orders"[77] to describe sin. The idea that the entire Creation was affected is expressed also in the Rabbinic literature according to which as soon as Noah was born many mysterious events ensued, all of which implied that the rebellion of animals and plants against man, which resulted from the Fall, had now come to an end.[78]

2.2.1.2.2 The Origin of the Evil Spirits
The Flood tradition is expanded so as to cover also the more specific question of the origin of evil spirits. This thought was developed already in the Book of the Watchers as is evident from 1En 15:8–12. The giants, who were the descendants of the angels and the earthly women, drowned in the flood. Their bodies, being human, died but their spirits, originating from the heavenly beings, are immortal. Thus they remain on earth without bodies. The understanding of the origin of evil spirits which is presented here was widely accepted and is reiterated by many authors.[79]

2.2.1.2.3 The Future and the Last Things
Because evil has been introduced and has seized power over it, the world must be destroyed. The Flood was God's first punishment of evil and is explained

---

[77] This expression, "change orders", is used as an "emblem". An "emblem" is (in literature) a word, an expression, or a sentence which is used to mark a certain idea (see further Kayser 1969, 75). The expression is used in different ways: the author of Jub accuses the entire Creation of "changing its orders", i. e. breaking the divine Law (Jub 5:2). In 1En 2–5 the readers are directed to look at the order of the subhuman Creation which has not changed its order and thereby testifies against the disorderly and thus sinful people (e. g. 1En 2–5). In both cases the expression "orders" denotes the same thing, God's Law for all created beings. This idea also seems to lie behind TNaph 3:5: "Likewise the Watchers departed (ἐνήλαξαν) from nature's order; the Lord pronounced a curse on them at the Flood".

[78] See Ginzberg I, 1947, 147; V, 168.

[79] E. g. Jub 10:5-13; Just. Apol. II, 5; Clem Hom VIII, 18f.; Athanag LegProChrist 25; Minucius Felix Octavius 26; Iren ConHer 5-28.

as the type of the final judgment already in the Apocalypse of Weeks (1En 93:1–10, 91:12–17).[80] The fallen angels are imprisoned under the earth until the final day of judgment[81] at which they will be condemned to the fire.[82] Evil people will share their fate.[83] On the basis of these thoughts a particular picture of the judgment is offered by the author of 1En 90:20–27. In this allegory of animals the righteous are pictured as white. Books are opened and the "Lord of the sheep" is about to judge the world, first of all the fallen stars, i. e. the fallen angels of the Flood tradition, are judged and thrown into the abyss "full of fire and flame" (90:24). Then all other sinners are judged. So the Flood tradition is used to demonstrate the certainty of the ultimate punishment for sin[84] and in Mt 24:37ff. (a little differently in Luk 17:26f.) testifies to the suddenness of the coming judgment. The thought of the Flood as a punishment made the author of 3Macc 2:4 use the motif of the Flood in a prayer, calling down the punishment of God on the intruder into the Temple.

Thus the Flood tradition foreshadows the coming destruction of the present world. In the *Apocalypse of Weeks* the Flood is termed "the first consummation" (93:4). This world will be destroyed in a catastrophe corresponding to the Flood. As the first so will be the final end of the rule of evil.[85] A different interpretation is found in PsPhilo. Convinced that God still punishes evil he declares that different disasters such as famine, earthquakes, pestilence and the like in the present time substitute for the Flood.[86] God's Covenant with

---

[80] The Qumran find, which contained fragments of this apocalypse, proves that this was the original sequence of the text (Milik 1976, 247).

[81] 1En 54:1–6.

[82] 1En 10:6, 12ff.; 67; 69:28; 90:20–27; 2En 18:6; Sir 16:7; 2Pt 2:4–5 SibOr II, 214–235; PsClem Hom IX,1.

[83] In Ez 32:27 Mesach and Tubal are pictured together with the fallen angels (Hendel 1987, 22 note 44). Cf. 1En 54:7–10; 65:6ff.; Mt 25:41.

[84] Se further CD II,14—III,1; 2 Pt 2:4–5; 3:6f.

[85] Cf. SibOr II:214–137; VII:6–15, 118–131; Mt 24:37, par. Luk 17:26–27; 4Ezra 3:8–11. The idea that the second judgment will be one of fire, but corresponding to the first by water, is present already in the story of the Watchers in 1En 6–11. The Watchers are detained until the final judgment when they will be trown into τὸ χάος τοῦ πυρός (1En 10:13). Cf. 2Pt 3:5–6; Jos *Ant* I, 70; Mekilta III,14: SibOr III, 690; Philo *Mos* II, 263. The idea that the first judgment was by water and the last will be by fire was further developed in LAE 49:3ff. (Lewis 1968, 15). The scheme of water—fire may have originated from the fact that Gen first presents the story of the Flood and immediately thereafter that of Sodom and Gomorrah. According to Stählin this picture functions as the basis of the preaching of John the Baptist."Wie gelegentlich schon im AT ist in der Täuferrede mit dem Bild des Feuers das der **Wasserflut** (vgl Hi 40,6) verschmolzen (vgl Ez 21, 36; 22, 31). Nahegelegt wurde diese Vereinigung der Bilder durch die Doppelüberlieferung von der Sintflut und von dem Feuerregen über Sodom und Gomorrha und durch die der bibl. Grundkonzeption 'Endzeit gleich Urzeit' entsprechende Erwartung eines großen Weltenfeuers und auch einer großen Weltenflut am Ende. In diese Zusammenhänge führt die Beobachtung, daß der Täufer nicht nur das Bild der Feuertaufe, sondern auch seine Wassertaufe mit der μέλλουσα ὀργή in Verbindung bringt (Mt 3,7)" (Stählin 1954, 437). The wrath of God is connected to the Flood in Sir 44:17 and Jub 5:6.

[86] PsPhilo *BibAnt* 3:9.

Noah that He would not send another Flood did not mean that He would stop punishing sin.

On the other hand the Flood tradition promises justice to the righteous. Thus the thought of their reward is accentuated in the Book of the Watchers.[87] Noah's salvation represents a guarantee that the righteous will survive the judgment and be rewarded by life in the new world (1En 10:17–11:2). The destruction will thus be followed by a new world. As the universe is involved into the evil brought about by the angels, so the new world which appears after the Flood is seen as a completely new Creation. A significant feature of the new world according to 1En 10 will be its righteousness.[88]

2.2.1.3 The Use of the Flood Tradition in Parenesis and Ethics

2.2.1.3.1 The Flood Tradition as Comfort

Apocalyptic literature, in which we find so many references to the Flood tradition, was created in order to give comfort and encouragement to people in times of danger and distress.[89] Therefore the Flood tradition is often moulded in forms suited to this purpose. Thus, when motifs from the Flood tradition are retold they are pregnant with sayings of comfort and encouragement. Noah may be remembered as an example of God's care (4Ezra 3:11). As we have already seen, the judgment will soon come, and the righteous will be saved and inherit the new world. In the present time the angels pray for the righteous and the suffering (1 En 9).

2.2.1.3.2 The Flood Tradition in Exhortations

In different ways the Flood tradition is used for exhortation. Punishment is prophesied if people do not turn away from sin. The use of the figure of Noah to show the gravity of the call to righteousness has a long tradition. Ezekiel 14:14–21 sharpens the prophecy of punishment for the country by saying that even if the three most righteous men known, Noah, Daniel and Job, were there, they would only be able to save themselves and not their families. In 2Clem 6:8–9 this passage in Ezekiel is turned into an admonition to " . . . keep

---

[87] The "righteous ones will escape" (1En 10:17); the earth will bear incredibly abundant fruit, 1En 10:18-11:2.

[88] 1En 10:18; 90:25-39; 91:17; Jub 5:12.

[89] This is shown in Hartman's study of 1En 10:16-11:2 under the headline "Comfort of the Scriptures" (1977, 87-96) and similarly in the study of 1En 1-5 entitled "Asking for a Meaning" (1979). Hanson describes the function of apocalyptic literature as follows: "Most of the apocalypses mentioned above [Dan 7-12, 1En, 4Esra, 2Bar,] seem to stem from settings of persecution within which they reveal to the faithful a vision of reversal and glorification (e. g. Dan 12:1)" (1976 "Genre", 28). This also seems to be the character of the story of the Watchers (1En 6-11) of which Nickelsburg writes: "It reflects a crisis in the faith of his [the author's] people, who ponder over the condition between God's complete foreknowledge and his inactivity in the midst of the present disaster" (1981, 51).

the baptism clean and unstained". The Zadokite document recalls the fate of the giants and admonishes the reader to live blamelessly in the sight of God.[90] As the Flood was God's punishment for sin it may be called the "wrath of God" (Sir 44:17).

In regard to a situation of oppression and suffering an author may try to encourage the listener/reader by material from the Flood tradition. Thus an imaginative use of the material appears in 4Macc 15:30–32 where a woman who encourages her sons to endure torture unto death for the sake of the Jewish faith is compared to the Ark resisting the roaring flood which stands for her maternal compassion.

If, on the one hand, Noah is described as an ethical pattern (on which see below), the angels and the giants are, on the other, exposed as warning examples. These warnings may be very explicit. According to 1En 65:6–11 the doom comes upon men

... because they have acquired the knowledge of all the secrets of the angels, all the oppressive deeds of the Satans, as well as all their most occult powers of those who practice sorcery, all the powers of (those who mix) many of colors, all the powers of those who make molten images; how silver is produced from the dust of the earth, and how bronze is made upon the earth—for lead and tin are produced from the earth like silver—their source is a fountain inside (which) stands an angel, and he is a running angel. ... Because their oppression has been carried out (on the earth), their judgment will be limitless before me. On account of the abstract things which they have investigated and experienced, the earth shall perish (together with) those who dwell upon her. And those (who taught them these things) will have no heaven forever, because they have revealed to them the things which are secret ...[91]

The readers are thus exhorted not to take part in any such things. Similarly in Jud v. 6 and 2Pt 2:4–5 the Christians are warned not to follow false teachers.[92] Furthermore, one should learn from the example of the giants not

[90] CD II, 17–III, 1. Cf. TNaph 3:5.

[91] Noah furthermore does not take part in such things: "but, as for you, my son, the Lord of the Spirits knows that you are pure and kindhearted; you detest the secret things" (1En 65:11). Further information about the angels' teaching is offered in 1En 69: "The third was named Gadar'el; this one is he who showed the children of the people all the blows of death, who misled Eve, who showed the children of the people (how to make) the instruments of death (such as) the shield, the breastplate, and the sword for warfare, and all (the other) instruments of death to the children of the people. Through their agency (death) proceeds against the people who dwell upon the earth, from that day forevermore. The fourth is named Pinem'e; this one demonstrated to the children of the people the bitter and the sweet and revealed to them all the secrets of their wisdom. Furthermore he caused the people to penetrate (the secret) of writing and (the use of) ink and paper; on account of this matter, there are many who have erred from eternity to eternity, until this very day. For human beings are not created for such purposes to take up their beliefs with pen and ink. For indeed human beings were not created but to be like angels, permanently to maintain pure and righteous lives. ... The fifth is named Kasadya; it is he who revealed to the children of the people (the various) flagellations of all evil—(the flagellation) of the souls and demons, the smashing of the embryo in the womb so that it may be crushed ... " (69:6–12).

[92] Jud v. 6 warns against false teachers, alluding to the Flood tradition in 1En. Similarly 2Pet 2 warning for false teachers reminds of the angels who were not spared but detained until the day of judgment (v. 4) and of the righteous Noah who was rescued (v. 5). God will act in the same way with righteous and unrighteous people (v. 9). (Reicke, 1946, 90).

to be arrogant, trusting only one's own strength (WisSol 14:6; Sir 16:7; 3Macc 2:4).

The story of the angels who fell in love with women naturally offers material for admonitions in regard to sexual behavior. So it is used in TReub 5:6 in warnings against promiscuity.[93] Men should avoid looking at women, behaviour which seduced the angels, and should have no close contact with them. Women are admonished not to approach men and not to adorn themselves.[94]

Noah planted the vine according to Gen 9:20. Using the Flood tradition the author of 3Baruch has certain difficulties with this motif. The garden of Eden was planted by two hundred thousand and three angels led by Michael. Satanael planted the vine. The waters of the Flood swept over the garden and uprooted the vine. Noah found it after the Flood and replanted it. The author asks how then can wine be used and is told that the drinking of wine in fact is a way for Satan to bring evil on earth (3Bar 4:6–17).[95]

Like the Greek and Roman philosophers the Jewish writers express their awareness of a natural Law, which actually makes a life in accordance with the will of God possible even without knowledge of the Mosaic Law.[96] The natural Law is expressed through the seven commandments given to Noah as the originator of mankind after the Flood. Evidently the Noachic Law played a certain rôle to the first Christians as an expression of the Will of God beside the Mosaic Law. According to Luke the Apostles and the Jerusalem Church imposed it on the Gentile Christians as minimal, but necessary, ethical rules.[97]

---

[93] Another parenetic use for the same area of life is found in CD V,1, where from the fact that the animals entered the Ark two by two the author draws the conclusion that God disapproves of polygamy.

[94] Cf. 1 Cor 11:10.

[95] The Greek version of this book gives it a Christian interpretation: " . . . its bitterness . . . will be changed into sweetness, and its curse will become a blessing, and its fruit will become the blood of God, and just as the race of men have been condemned through it, so through Jesus Christ Emmanuel in it (they) will receive a calling and entrance into Paradise" (3Bar 4:15). Gaylord remarks that the textual tradition of the Greek version is confused (Charlesworth 1983, 668, note y).

[96] R.Johanan said: "Had not the Torah been revealed to Israel, man would have learned modesty from the cat, honesty from the ant, chastity from the pigeon and manners from the rooster" (quote from Schultz, J.P. 1981, 360.) Paul uses the idea of the natural law in Rom 1:18-20; 2:14-16, 26–29 discussing the fallenness of both Jew and Gentile. The natural Law, the Rabbis called "the Law of the Sons of Noah". It contains seven roles: prohibition against 1) idolatry, 2) murder, 3) blasphemy, 4) sexual immorality, 5) theft, 6) avoidance of cruelty to animals, and 7) the injunction to establish courts of justice. *Op. cit.* 359.

[97] Acts 15:20, 23-29. The apostolic letter mentions only four of the seven commandments. According to Schultz "the Noahite Commandments were also seen by the Rabbis as an intermediate stage for Gentiles who were contemplating conversion to Judaism" (*op. cit.* 361).

2.2.1.3.3 Noah as Ethical Example

The righteous Noah is crucial in many writings using the Flood tradition.[98] We find Noah in different lists of the important ancient fathers.[99] Thus Noah plays a major rôle as an ethical example and, being a righteous man and a pattern of belief, is also seen as a preacher of righteousness and conversion from evil, e. g. in SibOr I:125–198; 2Pt 2:5; 1Clem 9:4–6.[100] In this case 1Clem 9:6 represents something new: certain people were saved because they listened to Noah's preaching and repented. In the story as it is otherwise told only Noah's family was saved.[101] According to the author of Heb 11:7 Noah through his building of the Ark "condemned the world". It is likely "that our author has in mind a more literal sense of Noah's condemnation, namely, the legend that he was commissioned to preach repentance. Because his contemporaries failed to accept his message, they were condemned".[102]

However, the effect of Noah's righteousness is usually seen as positive. Being righteous he was an ἀντάλλαγμα for the world (Sir 44:17). Furthermore, according to WisSol 14:6, the construction of the Ark and its voyage came about and were guided by divine wisdom, Noah became the "hope of the world", and the whole event is characterized as righteousness.[103]

2.2.1.4 The Flood Tradition as Used in Apologetics and Wisdom

The Flood myth contained material common to Jewish and Christian authors and writers from the surrounding world. So the SibOr I:97f. equates the

---

[98] Ez 14:14. 20; TBenj 10:6; Sir 44:17f.; SibOr I:148, 317; 1En 67:1ff.; Philo *Praem poem* 22f.; 2En 73:9; further VanderKam 1980; According to Philo (*Cogn* 90) Noah was the first righteous human being.

[99] In a list of "praise of the fathers" in Sir 44–50 Noah is listed as τέλειος δίκαιος. Philo *Praem poem* 11–14; Noah is mentioned in a short list of righteous fathers who married a relative in Tob 4:12; In Heb 11:7 among heroes of faith (cf. HelSynPr 12:58-60, see Charlesworth 1985); In 1Clem 7:6; 9:4 as a preacher of conversion; In HelSynPr 6:4 Noah is mentioned among people to whom God has listened, further in 9:10 he is even listed as priest together with Abel, Seth, Enos, Enoch, Melchizedek and Job.

[100] Cf. Jos *Ant.* I,3.1; GenR 30; EcclR 9.15 §1; TBSan 108a—b; Mekilta Shira 5 (38b); Ap-Paul 50. Clem Alex *Strom* 1.2.1.

[101] What is said in 1Clem actually is only a possible consequence of the general thought that Noah was a preacher of repentance. The targum of Pseudo-Jonathan to Gen 7:4 adds the information that God promised seven days to see if men would repent. If they did not, the water would come and destroy men and beasts. According to Targ Neofiti the 120 years mentioned in Gen 6:3 were given for repentance. Noah is made the preacher of righteousness who tries to convert the godless people (SibOr; 2Pt 2:4; 1Clem 7:5). According to Augustine the preaching continued for a hundred years (Augustine *De catech* 19.32). Josephus (*Ant* I,74) says that Noah's sermons were without result, but that he was threatened with death by the ungodly people. According to 1Clem 9:4 the faithful Noah through his service was found a herald of rebirth of the earth and through him the Lord saved the living beings who went into the Ark in conformity of mind (the latter detail is of course to be seen within the context of 1Clem which argues against divisions).

[102] Attridge 1989.

[103] Cf. HelSynPr 12:60f. where Noah together with his family is called "an end indeed of those who have passed on, but a beginning of those about to be born".

Watchers and the giants in Hebrew mythology and the titans[104] in the Greek. This common idea of a deluge made the Flood tradition suitable material for Jewish propaganda.[105] SibOr I–II retells the story of the Flood in the form of an oracle of which Noah's preaching is made the real centre. In proclaiming the Jewish God as the only God he commands the listener to repent (I:137–146). The listeners are called " . . . the abominable race of Rheia . . . " (I:184), which is probably to be understood as worshippers of pagan gods.[106]

The author of the *Wisdom of Solomon* interprets the history of Israel as evidence of God's wisdom.[107] He tries thereby to make the superior nature of the Jewish faith evident to the Hellenistic world. Thus the Flood too is interpreted. In the Flood God actually saved the whole world by very insignificant means (WisSol 10:4).[108]

In WisSol 14:5–6, mentioned above, the Flood tradition is used for a comparison, showing the wisdom of God in contrast to the vanity of idolatry. A man starting a voyage prays to his idol which is made of wood far inferior in quality to that of which the ship itself is built. In fact the ability to build a ship is given by the Lord (14:3, 5) and furthermore God guides the vessel on the journey: "Thus it also happened in the old days (i. e. of Noah) . . . your hand governed his journey" (14:6).

Christian authors used the Flood tradition in polemics against both Gentiles and Jews. Thus Justin adduced the motif of the righteousness of Noah as an argument against the Jews, saying that the uncircumcised Noah was saved in the Ark (Dial 19.4).[109]

2.2.1.5 The Flood Tradition as History

Certainly most of the authors from the ancient world, whose works are mentioned in this dissertation, believed the story of the Flood to be literally true even if they did not write history but used the Flood tradition for other purposes.[110] Some scholars, however, contemporary with the New Testament writers, use the story of the Flood as a source when writing history. Thus

[104] SibOr I,309; II,231; II,231f. mentions both giants and titans.

[105] In Jewish and Christian literature it is held that heathen mythology reflected a faint knowledge of the true God. In regard to the myths of the Flood and the surviving man the Gentile authors said that the Jews had only taken over the story from older non-Jewish literature (so e.g. Celsus).

[106] See J. Collins in Charlesworth 1983, 339 note p.

[107] WisSol 10.

[108] Cf. WisSol 14:6; 1En 90:30–42; 1En 91:16; 2Bar 15:7f.; 31:4; 40:3; Sir 44:17f.; 14:5–6; Sir 16:7; 44:17–18; Bar 3:26–28; Jos *Ant* I,74.

[109] There are several similar applications of the Flood tradition in the polemics against the Jews by Justin and other Fathers. See further Lewis 1968,110ff.

[110] Philo insists on the historicity of the story of the Flood: "And let no one suppose that what is here said is a myth" (about the angels who took earthly women as wives; *De Gig* 7). However, he uses the story from Gen to illustrate his philosophical teaching (see further 2.3.3.3).

Josephus in his *Antiquities* is writing the history of his people in a time when the greatness of its past needed to be recalled, and in I,2–8 he faithfully follows Genesis in retelling the Flood story.[111]

2.2.1.6 Transformation of the Flood Tradition into a New Myth

Hanson suggests that the presentation of the Flood tradition in 1En 6–11 testifies to a new introduction of myth into the old Jewish faith, because the motifs of the binding of the Watchers, their panic, and their imprisonment in the abyss draw upon a mythological complex foreign to Genesis.[112] Be this as it may, the mythical character of versions of the Flood tradition found in 1 Enoch and the Book of Jubilees was further developed in the Pseudo-Clementine writings in the fourth century C.E. PsClem *Hom* VIII contains the most detailed Early Christian version which is preserved.[113] The author rewrites the traditional story. In short *Hom* VIII, 11–19. can be summarized as follows:

The angels were grieved because men did not give thanks to God in a proper way. Having no comparable experience men did not recognise how blessed they were. Therefore the angels received God's permission to descend in order to convict those who were guilty of ingratitude. They changed themselves into precious stones, gold and pearls to see who would steal them, at which act they would transform themselves into human beings and convict the thief. By their own holy life they intended then to testify against the unrighteous sinners. However, when they transformed themselves into humans they became in all respects men and fell in love with the women. Having intercourse with the women they were defiled and lost their fiery substance. Thus weighed down they were unable to return to heaven.[114] As the women asked them for the jewelry and the precious stones they were forced to teach the people mining and art. Then they begot the giants who in their insatiable appetite began to eat all kinds of living beings and drink the blood. Therefore God sent the Flood to cleanse the earth. Like in Jubilees the Giants are said to have drowned but their spirits to have survived. Those spirits are ordered by God not to trouble the righteous but to punish the unrighteous people.

In this recounting of the Flood tradition the idea of the origin of evil spirits

---

[111] "The practice of beginning an ethnic history in primordial times was widespread, and is a mere extension of a practice extending from the Sumerian King list to Berossos and Mantheo, a practice which had already left its imprint on J and P in the Pentateuch. This impression is strengthened through comparison with Jubilees, Pseudo-Philo, and later Church historians like Eusebios and Africanus" (Hanson 1977, 196).

[112] See note 52.

[113] The Flood tradition is used in *Recognitions*, I,29–30; IV,12–13; *Homilies* VIII; IX, 1–3.

[114] τῷ γὰρ βάρει τῷ ὑπὸ τῆς ἐπιθυμίας εἰς σάρκα τελευτησάντος αὐτῶν τοῦ πόρος, τὴν ἀσεβοῦσαν ὥδευσαν ὁδὸν κάτω. σαρκὸς γὰρ αὐτοὶ δεσμοῖς πεπεδημένοι κατέσχηνται καὶ ἰσχυρῶς δέδενται, οὗ ἕνεκεν εἰς οὐρανοὺς ἀνελθεῖν οὐκέτι ἐδυνήθησαν (13,3).

plays a certain role. They result from the circumstance that heavenly beings were captured in human bodies. Thus the unclean spirits are the souls of the giants, separated from their bodies at the Flood. The reason for the sin of the angels was lust. These thoughts taken together, spirit captured in matter as a result of the sin of lust resulting in a fall from the divine order, seem to show a Gnostic colouring of the traditional story. According to Stroumsa the Pseudo-Clementine writings " . . . may indicate a transitional stage through which the myth reached Gnostic circles".[115] In the Gnostic writings most of the motifs from the Flood story are integrated into a new myth.[116]

The Gnostic book, *The Apocalypse of Adam*, is part of the development of the Flood tradition in Gnostic religion.[117] The author selected many of the motifs from the Flood tradition and mixed them with new thoughts.

3:1 "Now then, my son Seth, I will reveal to you what was revealed to me by those men whom I once saw before me. 2 After I have completed the times of this generation and the years of [the generations] have been fulfilled, the [. . . 3 lines missing]. 3 Rain showers of God the Almighty will be poured forth so that he may destroy all flesh from the earth because of the things it seeks after, including [those who] come from the seed of the men to whom the life of knowledge, which went out from me and Eve your mother, was passed on. For they were strangers to him.

4 "Afterwards great angels will come on high clouds to bring those men to the place where the spirit of life dwells [. . . 7 lines missing] from heaven to earth. 5 [But] the whole [multitude] of flesh will be left behind in the [waters]. 6 Then God will rest from his wrath. 7 He will cast his power upon the waters, and he will give power to (Noah and his wife and) his sons and their wives by means of the Ark, together with their animals, whichever he pleased, and the birds of heaven, which he called and placed upon the earth.

8 "And God will say to Noah—whom the nations will call Deucalion—'Behold, I have guarded you in the Ark, together with your wife and your sons and their wives and their animals and the birds of heaven, which you called [and placed upon the earth . . . 4 lines missing]. 9 For this reason I shall give the [earth] to you and your sons. In sovereignty you shall rule over it, you and your sons. 10 And from you no seed will come forth of the men who will not stand in my presence in another glory.'

11 "Then they will be like the clouds of great light. 12 Those men will come, the ones who were sent forth from the knowledge of the great aeons and the angels. 13 They will stand in the presence of Noah and the aeons. 14 And God will say to Noah, 'Why have you departed from what I told you? 15 You have created another race in order that you might scorn my power.'

16 "The Noah will reply, 'I shall bear witness before your might that it is not from me

[115] 1984, 31.

[116] According to Stroumsa the theme of *mixis*, which is contained in the myth of the angels' marriage to the daughters of men, constitutes the centre which was developed into Gnostic mythology. The thesis of Stroumsa is opposed by Layton (1987).

[117] See Stroumsa 1984, 82-88. According to MacRae it is possible that the ApAdam "reflects a transition from some form of apocalyptic Judaism to Gnosticism" (in Charlesworth 1983, 708). Dimant (1984, 472) finds ApAdam to be " . . . a Jewish Gnostic document in the sense of that its genre and its building-blocks are derived from Judaism. But in its intentionality it is anti-Jewish in the extreme, a product of the Gnostic revolt against the Jewish religion and the Jewish God".

that the race of these men has come, nor from [my sons . . . 5 lines missing] knowledge.'

[17]"And [he] will release those men and bring them into their proper land and build them a holy dwelling place. [18]And they will be called by that name and will dwell there six hundred years in a knowledge of imperishability. [19]And angels of the great light will dwell with them. [20]Nothing abominable will be in their hearts, but only the knowledge of God (ApAdam 3:1–20).[118]

The language in this text breathes a different religious atmosphere. It is filled with expressions which require knowledge of the religious system which is presupposed by the author.[119] Several thoughts are new and the new combinations of the motifs creates a new story. The revelation this time is given to Seth and not to Enoch. The reason for the Flood is changed. God the Almighty[120] wants to destroy mankind " . . . because of the things it seeks after". Demanding absolute observance of the Law, the inferior God wants to destroy all men because they seek things forbidden in the Law. But he also wants to destroy "those who come from the seed of the men to whom the life of knowledge, which went out from me and Eve . . . was passed on" (v. 3). The men who are in possession of this knowledge are the Gnostics. The Gnostics, however, are saved: "Afterwards great angels will come on high clouds to bring those men to the place where the spirit of life dwells . . . " (v 4). Thus the angels come not to execute the judgment ordered by God, as in 1 Enoch, but to save the Gnostics from the attack by the inferior god. Noah, however, is saved by the inferior god from the Flood in the Ark together with his family and the animals. The highest God accuses him saying: "You have created another race in order that you might scorn my power". Thus in the Apocalypse of Adam not only Noah but also some others, the Gnostics, survive the Flood. Two "races" which are separated from each other are present on earth. This is illustrated in Noah's words: ". . . it is not from me that the race of these men has come . . . ". Noah is set to rule over the earth not because of his righteousness but because God guarded him in the Ark (v. 8f.). In this way the old material from the Flood tradition has been incorporated as an essential part into the new Gnostic mythology.[121]

---

[118] Transl. MacRae in Charlesworth 1983.

[119] E. g. God "will cast his powers upon the waters" (v. 7), "stand in my presence in another glory" (v. 10), "be like the clouds of great light" (v. 11), "another race" (v. 15), "life of knowledge" (v. 3), "knowledge of imperishability" (v. 18), "knowledge of the great aeons and the angels" (v. 12).

[120] God the Almighty is also called God the ruler of the aeons (e. g. 1:4) and Sakla (e .g. 5:1). This God is the creator but he is inferior to the "eternal God". Eve had knowledge of this eternal God and taught Adam (1:3) who now teaches Seth.

[121] Further developments along the same line are to be found in *Apocryphon Johannis* and *The Hypostasis of the Archons*.

2.3 Techniques in the Use of the Flood Tradition

2.3.1 On the Use and Interpretation of Received Material

Every writer who uses a received material in some way interprets it so that it may be more or less changed in terms of form and meaning. Sometimes the received material is only slightly revised but sometimes it is transformed to such a degree that the original material is hardly recognizable. The use of the traditional or received material may be open, with references to the origin, or even with explicit quotations, but sometimes an author may only allude to it so that we may not recognize the material echoed even if it was discerned by the original readers.

In order to fit a new literary situation the received material is usually adjusted. In order to understand which rôle the traditional material of the Flood plays in the texts we should also scrutinize how the material is used. In this section I shall consider how the Flood tradition was handled in different writings and do so from two points of view; a) the author's treatment of his material, in terms of selection, combination, and shaping, and b) the way he applies it in his writing, i. e. in what form[122] he presents the received material so as to create the intended effect on the reader.

In the last part of this chapter I shall discuss some texts which use the Flood tradition indirectly or covertly. As, in my opinion, Paul in Rom 8:18ff. uses the Flood tradition in such a hidden way, I find it important to examine two examples of this use.

2.3.2 Selection, Combination and Modification of the Flood Tradition

2.3.2.1 Selection

The most obvious technical aspect of the use of already existing material consists in selecting which parts to utilize. Just as a photographer can change the view of his object by altering the angle from which the picture is shot, the writer by selection of the motif makes the reader see different points of the story. Of course the phenomenon is the same as the way in which both Jews and Christians use the Bible, selecting passages for different purposes. Some examples may illustrate how an author by selection can change the impression received from the Flood Tradition.

Biblical Antiquities 3 by Pseudo-Philo uses most of the material in Gen 6–

---

[122] Although I shall not discuss the forms in the way the form-critics such as Dibelius, Bultmann and others use the term I shall employ such concepts as allegory, comparison, myth, historical report and so on to concentrate how an author delivers the recounted material to his readers.

9.[123] CD V,1 on the other hand, for a precise ethical argument (against polygamy) uses a single element from the same text: "Also those who entered the Ark went in two by two",[124] a quotation from Gen 7:9.

The author of Sir 16:7 brings the whole story of the Flood to life in the mind of the reader by a few words: "he did not pardon the giants who were in ancient times, those who revolted [trusting] in their strength".[125] The reader is led to view the story of the Flood focusing on the giants. The accent falls on God's ruthlessness towards those who because of their trust in their own strength fell away.[126]

Again, the author of 1Clem 7:5f. makes this particular selection from the tradition:

Let us go through all the generations and learn that in generation after generation the Lord gave an opportunity of repentance to those who wanted to turn to him. Noah preached repentance and those who obeyed were saved.

The focus here is on God's giving the opportunity of repentance through Noah's preaching, which as well suits the overall message in 1Clem.

In the context of *TReu* 5:6 the author is about to warn his sons against fornication, and maintains that their wives and their daughters should not adorn themselves, in order to avoid tempting men. He refers to the Flood tradition as support for his statement, selecting one motif from it, i. e. the Watchers who saw the women and desired them:

For it was thus that they charmed the Watchers, who were before the Flood. As they continued looking at the women, they were filled with desire for them and perpetrated the act in their minds. Then they were transformed into human males, and while the women were cohabiting with their husbands they appeared to them. Since the women's minds were filled with lust for these apparitions, they gave birth to giants. For the Watchers were disclosed to them as being as high as the heavens.[127]

By selecting this single motif the author changed the accents of the traditional material.[128]

---

[123] The text of Gen is strongly compressed. Repetitions are deleted and so is the difficult verse 6:4.

[124] Transl. Vermes, 1987. The Qumran text reads וכאי התבה שנים שנים באו אל התבה (Lohse 1971).

[125] In this version both the appetite and the falling away from the right order, which is usually attributed to the angels, are ascribed to the giants.

[126] Similarly 2Pt 2:4f. In CD II,17–III,1 the stubbornness of the Watchers is emphasized, in Bar 3:26–28 their ignorance.

[127] Transl. Kee (in Charlesworth I 1983).

[128] The perspective is adjusted to the foregoing story where Reuben recounts his sin with his father's wife, Bilhah. According to the text Bihlah deceived him.

2.3.2.2 Combination

Sometimes authors combine material from different sources and thus create something new. A combination may be made either by apposing different sources in the text or by fusing them. We have already seen how Jubilees combines the story of the Fall of Adam and Eve with that of the Fall of the angels in 1En 6–11.[129]

In CD IV, 20–V,6a, already discussed, the adversative priest, Zaw, is accused of having two wives, which is fornication in the eyes of the author.[130] In support for his judgment he refers to Gen 1:27 (CD V, 21) combined with Gen 7:9 (CD IV,1).[131] Gen 1:27 says: "God created man in his own image, in the image of God he created him; male and female he created them" and Gen 7:9 "two and two, male and female, went into the Ark with Noah, as God had commanded Noah".[132] The combination of Gen 1:27 and Gen 7:9 results in the idea that God wanted matched couples in the Ark in order to have only complete individuals. The author of CD infers that the Flood tradition implies that God has imposed a law against having more than one partner. Gen 7:9 thus is shown to contain something of which a reader would not think just by reading this particular text.

Another combination is to be found in a text which unites the Genesis version of the Fall (the Fall of man) and that of the Flood tradition (the Fall of the angels), namely 2Bar 56:5–16:[133]

And as you first saw the black waters on the top of the cloud which first came down upon the earth; this is the transgression which Adam, the first man, committed. For when he transgressed, untimely death came into being, . . . the conception of children came about, the passion of parents was produced, the loftiness of man was humiliated, and goodness vanished. . . . And from these black waters again black were born, and very dark darkness originated. For he who was a danger to himself was also a danger to the angels. For they possessed freedom in that time in which they were created. And some of them came down and mingled themselves with women. At that time they who acted like this were tormented in chains. But the rest of the multitude of angels, who have no number, restrained themselves. And those living on earth perished together through the waters of the flood. Those are the first black waters.[134]

The two traditions[135] are fused by the sentence: "For he who was a danger to

---

[129] See 2.1.5.

[130] הם ניתפשים בשתים בזנות לקחת שתי נשים בחייהם " . . . shall be caught in fornication twice by taking a second wife while the first is alive" (transl. Vermes 1987).

[131] This way of combining passages from Scriptures is in accordance with Hillel's fourth rule, *Binjan ab mi-schne ketubim*. For this rule see Strack-Stemberger 1982, 29.

[132] Cf. note 124.

[133] The text is part of the interpretation of Baruch's dream in which he saw rain falling, first black and then bright (53:1–12). This happened and then he awoke "because of fear". After a prayer (54:1–22) the angel Ramuel reveals the meaning of the dream (55:1–74:4).

[134] Transl.Klijn (Charlesworth 1983).

[135] Genesis cannot be the only source because it does not speak of the detainment of the angels as does this author. The text therefore must build on the Flood tradition. The version of

himself was also a danger to the angels". The second part of the text consists of a short summary of the relevant tradition. The author has made a selection of motifs which are mentioned in a few words. He does not refer to the teaching of the angels. Nor does he use the story of Noah and the Ark.[136]

2.3.2.3 Modification

The technique used by Josephus in retelling the Old Testament as history combines different approaches: such parts of his source material as do not suit his purpose are omitted,[137] the text is emended by material from other sources,[138] and the material from the Scripture is explained in rational terms.[139] Thus he can be said to modify the material used. By the term modification I thus refer to literary methods as a) rephrasing of a sentence, b) altering concepts in the texts for such concepts as represent a different theological understanding, and c) expansion of the text.[140]

a) Rephrasing of sentences are numerous in the old translations and in the targums. Statements may be made more sweeping: the expression "upon the earth" in Gen 7:23 the LXX renders "upon the face of all the earth";

---

the Flood tradition underlying the text may be that which speaks of the angels as bearers of knowledge and light into the world (cf. Jub 4:15). The version of the Flood tradition underlying the text was also different from that present in the Book of the Watchers because according to 2Bar evil did not come into the world through the angels but rather man caused the fall of the angels.

[136] The combination of the two sources follows the pattern from Jub. Similarly the story of the fall of Adam and the one of the fall of the angels are combined in PsClem *Hom* VIII.

[137] The feature of God's concern for the animals (Gen 7-9) is diminished.

[138] Josephus (*Ant* I, 70) says that Adam predicted the Flood, information which did not come from Gen but is known from other sources, e.g. TAdam 3:5; About the giants Josphus (*Ant* 1:71) says " . . . the deeds that tradition ascribes to them resemble the audacious exploits told by the Greeks of the giants" and that Noah "urged them to come to a better frame of mind and amend their ways; but seeing that, far from yielding, they were completely enslaved to the pleasure of sin, he feared that they would murder him and, with his wife and sons and his sons' wives, quitted the country" (*Ant* I, 73f.). This information he may have obtained from SibOr to which he refers in *Ant* I,118 (According to Thackeray 1978, 56, Josephus used the text of Alexander Polyhistor.)

[139] Names of months and festivals are compared with other languages to make the story understandable to the non-Jewish reader. Josephus also refers to other historians (see note 1) He even mentions testimonies from sources saying that the Ark was still visible in Armenia. The building of the Ark is explained: "God put into his [Noah's] mind" that he should build an Ark (I,76). That God gave the instructions for the building is left out. Similarly the covenant is explained: Noah, being afraid that the deluge would be perennial, prays to God. God answers by promising that the deluge would never occur again. About the rainbow Josephus says: "He meant the rainbow, which in those countries was believed to be God's bow" (*Ant* I, 103). Thus also the story of God's covenant with Noah is made more rational. Likewise Noah's great age is explained with the statement that the Ancient people " . . . were beloved of God and the creatures of God Himself; their diet too was more conducive to longevity", and furthermore, because men of old were astronomers God granted them longer life to give them time for more accurate observations (*Ant* I, 105f).

[140] TAdam 3:5 has combined the Flood tradition with material speaking of the daughters of Cain which can be found also in Rabbinic literature, e. g. GenR 22.2, 7; Yeb 62a.

sentences may be rephrased in order to fit to other parts of the text: in Gen 7:17 LXX rephrases "forty days" as "forty days and forty nights" in harmony with 7:4.

The picture of the Ark is changed in WisSol 14:5–6. The Ark, rather impressive in Gen 6, is here made very insignificant. The giants are said to be big and strong but presumptuous. The character of Noah is not changed but he is characterized by a new interpretation of his name, "The hope of the world", thus signifying Noah as the one who saved both the subhuman and the human Creation for the new world after the Flood. By these means Wisdom, of whom the author speaks, becomes the more impressive figure.

b) Already the old translations of Genesis made alterations in the text recounting the Flood story. The LXX shows several divergences from the Hebrew text.[141] Thus the Codex Alexandrinus in Gen 6:2 translates בני-האלהים with ἄγγελοι τοῦ θεοῦ but in v. 4 with υἱοὶ τοῦ θεοῦ.[142] On the translation of Gen 6:6f. Lewis remarks: "Interested in avoiding the anthropomorphisms, the translators have God to be 'provoked' (θυμοῦσθαι), instead of 'repenting' that he made man (Gen 6:7). He 'reflected' (ἐνθυμεῖσθαι) and 'bethinks himself' (διανοεῖσθαι, Gen 6:6)".[143]

c) The text is expanded in Ps-Philo's *Biblical Antiquities* 3,9–10 which otherwise follows the text of Gen closely.[144]

But when those inhabiting the earth sin, I will judge them by famine or by the sword or by fire or by death; and there will be earthquakes, and they will be scattered to uninhabited places. *But no more will I destroy the earth by the water of the flood. And in all the days of the earth, seedtime and harvest, cold and heat, spring and fall will not cease day and night* until I remember those who inhabit the earth, until the appointed times are fulfilled.

But when the years appointed for the world have been fulfilled, then the light will cease and the darkness will fade away. And I will bring the dead to life and raise up those who are sleeping from the earth. And hell will pay back its debts, and the place of perdition will return its deposit so that I may render to each according to his works and according to the fruits of his own devices, until I judge between soul and flesh. And the world will cease, and death will be abolished, and hell will shut its mouth. And the earth will not be without progeny or sterile for those inhabiting it; and no one who has been pardoned by me will be tainted. And there will be another earth and another heaven, an everlasting dwelling place.[145]

The quotation from Gen 8:21f. (italicized above) has been expanded by two additions, one before and one after. The first addition may be a rather free

---

[141] Lewis, who makes a very thorough examination of the different translations, counts no less than nine kinds of divergence (1968, 82–88).

[142] Other MSS have ἄγγελοι throughout.

[143] Lewis 1968, 87.

[144] The author compresses the text by omitting the repetitions. The difficult verse 6:4 is also excluded.

[145] Transl. Harrington in Charlesworth 1985.

compilation from the lists of curses for those who do not obey the Law (Lev 26:3ff.; Deut 28:15ff.). This insertion into the text seems to say that, although God will not send a Flood any more, He still will punish sin. The second extension introduces an eschatological perspective and the author can continue by adding a whole paragraph on the end of time. There will be the resurrection of the dead, the judgment, and finally a new heaven and a new earth (3:10).

Interpretative additions are of course frequent also in the targums. Targum Onkelos rendered Gen 6:3 as: "This evil generation shall not endure (יתקים) before me forever because they are flesh and their works are evil".[146] The expansion of the text makes the reason for God's limitation of a life-time evident. Sometimes mythological material was added to the text. The targum of Pseudo-Jonathan adds to Gen 6:2: "The daughters of men were fair, with painted eyelids, rouge, and were walking about nude, which led the sons of the great ones to conceive impure thoughts".[147] In 6:4 the targum reads: "Shambaza'i and 'Uzi'el who were fallen (נפלים) from heaven, were on the earth in those days".[148]

I shall return for a moment to TReu 5:6. We have already seen that the author selected only a few words from the traditional material. The possibility of the use made of the Flood tradition rests on the statement that the Watchers "saw them [i.e. the women who are described as 'handsome and beautiful'] and desired them" (Gen 6:2; 1En 6:2). This point is intensified by the author of TReu through rephrasing the verb "they saw" into κἀκεῖνοι συνεχῶς ὁρῶντες αὐτάς, ἐγένοντο ἐν ἐπιθυμίᾳ ἀλλήλων. The author further inserts the interpretative element "For it was thus that they charmed the Watchers". That the Watchers were charmed is taken as implicit in the statement that they lusted after the women.[149] By these means the author has shown the story to contain a meaning which the ordinary reader would not find there.

In 2.2.1.2.1 I already remarked on the development of a doctrine of the unclean spirits. They are the spirits of the giants who died in the Flood. In PsClem *Hom* VIII the thought is taken up, and a new element is added. God sends an angel to the unclean spirits with the following message:

These things seem good to the all-seeing God, that you lord it over no man; that you trouble no one, unless any one of his own accord subject himself to you, worshipping you, and sacrificing and pouring libations, and partaking of your table, or ac-

---

[146] Lewis 1968, 93.

[147] *Op. cit.*, 95.

[148] Lewis 1968, 96. We recognize the names of the two leading angels from 1En. However, 1En does not say that they were "fallen from heaven". It is clear that at least the authors of Pseudo-Jonathan and Neofiti knew some version of the Flood tradition beside that of Gen and were influenced by it.

[149] This way of using a word of Scripture is in accordance with Hillel's fifth principle of interpretation, *Kelal u-ferat u-ferat u-kelal* whereby a meaning which is inherent in a text may be used (Strack-Stemberger 1982, 29).

complishing aught else that they ought not, or shedding blood, or tasting dead flesh, or filling themselves with that which is torn of beasts, or that which is cut, or that which is strangled, or aught else that is unclean. But those who betake themselves to my law, you not only shall not touch, but shall also do honour to, and shall flee from, their presence. . . . But if any of those who worship me go astray, either committing adultery, or practising magic, or living impurely, or doing any other of the things which are not well-pleasing to me, then they will have to suffer something at your hands or those of others, according to my order (*Hom* VIII, 19).[150]

The direct purpose of this addition seems fairly clear. The heavenly message to the unclean spirits is actually addressed to the human readers who should draw conclusions for their own life.[151]

2.3.3 Reapplications of the Flood Tradition to New Situations

When the author has selected his material and given it the shape he wants, he can present it to his reader in many forms. I will try to illustrate some of these different ways of applying the tradition.

2.3.3.1 Example

As we have seen, Noah is made an example of righteousness in both Jewish and Christian writings.[152] The author of 2Pet 2:4f., 10f.[153] simply mentions a series of motifs from the tradition which he turns into examples and uses as arguments for exhortation. The context is a warning against false teachers who will deceive the believers with false words. They are people "whose condemnation from old is not idle and whose destruction is not asleep" (2Pet 2:3). The author has chosen the following motifs from the Flood tradition: the sinful angels who are detained in the dark prisons for the final judgment, further, the old sinful world was destroyed by the Flood, whereas Noah, the righteous, and his house were saved.[154]

The author contrasts the angels with Noah. In the Flood tradition the angels teach perversive knowledge, whereas Noah is a preacher of repentance (Νωε

---

[150] Transl. Peterson (in Roberts and Donaldson Eds. *ANF* 8 1951.

[151] A further example of the use of interpretative elements incorporated in the text may be taken from Sir 44:17 where a series is inserted: "Noah was found perfect in righteousness. In the time of wrath he became a ransom. Because of this there was a remnant on earth when the Flood came. An eternal covenant was made with him in order that not all flesh would be wiped out by a Flood".

[152] See 2.2.1.3.3 "Noah as ethical example".

[153] Verses 4f. constitute the protasis of an conditional clause. The apodosis is missing and the clause must be considered an anacoluthon.

[154] To this he adds the destruction of the two cities on the plain. The connection of Sodom and Gomorrah to the Flood is rather frequent, see e. g. Sir, 16:7-8; III Macc 2:4f.; TNaph 3:4; HellSynPr 12:58-61; Lk 17:26f.; WisSol 10:4-8; Philo *VitMos* 2:10 § 52-56.

δικαιοσύνης κήρυκα v. 5). The picture of the false teachers is parallel to that of the fallen angels from the Flood tradition. Thus people follow them in their lust (ταῖς ἀσελγείαις v. 2), but punishment awaits them (v. 3). Apparently vv. 4 ff. sought to explain (γάρ) this statement and has the form of the author's citation of the analogies from the Flood tradition: God did not spare the sinners. The analogy of v. 4f. is a *Qal wa-chomer* argument.[155] If God did not spare the angels and the old world He certainly will not spare these false teachers.[156]

By using the tradition thus the author made it a mirror of his contemporary situation. The threat of destruction for those following the false teachers is forcefully stated and at the same time the promise of salvation to those who keep to the right way is articulated.

2.3.3.2 Comparison

Mt 24:37f. and Lk 17:26f. have preserved an apocalyptic saying of Jesus from the Q material which is built on the story of the Flood.[157] The comparison is introduced (v. 37) by the comparative ὥσπερ . . . οὕτως and continued (v. 38) by ὡς . . . οὕτως (v. 39).[158] The saying is used slightly differently by the two Evangelists. Matthews' message is that no one knows the day of the Parousia of the Son of Man, not even the Son (Mt 24:36). This statement is illustrated by its comparison with the days of Noah: "As the days of Noah so will be the Parousia of the Son of Man" (v. 37). The comparison is developed in the following verse.[159] The mention of the eating and drinking, the marrying and giving in marriage[160] signifies the ordinary way of life. The *tertium comparationis* lies in the expression καὶ οὐκ ἔγνωσαν (v. 39). So will be the Parousia of the Son of Man; people will be living their ordinary lives, not knowing their danger. The Flood comes as a surprise. Thus the story of the Flood is used to illustrate the unpreparedness of the people before the Parousia and therefore the disciples must be on their guard.

---

[155] Another *Qal wa-chomer* argument using the Flood tradition is to be found in Paul's application of the Flood tradition in 1Cor 6:2f. Referring to the "teachings of the primitive Christian catechism" (Conzelmann 1975, 104) Paul scourges the Corinthians for bringing each other before the civil court. They ought to be able to settle their disagreements within the Church. "Do you not know that we are to judge angels. How much more matters pertaining to this life!".

[156] Similarly the author of 2Clem 6:8f. uses the story of the Flood to illustrate the need to "keep the baptism clean".

[157] Bultmann has listed this text as an "apocalyptic saying" of Jesus containing a "Warning of the Parousia" (1968 "History", 117).

[158] The parallel in Lk has καθώς . . . οὕτως (17:26) .

[159] Neither Mt nor Lk mention the sin of the generation before the Flood nor the righteousness of Noah. They both stress the current activity (Mt uses the present participles, Lk the imperfect) during which an event occurred, viz. that Noah went into the Ark (εἰσῆλθεν aorist).

[160] The aspect of the action as continuing is expressed by Mt by the present participle and by Lk by the imperfect tense.

Luke does not speak of the "Parousia of the Son of Man" but of "the days of the Son of Man".[161] He is about to warn his disciples against false prophets who will point out the place and the time when the Son of Man will come. But as at the days of the Flood people lived their ordinary daily life unaware of anything unusual so will be the days of the Son of Man. The Flood illustrates that no specific sign tells when the Son of Man will come. The message can be condensed: "Above all, disciples are not to be misled by bogus prophets trying to declare the signs of the times and to indicate the time and place of revelation. Jesus makes it clear that the arrival of the Son of Man will be sudden and unmistakable; it will not require other human beings to call attention to it".[162]

In PsClem *Hom* IX,2 the author compares the sins of the Flood generation with the sins of the then living people: "And yet their sin was much less than that which is chargeable against you. For they were wicked with respect to their equals, murdering or committing adultery. But you are wicked against the God of all, worshipping lifeless images instead of him or along with him and attributing his divine name to every kind of senseless matter".

2.3.3.3 Allegory

Among the authors who have explained the Flood tradition or single motifs thereof allegorically Philo of Alexandria is the most expansive.[163] In *De gigantibus* Philo treats Gen 6:1–4 from which I shall illustrate his manner of exposition.

Philo insists that the story of the Flood is historical. Yet, in his exposition each detail of the story is given an interpretation in the manner of an allegory of some philosophical truth.[164] Gen 6:1, says that ". . . men began to multiply on the face of the ground, and daughters were born to them". Why did

---

[161] " 'The days of the Messiah' was a technical expression for the Messianic period [Cf. Shabbath 113b, Sanhedrin 91b, and 1En 61:5 'the day of the Elect One']" (Allen 1957,). It is possible that Q read "the day of the Son of Man" (Schulz, S. 1972, 279; Marshall 1989, 661)

[162] Fitzmyer 1985, 1167.

[163] See especially Lewis 1968, 42–81. On page 183-185 Lewis lists all the references to the Flood tradition in Philo's works. Philo wrote many books which are presented as explanations of parts of the Flood story, i. e. *De Gigantibus, De Agricultura, De Ebriate, De Sobritate, De plantatione.* Several treatises which have titles connected to the Flood story prove disappointing as regard a study of Philo's treatment of Flood tradition. "His conception of the flood even must be drawn from passages scattered here and there where he uses it as an illustration of some other point. The most complete treatments are to be found in *De Abrahamo, De Vita Mosis, Quod Deus immutabilis sit,* and finally in even greater detail in *Quaestiones et Solutiones in Genesin*" (Lewis 1968, 43).

[164] "With the aid of allegorical interpretation he [Philo] could see how to read profound philosophical theories out of the early history of Genesis, especially in the fields of psychology and ethics, theories which actually had their true roots in Greek philosophy. In his hands, the surface events of biblical narrative became profound lessens in the supreme problems of human existence" (Schürer 1987, 878).

men multiply and why were daughters born to them, Philo asks. The reason for this is that rarity always has an opposite. This statement is a philosophical premise which Philo now applies to the text: Noah, being the only righteous man, must have a plenitude of unrighteous men opposed to him. Virtue is a masculine quality. Noah consequently has sons but the unrighteous give birth to daughters. This does not mean that they were all women but it is the way Moses, according to Philo, characterizes ungodly men.

Gen 6:2 says that the angels saw that the daughters of men were fair and took wives from them. Philo interprets the sons of God as angels and to him "souls, and demons and angels are but different names for the same one underlying object".[165] Some angels serve God as ministers and helpers of men, but other angels (i. e. souls) descend into human bodies, which is the spiritual meaning of the statement that the angels went to the daughters of man and begat the giants. The souls which descend into human bodies are of three kinds and create three different kinds of people: "some men are earth-born, some heaven-born, and some God-born".[166] "The earth-born are those who take pleasures of the body for their quarry ... The heaven-born are the votaries of arts and of knowledge, the lovers of learning ... But the men of God are priests and prophets who have refused to accept membership in the commonwealth of the world ... but have risen wholly above the sphere of sense perception and have been translated into the world of the intelligible and dwell there registered as freemen of the commonwealth of Ideas, which are imperishable and incorporeal".[167] Philo thus makes Gen 6:1-4 an allegory of the true philosophical life.

Christians only seem to have applied the allegorical interpretation on a large scale after NT times.[168]

2.3.3.4 Typology

As we saw already when outlining the elementary Flood tradition,[169] its use according to 1 Enoch expresses the belief in a coming judgment on all evil, and the promise and hope of deliverance of the elect into a new world. The Flood tradition functions as a "type" of the Last Judgment. This in fact seems to be a primary use of the tradition from early on. Motifs from the Flood tradition are used typologically already in the Apocalypse of Weeks

---

[165] *De Gig* 16.

[166] *De Gig* 59.

[167] *De Gig* 60f. Of the philosopher's soul he says: "Those last, then, are the souls of those who have given themselves to genuine philosophy, who from the first to the last study to die to the life in the body, that a higher existence immortal and incorporeal, in the presence of Him who is Himself immortal and uncreate, may be their portion" (*De Gig* 14).

[168] See Lewis 1968, 156-180.

[169] See above 2.1.3.3.

(1En 93:1–10, 91:12–17). The traditional material alluded to is compressed in a few words: "Therein the first consummation will take place" and "therein also a certain man shall be saved".[170] It is uncertain whether the original text referred to the fallen angels.[171] The giants are not mentioned. To recognize the application of the Flood tradition clearly one has to regard the structure of the whole apocalypse. The entire history of the world is divided into ten "weeks". The beginning and the end correspond to each other, both being described as righteous and peaceful.[172] There is also one great judgment at the beginning of history corresponding to the last "eternal" Judgment. The expression "the first consummation" makes the Flood the prototype of the final Judgment. Not the origin of evil but only its reality is of interest to the author. The centre of interest falls on the final Judgment and end of evil, of which the Flood is the typos.

"Noah for the later church is chiefly a type of Christ".[173] The idea of Noah as the τέλος of one world and the ἀρχή of another[174] made him a prototype of Christ.[175]

In 1Pet 3:18–22 the author uses the motif of the imprisoned angels as a type for the sinners at the Last Judgment, and makes clear "that he thinks of the Christian Church as the 'antitype' or fulfilment of the Ark, and of the waters of Christian baptism as prefigured by those of the Flood".[176] This typological use of the Flood tradition is found in many passages in the writings of the Church Fathers.

---

[170] A common feature in the Flood tradition, although not typical only of it, is the mention of evil times preceding the judgment, the thought that the final judgment "shall be executed by the angels of the eternal heaven—the great judgment which emanates from all of the angels" (91:15) and that the new creation "shall be a time of goodness and righteousness and sin shall be no more heard of forever" (91:17).

[171] Isaac (in Charlesworth 1983, 73, note q2) comments on the text: "Text may be corrupt. B reads 'and it shall be executed from the Watchers; and a great, eternal peace which emanates from the midst of the angels.' C reads 'and it shall be executed from the Watchers of the eternal heaven; the great (judgment) in which he will execute vengeance among the angels'". Knibb (1978) translates: " . . . there will be the eternal judgment which will be executed on the watchers, and the great eternal heaven which will spring from the midst of the angels". The seriously damaged text of the Qumran fragments is restored by Milik (1976, 267) and translated: " . . . an eternal judgment and the (fixed) time of the Great Judgment [shall be executed in vengeance, in the midst of the Holy Ones]".

[172] The first week is described: "I was born the seventh during the first week, during which time judgment and righteousness continued to endure" (93:3b). Correspondingly the time after the last judgment ends with the words: "Then after there shall be many weeks without number forever; it shall be a time of goodness and righteousness, and sin shall no more be heard of" (91:17).

[173] Lewis 1968, 158.

[174] Thus Philo *QuestGen* I.96; cf. PsClem *Hom* VIII,17.

[175] Tertullian *De monog.* 5.

[176] Selwyn 1961, 334. For the motif of the imprisoned angels as a type for the sinners at the jugment see Reicke 1946, 19.

2.3.3.5 Indirect and Hidden Uses of the Flood Tradition

Up till now I have discussed texts where the authors have applied the received material directly or openly. I now turn to some texts where the Flood tradition was used in a more indirect or hidden way.[177] By the term "hidden use" I mean that the author does not make any clear reference to the story of the Flood but still uses material from it.[178] Of course, the borderline between an open and a hidden use of a received material is difficult to keep absolutely clear.[179]

In 1En 106f. the author makes an indirect but not hidden use of the Flood tradition. The text contains the birth story of Noah which presupposes that there were giants on earth, born of earthly women but begotten by angels. The event is described in the following way: Noah's wife gives birth to a child of extraordinary appearance:

And his body was white as snow and red as a rose; the hair of his head as white as wool and his *demdema*[180] beautiful; and as for his eyes, when he opened them the whole house glowed like the sun—(rather) the whole house glowed even more exceedingly. And when he arose from the hands of the midwife, he opened his mouth and spoke to the Lord with righteousness. And his father, Lamech, was afraid of him and fled and went to Methusalah his father; and said to him, 'I have begotten a strange son: he is not like an (ordinary) human being, but he looks like the children of the angels of heaven to me; his form is different, and he is not like us. His eyes are like the rays of the sun, and his face glorious. It does not seem to me that he is of me, but of the angels; and I fear that a wondrous phenomenon may take place upon the earth in his days (1En 106:2-6).[181]

Now Methusalah in turn went to his father, Enoch, to ask about the child. Enoch, who is in heaven, explained the matter:

The Lord will surely make new things upon the earth; and I have already seen this matter in a vision and made it known to you. For in the generation of Jared, my father, they transgressed the word of the Lord, (that is) the law of heaven. And behold, they commit sin and transgress the commandment; they have united themselves with women and commit sin together with them; and they have married (wives) from among

---

[177] It is possible that authors sometimes hide their references to a background text so that only the initiated readers comprehend them. However, when I speak here of hidden use I intend allusions to the traditional material which are unclear to us although they were probably evident to ordinary original readers, i. e. without any need of special information.

[178] Sometimes it is difficult to prove that the story of the Flood really underlies a certain text. So for example it has been proposed that the story of the Flood lies behind Peter's vision in Acts 10 :11-16 but this has never been proved (see Selwyn, 1961, 333f.). I shall indicate some texts where it is fairly certain that the story of the Flood is used, be it the Genesis version of the story or the more developed Flood tradition.

[179] The Apocalypse of Weeks is an example of a non-explicit but nevertheless half-way hidden use of the tradition.

[180] "This Eth. word has no equivalent in English. It refers to a long and curly hair combed up straight, what one calls gofare in several modern Ethiopian languages, or "afro" in colloquial English" (Isaac in Charlesworth 1983, 86, note g).

[181] Transl. Isaac (in Charlesworth 1983, 86f.).

them, and begotten children by them. There shall be a great destruction upon the earth; and there shall be a deluge and a great destruction for one year. And this son who has been born unto you shall be left upon the earth; and his three sons shall be saved when they who are upon the earth are dead. And upon the earth they shall give birth to the giants, not of the spirit but of flesh.There shall be a great plague upon the earth, and the earth shall be washed clean from all the corruption (1En 106:13-17).

The newborn son is declared righteous, and Enoch orders that he be named Noah. After Noah's time there will be a time of still greater oppression. But finally there will come a great generation of righteous ones and then wickedness will perish from the earth. With this message Methusalah returns home, and the name Noah is given to the child.

In this text the Flood tradition is used as the scene against which the whole play is set. Although it is not the Flood story which is told, the story functions only when the scenery from the Flood tradition is clear to the mind of the reader. The reader is placed in a situation where children are born who have angels as their fathers.[182] The suspicion that this is the matter with the newborn child is first uttered by Lamech. Then the question goes to Enoch, who is presupposed to be known to the reader. Enoch foretells the Flood, the rôle of Noah and, finally, the final salvation of the world.

The aim of the author seems to be to present the hero of his text.[183] The story keeps to the apocalyptic pattern of seeing the Flood as the first consummation which will have a counterpart at the end of history.

In 1QH X,33-35 some few lines seem to allude to the Flood tradition.[184] In a prayer the author expresses his anguish:[185]

> My heart is stricken with terror,
>   and my loins with trembling;
> my groaning goes down to the Abyss,
>   and is shut up in the chambers of Hell.
> I am greatly afraid when I hear of Thy judgment
>   of the mighty Heroes,
> and of Thy trial of the host
>   of Thy Holy Ones.[186]

By the expression Holy Ones the author of the Book of Hymns usually means the angels.[187] The allusion to the Flood tradition is achieved through placing

---

[182] In Genesis Apocryphon col I-V we find a birth narrative which is very close to that of 1En 106-108. It has been classified by Fitzmyer as "a haggadic elaboration of Gn 5.28-29" (1966, 69). In Gen Ap the story is more elaborate than in 1En 106ff. but still follows the same fundamental pattern.

[183] This text may have been part of the Noah Book. Cf. note 35.

[184] Maier refers to following parallels: CD II, 18; 1QM XIV, 14; Jub 5,6; 10:7-11; 1En 6ff.; and comments: "Der Beter erschrickt, da er durch dieses Beispiel an den Schrecken des eschatologischen Gerichtes denken muß" (1960, 104).

[185] One may have the reservation that the punishment of angels is reported also outside the Flood tradition.

[186] Transl.Vermes 1987.

[187] Gaster translates "Thine angels" (1964, 176). Similarly Lohse speaks of "Das Gericht, das Gott an den schuldigen Engeln ... " (1971, 293 note 50).

into the text some expressions which have a background in the Flood tradition. Those elements taken together create the specific picture recognizable from the story of the Flood. There are the "groaning", "the chambers of Hell" and the "trial of the host of Thy Holy Ones" (the angels). The author thus alludes to the motif of the angels kept in confinement under the earth awaiting the final judgment. The picture creates a strong expression of anguish since the author thus in some sense places himself in a drama equivalent to the Flood.

In ApAb 14 the Flood tradition, albeit vague, is still recognizable.[188] Abraham's dream, contained in Gen 15:12–16, has been developed by the author of ApAb into an apocalyptic vision.[189] When Azazel appears in the form of an unclean bird (cf.Gen 15:11) the *angelus interpres* rebukes him (v. 13) and adresses Abraham:

Be bold and do through your authority whatever I order you against him who reviles justice. Will I not be able to revile him who has scattered about the earth the secrets of heaven and who has taken counsel against the Mighty One? Say to him, "May you be the firebrand of the furnace of the earth! Go, Azazel, into the untrodden parts of the earth. For your heritage is over those who are with you, with the stars and with the men born by the clouds, whose portion you are, indeed they exist through your being. Enmity is for you a pious act. Therefore through your own destruction begone from me!"[190]

In the text we recognize a series of elements from the Flood tradition: Azazel has "scattered about the earth the secrets of heaven";[191] he "has taken counsel against the Mighty One";[192] he is deemed to be "the firebrand of the furnace of the earth";[193] he is a leader and has with him "stars and men born by the clouds".[194] The motifs from the tradition are used only to characterize one of the figures in the text, which has a centre of interest unrelated to the Flood tradition.

There is an allusion to the Flood tradition also in ApAb 24, although so vague that the author must count on a reader who knows the Flood tradition very well. In the vision Abraham sees Adam and Eve, Cain and Abel and says:

---

[188] "It is not difficult to find here the traditions of Genesis 6:1–4 developed according to the tradition of 1 Enoch. Azazel is the head of the angels who plotted against the Lord and who impregnated the daughters of men. (ApAb 14:4; 1En 6:4 and ApAb 14:6; 1En 6:1f., 10:4). These angels are compared to the stars (ApAb 14:6; 1 En 86:1). Azazel revealed the secrets of heaven and is banished to the desert (ApAb 14:4; 1 En 8:1 and ApAb 14:5; 1En 10:4). Abraham, as Enoch, receives the power to drive away Satan (ApAb14:3; 1 En 14:3)" (Rubinkiewicz in Charlesworth 1983, 685).

[189] The vision, which ends in a discussion of the situation after the destruction of the Temple and the dispersion of the people, centres in the question: "Will what I saw be their lot for long?" (28:2) and thus, as most apocalypses, has a comforting purpose.

[190] ApAb 14:4–7. Transl. Rubinkiewicz (in Charlesworth 1983).

[191] Cf. 1En7–8; 9:6f.; 13:2; 16:3; 64; 65:6ff.; 69:1–15, 28.

[192] Cf. 1En 6.

[193] Cf. 1En 10:6, 13; 21; 54:6; 67:4.

[194] In the Flood tradition Azael is the leader of the angels. The angels are sometimes called stars, as in 1En 21:2–4; 86:1ff.

And I saw there fornication and those who desired it, and its defilement and their zeal; and the fire of their corruption in the lower depths of the earth. And I saw there theft and those who hasten after it, and the system of their retribution, the judgment of the great court. I saw there naked men, forehead to forehead, and their shame and the harm (they wrought) against their friends and their retribution (ApAb 24:6-9).[195]

The first lines seem to depict the story of the Flood[196] and the last that of Sodom and Gomorrah. In this case the author describes events from an apocalyptical view of history. His technique is to give some key concepts, thus recalling the traditional material to the mind of the reader. Thus the Flood story is suggested by the mention of the "fornication" and the "desire" of the angels. He also refers to "the lower depths of the earth" and their "retribution, the judgment of the great court" thus alluding to Gods judgment which was performed by the angels.[197]

Of the man who had no wedding garment Jesus says: "Bind him hand and foot, and cast him into the outer darkness; there men will weep and gnash their teeth" (Mt 22:13). Whence did this motif come? According to Rubinkiewicz the background is 1En 10:4.[198] The technique used is again that of quoting some key words which for the reader who knows the Flood tradition add color to the picture. The aim is not to bring up the tradition as such but create in the mind of the reader an awareness of the fate which he must share with the cursed fallen angels if he will not lead an obedient life in the Church.

The author of Revelation created his vivid scenes from many different sources. Having painted in the preceding context the picture of Christ's victory over the godless state, in Chapter 20:1-10 he presents the final end of Satan and the victory of the Kingdom of God.[199] Scholars have long

---

[195] Transl. Rubinkiewicz (in Charlesworth 1983).

[196] The reference seems to be to the Flood tradition and not to Gen 6-9, as there is no mention in Gen of corruption or defilement in regard to the sons of God taking daughters of men as wives. Furthermore, Gen 6-9 contains no picture of the "court" of God which is, on the other hand, a rather prominent part in several accounts of the Flood tradition (e. g. 1En 9:1, 3; 14:8-25; 40).

[197] The author of 1QS IV,15-17 adopts a similar approach. According to Nickelsburg this text is "reminiscent of motifs in the description of the eschaton in Enoch 10:16-22" (1981, 136). The connection to the Flood tradition can only be surmised from the large complex of ideas involved in this text. In vv 22ff. the author mentions the sons of Heaven, and the "inheritance '' in either the evil spirit or the spirit of truth; further he also speaks of the new Creation which will make an end of evil.

[198] Rubinkiewicz 1984, 97-113. According to Rubinkiewicz the connection was made through the association in later Jewish thought between Azazel, driven into the desert on the Day of Atonement, and the Fallen angel Azael and, further, through the idea expressed in ApAb 13:14 that when Azael left his place in heaven his "garment" was given to Abraham. This Rubinkiewicz connects to Sech 3:3-5.

[199] Bousset (1906, 436) sees relations to Ancient Iranian and Babylonian myths. Charles (1959, 141f.) refers to the idea in Isa 24:22f; and several places in 1En, where Azael is bound and cast into the abyss to await the final judgment; Beasley Murray similarly refers to Ancient Iranian, Babylonian etc. mythology and mentions especially Jes 24:21f., and 1En 10:4ff as a background of Rev 20 (1981, 286). Most scholars believe Isa 24 to be the direct background of Rev 20:1-10.

recognized the similarity to what I here call the Flood tradition behind this text. The conformity in a series of ideas suggests that in this passage Rev is somehow dependent on the Flood tradition. Rubinkiewicz makes the following comparison between similarities and dissimilarities:

	Rev 20:1–10	1En 10:4–6	1En 10:11–13
1) Angels	+	+	+
2) Fettering of Satan	+	+	+
3) Imprisonment	+	+	+
4) Duration of imprisonment	+	+	+
5) Release	+	—	—
6) Judgment and punishment	+	+	+

Of the six motifs mentioned five are found in 1En. Each of these five motifs recur also in other passages containing material from the Flood tradition.[200] Rubinkiewicz concludes "daß wir es in Offb 20,1–10 mit der Verwendung des 'Klischees' von Hen 10 zu tun haben".[201]

2.3.4 Conclusions

It has become clear that the richness of the motifs of the Flood tradition made it useful for different purposes.[202] I now turn to the text which is the central interest of this study, Rom 8:18ff., and try to demonstrate its relations to the Flood tradition.

---

[200] The first point, that this is an act performed by angels, need hardly be proved by special quotations. The evil angel is bound and detained e.g. 1En 13:2; 14:5; Jub 5:6, he is judged and destroyed in fire, 1En 67:4; 90:23f.; Jub 5:10. The timespan between the imprisonment and the judgment is made clear. (This was emphasized by Bousset 1906, 436f.). The chains are also mentioned in some texts as 1En 54:3–6; 69:28.

[201] Rubinkiewicz 1984, 135.

[202] There may be other passages in Rev as well as in other writings where motifs from the Flood tradition influenced the text. However, these instances are so vague that they are beyond any certain identification. According to Milik, commenting on 1En 14:18, several other passages in Rev show influence from the Book of the Watchers: "The image of the throne of God, the appearance of which is like ice (ὧσυ (sic) κρυστάλλινον; perhaps read ὡς ὕ⟨δωρ⟩ κρυστ. 'like frozen, icy water' or even ὡς ὕ⟨αλος⟩ κρ. 'like glass in rock—crystal') certainly influenced the image in Rev.4:6: καὶ ἐνώπιον τοῦ θρόνου ὡς θάλασσα ὑαλίνη ὁμοία κρυστάλλῳ. The author of Revelation is no doubt thinking of the pavement in front of the throne, a pavement in transparent ice like that in the antechamber of the throne-room in En. 14:10 .... A number of other elements common to the Book of Revelation and to En. make it clear that the Christian writer had first-hand knowledge of the Book of Enoch, probably the Greek translation of it; cf. En 22:12 and Rev 6:9–10; En 86:1 and Rev. 9:1 and 11 and 8:10; En 91:16 and Rev.12:1" (1976, 199).

Chapter 3
The Religio-Historical Background of Rom 8:18–27

3.1 Line of Thought

3.1.1 Wide Context

The theme of Romans is given in 1:16–17:[1] In the Gospel God in accordance with Scripture has revealed His righteousness which He gives to each one who responds with faith. Therefore the Gospel means salvation for both Jew and Gentile. Although Paul places both Jew and Gentile under the same condition,[2] viz. that salvation depends on faith and not on obeying the Torah, ". . . there is a certain undeniable priority of the Jew".[3] The location of the expression " . . . to the Jew first and also to the Greek" in the very centre of the thematic verses should be carefully considered. Paul has thereby indicated that it is of importance for the issue of the letter, not just as an illustration of the theme "righteousness through faith".[4]

---

[1] Vv.16f. is seen by almost every commentator as the theme of the letter. On the other hand, Friedrich regards vv.1–5 as the theme (1961, 1139), and similarly Balz terms those verses "ein geheimes Thema" (1971, 28f.). Wuellner (1977, 345 ff.) finds 1:16f. to be a "transitus" from the *exordium* (1:1–15) to the *confirmatio* (1:18–15:13) which "lays out the central argument".

It is clear that verses 16f. can be understood in different ways. To the overwhelming majority of exegetes their point is the expression δικαιοσύνη . . . ἐκ πίστεως v.17; salvation is available only through faith. Thus Nygren concentrates the theme to the line: ὁ δίκαιος ἐκ πίστεως ζήσεται (1947, 89). At the same time he can say that 1:4 contains the entire letter *in nuce* (page 59) because the resurrection is the beginning of a new world, in Nygren's terms a new "aeon". However, there are indications in the letter that the centre of interest is the relationship between Jew and Gentile. Paul seems to allude to this topic already in the opening of the letter (1:1–7) by quoting a confession formula (v. 3f.), which apparently originated in the early Semitic-speaking Church (Bultmann 1968, 49; Schweizer 1962, 91; 1963, 180–189), but which by the time of the letter probably was used also in hellenistic Churches (Kramer 1963, 108).

Paul's statement in the introduction of the thematic verses, "I am not ashamed" seems to imply that he was supposed to have a reason to be ashamed of his Gospel. His statement is explained (γάρ): the Gospel is God's power to salvation for everybody who believes in it, "everybody" being further defined as Jew and Gentile. This theme of Jew and Gentile is followed up in the rest of the letter (besides chapters 9–11 which especially discuss the subject: 2:9ff.; 3:9, 29f.; 4:9; 9:24, 30f.; 10:12; 15:8f.).

[2] "The phrase as a whole underlines and explicates the preceding παντί. The word τε (though its presence is simply ignored by RV, RSV, NEB and JB) is suggestive of the fundamental equality of Jew and Gentile . . . " (Cranfield 1980, 91).

[3] Cranfield, 1980. Cf. Boers (1982, 187): " 'Jews first!' That is what carries the argument in the rest of this letter".

[4] According to Beker the theme of the letter (Rom 1:16–17) revolves around four interrelated issues: (1) the righteousness of God, (2) apprehended by faith, (3) is salvation to everyone who

In 1:18–8:39 Paul develops the theological idea of the new righteousness. No man can become righteous through the revelation by Creation and nobody can become righteous by fulfilling the Law (1:18–3:10f., 20). Righteousness is given by God through Jesus Christ (3:21–31). God makes both Jew and Gentile righteous through faith (3:29f.). In this righteousness the Law is not abandoned but fulfilled. Therefore Abraham is the father not only of the Jew but of the Gentile believer as well (4:1–25).

Having settled these fundamental ideas Paul explains the life in the new righteousness (5:1–8:39). In Chapters 9–11 Paul applies these theological ideas to the relationship between Jew and Gentile.[5] Chapters 12–15, being parenetical, contain practical applications of the message. Chapter 15 also offers information on the Apostle's travel plans. Chapter 16 concludes the letter with a list of greetings.[6]

3.1.2 The Closer Context, Rom 5–8

In consequence of his understanding of righteousness Paul presents an exposition of the life according to the new righteousness (5–8).[7] We are at peace with God and therefore proud (καυχώμεθα) of our hope of the coming glory, yea, even of the present sufferings (5:1–5). The certainty of salvation is evident through the gift of the Holy Spirit which represents God's love poured out into our hearts (5:5). This is all built on God's act in Christ, Who is the second Adam, incorporating a new mankind (5:6–21).

If righteousness is not attained through keeping the Law, a righteous life

believes, to the Jew first and also to the Greek', (4) and is the confirmation and the fulfilment of the Old Testament promise of Hab 2:4 (1986, 13). This scheme makes clear the equality of Jew and Gentile in the new righteousness as well as the priority of the former.

[5] To some expositors chapters 9–11 appear to be an excursus: J.A.T. Robinson (1979, 108), Vielhauer (1975, 183), Bruce (1971, 181). To others the chapters are a new section of the letter which is not integrated into the main theological discussion but presents a new theme, viz. the question of the place of Israel in the history of salvation, e. g. Lietzmann (1933, 89). Chapters 9–11 have also been seen as a sermon formulated earlier but incorporated into the letter, probably by Paul himself: Dodd (1963, 161ff.), Black (1984, 128). Contrary to this Stendahl (1976, 29), following Munck (1959), calls chapters 1–8 a "preface" to the "central revelation" of chapters 9–11, which are maintained to be "the climax of the letter" (op. cit., 85). Beker similarly: "Romans exhibit a basic apology for Israel. Therefore, chapters 9–11 are not an appendix but a climactic point in the letter" (1984, 87). Thus also Hellholm: "Når det gjelder *probatio*-delens oppbygning mener jeg meg å kunne vise at den første delteksten utgjøres av en *quaestio infinita*. Dette avsnitt omfatter 1,18-8,39, som behandler det prinsipielle spørsmål om rettferdiggjørelsen av *mennesket*; den andre delteksten på samme nivå utgjøres av en *quaestio finita*. Dette avsnitt omfatter den resterende delen av *probatio*-avsnittet, dvs. 9,1-11,36, som behandler det specifikke spørsmålet om rettferdiggjørelsen av jødene" (1989, 271).

[6] The originality of chapter 16 is debated. See Kümmel (1987, 314-320), Manson (1977, 1-16), Donfried (1977, "Notice" 50-60), Wuellner (1977, 152-174).

[7] The close parallels running through chapters 5–8 show this section to be tightly knit. See Rolland (1980 and 1988).

is to be lived outside the Law. This raises serious questions in regard to the Law. Does the new righteousness mean a freedom from the Law in the sense that we can now persist in doing what the Law condemns and thus even multiply the grace (τί οὖν ἐροῦμεν; ἐπιμένωμεν τῇ ἁμαρτίᾳ, ἵνα ἡ χάρις πλεονάσῃ; 6:1)? This is not the case. In baptism we have died together with Christ in order that we may also live together with Him. Therefore we should no longer continue the old way of life (6:1–14). The same point is then demonstrated through an example from the slave market (6:15–23) and one from marriage (7:1–6).

A second question arises: what has been said seems to lead to the opinion that the Law is evil (τί οὖν ἐροῦμεν; ὁ νόμος ἁμαρτία; 7:7). This thought is explicitly denied (7:7–25a). When we break the Law our conscience tells us that we act against the will of God. Thus we agree that the Law expresses the will of God and is therefore good and divine.[8]

The argument for the divine character of the Law ends in the exclamation: ταλαίπωρος ἐγὼ ἄνθρωπος· τίς με ῥύσεται ἐκ τοῦ σώματος τοῦ θανάτου τούτου; (7:24).[9] The answer is given immediately: χάρις δὲ τῷ θεῷ διὰ Ἰησοῦ Χριστοῦ τοῦ κυρίου ἡμῶν (7:25a).[10] This question and answer mark the transition to the next section of the letter.

Up till now Paul has shown the negative side of salvation. The argument in 7:7–24 could even imply that a righteous life is impossible. Although the righteousness of God is revealed in Christ, man in his own power cannot lead this righteous life. The possibility of a righteous life is opened up in Christ through the Holy Spirit (8:3ff.). The description of the life in Christ therefore must be a description of the work of the Spirit.[11] In Jesus Christ the believer has passed from the dominion of the old Law, which was characterized by sin and death, to that of the new Law of the life-giving Spirit in Jesus Christ (8:2). What was impossible in the old life is now possible through the Holy Spirit.

[8] With Stendahl who argues that the whole section 7:7-24 is formed, in line with the usual reasoning in philosophic tractates, as an argument for the statement that the Law is good (1976, 27f.).

[9] One major question in the exegesis of chapter 7, especially vv.7-24, concerned whether Paul speaks of the Christian (Cranfield, 1980, 330f.) or of the non-Christian (Dodd 1963, 123-133; Kümmel 1987, 307). The question is somewhat inept, as Paul does not discuss man but the Law. Thus Fuchs (1949, 55-83), J. A. T. Robinson (1979, 82-95).

[10] Several exegetes find difficulties in placing vv. 7:25b-8:1 in the line of thought. This is especially the case with those who see 7:7-25 as expressing the experience of the non-Christian. They believe these verses not to be original (Müller 1941; Bultmann (1967); Fuchs (1949, 82f.), Michel (1978), Käsemann (1973, 202) or to be misplaced Moffat (1926), Dodd (1963).

[11] No chapter in the NT speaks more intensively of the Spirit, which is already statistically evident: in Rom 8 πνεῦμα occurs no less than 21 times (to be compared, in Romans, with five times in chapters 1-7 and seven times in chapters 9-16).

3.1.3 The Immediate Context, Rom 8:12–39

Beginning in v. 12[12] Paul sums up what has been said hitherto (ἄρα οὖν, ἀδελφοί): we have obligations, but not to the flesh so that we should live according to the flesh (cf. 8:3), for a carnal mind means death (cf. 8:6). The Law could not lead to righteousness because it was weakened by the flesh. However, God has liberated us from death through Jesus Christ. This expresses, so to speak, the negative side of the new righteousness; the believer is set free from the power of the flesh.

The conclusion in v. 12 is further developed in v. 14. Paul, however, interrupts the thought by inserting the two conditional clauses in v. 13, to which I shall return. The idea of being driven by the Spirit in v. 14 corresponds to the "we have obligations" of v. 12. The positive meaning of the argument is emphasized: those who are driven by the Spirit have certain obligations—i. e. to kill the works of the body. As sons of God they are no longer subject to the destructive powers as slaves, but are free. The Spirit of God lives within them, as Paul has said already in vv. 9–11. The real power of the Christian life thus is the Spirit. So v. 14 appears to be the very kernel of the entire concluding passage, vv. 12–17.

We should observe two small nuances in Paul's language. The first concerns the wording of the sentence. Paul does not say: "We have no obligations to the flesh",[13] but rather: "We have obligations, [but] not to the flesh" (8:12).[14] The difference is important. Paul does not speak of our being free from obligations. On the contrary he says that we have obligations.[15] The second observation pertains to the place of the negation. One would have expected a positive statement to follow the negative of v. 12 but it does not. Instead the statement is followed by two conditional constructions, which are contrasted to each other. Paul seems to have stopped short in v. 12, hurrying to the warning in v. 13 and leaving the sentence incomplete.[16] The impres-

---

[12] Different divisions of the text have been suggested, e. g. Dodd (1963,133ff.) 8:1-4, 5-13, 14-17, 18-25, 26-27, 28-39. J. A. T. Robinson (1979, 96) divides the text 7:7-8:4, 5-13, 14-17, 18-25, 26-30, 31-39, and von der Osten-Sacken (1975, 60-62) differently, seeing 8:1-13, 14-30 and 31-39 as its natural structure.

[13] Thus e. g. NEB "It follows, my friends, that our lower nature has no claim upon us; we are not obliged to live on that level"; similarly e. g. the Swedish Bible 1917, Lietzmann (1933), Schlier (1977).

[14] Thus for instance according to RSV, Swedish transl. 1981, Barrett (1957); Dodd (1963), Cranfield (1980) Paul does not really intend to introduce practical or ethical implications of his reasoning. He rather concentrates on the thought of eternal life for those who mortify the flesh; thus Nygren (1947), Sanday and Headlam (1962). Paulsen (1974, 81-83) concludes that Paul introduces the ethical implications of what is said but that the explication is postponed until chapters 12-15.

[15] Wilckens remarks: "Das Wort ὀφειλέτης findet sich nur bei Paulus in der Bedeutung 'verplichtet' " (1978, 134) and further, "Sonst im NT wird das Wort in der ursprünglichen Bedeutung 'Schuldner' gebraucht" (*ad loc.* note 553).

[16] Cranfield (1980), Paulsen (1974, 85); Pallis (1920) rewrites the sentence as ὀφείλομεν ζῆν οὐ τῇ σαρκί, ἀλλὰ τῷ πνεύματι.

sion that he broke off is strengthened by the two conditional clauses: the first refers to the "negative" statement of v. 12 but the second sounds less logical as a reference to the same sentence. It fits only a "positive" statement which could have been offered after v. 12. Cranfield reconstructs the expected sentence in v. 12 along the lines of ἀλλὰ τῷ πνεύματι τοῦ κατὰ πνεῦμα ζῆν.[17] The second conditional clause then concludes the intended "positive" part of Paul's exposition: the Spirit makes possible the new life outside the Law, although it is not against the Law. Together the two conditional clauses form a wordplay[18] whereby Paul emphasizes two aspects of the message: a life according to the flesh leads to death but a life according to the Spirit, which puts to death that of the body, leads to life.[19] This is equivalent to what Paul has just said in v. 9: you are no longer in the flesh but in the Spirit, and if somebody does not have Christ's Spirit, he does not belong to Christ. By the language of dying and living and receiving the Spirit Paul seems to refer to the experience of baptism as dying from sin and receiving the Spirit.[20]

When in v. 14 the concept of sons of God is introduced, this is in fact a new thought. Before Chapter 8 Paul has spoken of the Son of God (1:3f.; 5:10; 8:3) but not of the sons, nor of the children, of God. This may be due to the fact that Paul connects the idea of sons to the idea of the Spirit. Those who are driven by the Spirit are the new people, the sons or children, of God.[21] Thus, when Paul has introduced the Spirit into the discussion, he can

---

[17] *Ad. loc.*

[18] The chiastic pattern of this verse (ζῆτε ... ἀποθνήσκειν — θανατοῦτε ... ζήσεσθε) may indicate that Paul uses traditional material, in the form of what has been called "Sätzen heiligen Rechts". The change of subject from "we" to "you" may be evidence of such quotation (Bindemann 1983, 33f.). Käsemann (1973, 215) sees the construction as an example on antithetic parallelism.

[19] The difference between σάρξ and σῶμα goes back to v. 9f. Käsemann interprets the two διά (v.10) differently: διὰ ἁμαρτίαν " ... sofern die Sünde in Frage steht ... ", διὰ δικαιοσύνην " ... was Gerechtigkeit angeht ... " (1973, 214). Cf. "Die bewußte Stilisierung, die V. a und V. b sich genau entsprechen läßt, ist nicht zu übersehen. Dann erkennt man jedoch, daß der doppelte Gebrauch des διά irreführend ist; er verschiebt sich nähmlich. Heißt διά in 10b 'wegen, weil', besagt es dort die notwendige Zusammengehörigkeit von Gerechtigkeit und Leben, so bedeutet es in 10 a limitierend: 'soweit'. Soweit der Leib sündig ist, ist er wie das Fleisch als sündige Weltlichkeit tot und bleibt auch der Tatsache der Auferstehung gegenüber tot" (Käsemann,1933, 123).

[20] 8:11 seems to allude to 6:9-11. Cf. 1Cor 12:13. V. 15 may also refer to the baptism: "The reference of the aorist ἐλάβετε is no doubt to the beginning of their Christian life—in particular, probably, to their baptism" (Cranfield 1980). Similarly e. g. Sanday and Headlam (1962), Käsemann (1973), Paulsen (1974, 87).

[21] It seems most likely that Paul here speaks of "sons of God" in the usual Jewish meaning of belonging to God's people (thus Bindemann 1983, 34). The distinction made by Sanday and Headlam, " ... τέκνον denotes the natural relationship of child to parent, υἱός implies, in addition to this, the recognized *status* and legal privileges reserved for sons" (1962, 202), does not hold, since the words are used vice versa in 8:17. Bruce is more right saying: "Nowhere in the New Testament can a valid distinction be made between being 'children (*tekna*) of God' and 'sons (*huioi*) of God' " (1971, 167). However, in Rom 8:19 Paul uses the word υἱοί in a different way, denoting angels.

talk of the sons, or of the children, of God. In v. 15 Paul elaborates these ideas: the Spirit is the Spirit not of slavery but of sonship. This is presented as an explanation (γάρ): we are sons of God, because we posess the Spirit of sonship. The contrast of slavery to sonship, not to freedom, is logical, since slave and son are opposites. The slave fears his master but the son cries Ἀββὰ ὁ πατήρ. This cry seems to be a well known phenomenon, to which Paul refers as further evidence of the indwelling of the Spirit: the one who cries "Abba, father" is, of course, the son.

From here the thought of sonship is developed, but in such a way that Paul in a few of steps leaves the σάρξ—πνεῦμα theme and advances to another contrast, namely that of present sufferings and future glory. The steps are: as sons we are heirs, but, as Christ is *the* Son, we are heirs together with Him, insofar as on the one hand, we now suffer with Him and, on the other, will one day be glorified with Him. Thus Paul returns to contrasting present and future, which he actually introduced in 5:1–11, and in v. 18 begins a detailed exposition of this aspect. Two general observations may be made: a) The strange apocalyptical language is limited to 18–27.[22] b) By v. 28 the theme of groaning yields to more explicit talk of God's care for those who love Him. Paul thereby returns to the reasoning of vv. 14–17. What follows after v. 27 reiterates the idea of a worldwide salvation. Vv. 28–30 concludes the section begun in v. 17f. by saying that for those who love God (a definition which overrules the classifications Jew and Gentile) everything works out well (v. 28a). They are in the plan of God, which from His foreknowledge of them works to their glorification (vv. 28b—30).

In vv. 31–39 Paul concludes the entire first half of the letter in a rather elevated tone and at the same time prepares the mind of the readers for the second part. Chapters 9–15 apply the faith to the relationship between the two major groups of the Christian community at that time, Jews and Gentiles. Thus no power in the universe will be able to separate the believers from the love of Christ. This is a conclusion, but also functions as an opening of the following discussion on Jews and Gentiles, which is terminated in 11:32[23] by a sentence which connects to this universalistic perspective of Rom 8: συνέκλεισεν γὰρ ὁ θεὸς τοὺς πάντας εἰς ἀπείθειαν, ἵνα τοὺς πάντας ἐλεήσῃ.

---

[22] That this section is marked by apocalyptical colouring is generally agreed. von der Osten-Sacken differs: "So scheint die Annahme näherliegend, daß die Überlieferung von Röm 8,19-27 eine christliche Schöpfung ist, die am ehesten hervorgerufen ist durch enthusiastische Strömungen, wie sie sich nach dem Zeugnis der paulinischen Briefe im griechischsprachigen Christentum gebildet haben" (1975, 101).

[23] Foerster terms this verse " . . . das Ziel der Erörterung von R 1-11 . . . " (1938, 1031).

3.1.4. Line of Thought in 8:17–27

In the following outline of the thought elements (hereafter abbreviated TE) of the text I do not primarily look for a possible structure which could be theologically motivated. I wish only to bring out the line of thought. By so doing we shall find some breaks or holes which I hope to fill in the second part of this Chapter.

The division of the text into TEs is somewhat problematic. The text does not present only one clearcut element of thought at a time, but thoughts of different kinds are sometimes fused. In these cases I first regard the whole complex in order to discern the main idea and then divide the TE into smaller parts.

The main issue of this dissertation concerns Rom 8:18–27. However, v. 17 is so closely bound to this text that it is necessary to begin the exposition of the line of thought in this verse. I shall number it as TE 0.

TE 0 (v. 17)

εἰ δὲ τέκνα, καὶ κληρονόμοι· κληρονόμοι μὲν θεοῦ, συγκληρονόμοι δὲ Χριστοῦ, εἴπερ συμπάσχομεν ἵνα καὶ συνδοξασθῶμεν.

Starting with the idea of the children of God Paul in TE 0 presents a chain of thoughts: as children of God we are also God's heirs, we are heirs together with Christ, and consequently will be glorified together with Him. Rather surprisingly, Paul in this chain of thought inserts a condition: if we suffer with Christ. This thought falls outside the conclusion which was begun in v. 12. In fact it introduces something new,[24] although Paul speaks of suffering in a similar way in 5:3.[25] The force of the εἴπερ clause, however, should not be taken as conditional ("provided that") but rather as reminding the readers of the consequence of faith in Christ.[26]

Leaving the topic of life in the power of the Spirit Paul takes up the theme

---

[24] Paul has spoken before of being united with Christ, viz. in chapter 6. There the prefixed συν is used in a similar way, but the topic is baptism as dying together with Christ: συνετάφημεν αὐτῷ (v.4); σύμφυτοι ... τῷ ὁμοιώματι τοῦ θανάτου αὐτοῦ (v.5); συνεσταυρώθη (v.6); συζήσομεν αὐτῷ (v.8). The sufferings mentioned in TE 0 (v.17) thus differ from the dying with Christ, mentioned in chapter 6, and also from the anguish described in the immediately preceding context, which has been directed to the question of dying from sin and living in Spirit together with Christ (8:1-11, 13).

[25] Balz seems to make a mistake when he sees "wörtliche Anklänge" between chapter 5 and chapter 8, mentioning as examples συμπάσχειν and παθήματα (1971, 31). In 5:3 Paul uses the word θλῖψις and not παθήματα. It should be observed that in 5:3 Paul does not explicitly define the sufferings as sufferings for Christ. From these observations it can be inferred that the Apostle does not write to a Church where persecution is the major problem. I therefore also believe it to be a mistake to outline 8:18-27 as a teaching of sufferings for Christ (thus Nygren 1947, 335; Sanday and Headlam 1962, 204-210).

[26] Thus Zahn (1865, 513), Lietzmann (1933), Schlier (1977), Cranfield (1980), Michel (1978). Differently Michaelis (1954, 925), who takes the clause as conditional. So also Käsemann (1973, 219).

of δόξα.[27] The present time is marked by suffering but the future will be characterized by glory. Paul thus introduces a thought of opposition, the present time as opposed to the future, and sufferings opposed to glory. Thus TE 0 plays the rôle of transition from the discussion of the present Christian life into a discussion of its eschatological perspective.[28]

TE 1 (v. 18)

Λογίζομαι γὰρ ὅτι οὐκ ἄξια τὰ παθήματα τοῦ νῦν καιροῦ πρὸς τὴν μέλλουσαν δόξαν ἀποκαλυφθῆναι εἰς ἡμᾶς.

λογίζομαι marks a new section.[29] By the change of the subject from plural to singular Paul makes the statement express a personal theological conviction.[30] TE 1 (v. 18) is formed as a plain statement which functions as an explanation (γάρ) of TE 0 (v. 17). Whereas in TE 0 (v. 17) the σὺν Χριστῷ is the central issue,[31] TE 1 (v. 18) concentrates on παθήματα and δόξα. The two words develop the idea of TE 0 (v. 17), noting on the one hand the contrast between "now" and "then", but stressing, on the other, the dominance of the hope of glory.

By the expression τοῦ νῦν καιροῦ Paul probably means " . . . the period of time which began with the Gospel events and will be terminated by the parousia".[32] It is characterized by suffering, παθήματα. The future is

---

[27] The theme of δόξα is introduced in 1:18-32. Because people did not honour God, they became futile in their mind, and God gave them up to various dishonourable habits. Paul continues in an apocalyptic perspective saying that there will be a day of wrath (2: 5), when God's wrath will be revealed, a day in which God will give honour (δόξα) to those who have done good and wrath to those who have done evil things, "the Jew first and also the Greek" (2:7ff.) . Everybody has lost the glory of God (3:23), but those who have peace with God through Christ rejoice in the hope of God's glory (5:2). This glory is available because of the union with Christ who was resurrected from the dead through the glory of God (6:4). Abraham, because of his faith, is the outstanding example of the right glorification of God through faith (4:20). The sonship and the glory in reality belong to Israel, but Israel did not understand this (9:4). However, this glory was promised also to the Gentiles (9:24).

[28] The rôle of v.17 as transition is rightly seen by e. g. Käsemann (1973), von der Osten-Sacken (1975, 54), Paulsen (1975, 80f.), Cranfield (1980, 404), Eareckson (1977, 66). Gager (1970, 327), understands vv. 18-27 as an exposition of v. 17, similarly Balz (1971, 33), (Paulsen 1974, 112), Bindemann (1983, 67).

[29] The οἴδαμεν of TE 4 (v. 22) has a similar function. Therefore it is natural to regard TE 1-3 as a coherent section of the text.

[30] "Es [λογίζομαι] bezeichnet nicht nur einen logischen Neuansatz, sondern auch einen hervorgehobenen theologischen Schluß (M. Luther: 'ich halte dafür')" (Michel 1978, 265); " . . . feststellendes Urteil . . . nicht Überzeugung . . . " (Käsemann 1973, 221).

[31] The preposition σύν plays a decisive rôle not only in Chapter 8 but also in the rest of the letter. It is evident that righteousness is only accessible through union with Christ in death and resurrection (chapter 6). In this Jew and Gentile are equals and must consequently accept each other as members in the body of Christ, which is in contrast to being formed according to this present world (12:1ff.).

[32] Cranfield (1980), Stählin (1942, 1108) writes: "Für Paulus ist eine Wendung charakteristisch, die er fast immer auf die Periode zwischen den Aeonen bezogen gebraucht: ὁ νῦν καιρός. Es ist für Israel die Zeit des Gnadenrests zwischen seiner Periode als Gottesvolk und seiner Wiederannahme am Ende (R 11,5), für die Christen aber einerseits die Leidenszeit zwischen der

characterized by the glory which will be revealed (ἡ μέλλουσα δόξα ἀποκαλυφθῆναι). In his development of the scheme present—future Paul thus resorts to apocalyptic language.[33] In apocalyptic thought God in the last days will reveal a reality of which the world is at present unaware.

A coming glory will be revealed "to us". What is meant by the εἰς ἡμᾶς is not immediately clear. In this context the most natural understanding of the expression is that "to us" something will be revealed which we, the believers, do not see now.[34] What will be revealed is perhaps explained in the next sentence, i. e. the sons of God. However, most interpreters accept the presupposition that the "sons of God" in TE 2 (v. 19) has to be the believers themselves. Consequently God will reveal His glory not *to* the believers but *in* or *through* them.[35] The believers themselves thus in some sense are the direct object which will be revealed. This idea of the revelation of the glory as a revelation in or through the believers also affects the concept of δόξα. Jervell consequently writes: "Die δόξα der Gläubigen, V. 18 und 21, ist natürlich die Christusgleichheit, V. 29–30".[36]

In regard to the following text TE 1 (v. 18) functions as a thesis followed by further explanations. Thus the γάρ may be considered to cover the entire section vv. 18–27.[37]

It is difficult to see how TE 0 (v. 17) is explained by that which follows in

---

Freudengegenwart des Bräutigams und seinem Wiedererscheinen (R 8,18), anderseits eine Zeit eigentümlicher göttlicher Gerechtigkeitsoffenbarung zwischen der Periode der ἀνοχὴ τοῦ θεοῦ und dem Endgericht (R 3,26)". Similarly Schlier (1977), Zeller (1985). Nygren understands the expression as equivalent to ὁ αἰὼν οὗτος, denoting not the time inaugurated by Christ but the old evil world (1947, 336).

[33] In fact, Paul has used this kind of language also in 1:18ff. The present world, seen through apocalyptic glasses, is a revelation of God's wrath.

[34] Newman and Nida (1973): " . . . God is going to reveal it to us . . . The most natural meaning of the Greek preposition εἰς (TEV to) would seem to be that of 'to' or 'for', although there are definite instances in the New Testament where it does have the force of 'in'. If the usual meaning is given to this preposition, the present passage indicates that at the end of time God will reveal his glory 'to' or 'for the benefit of' his people (note Segond 'for us'). Otherwise, the focus is on the truth that at that time God's people will share in and reflect God's true glory. No dogmatic conclusion can be made, and translators may follow either exegesis".

[35] Sanday and Headlam (1962) paraphrase v.18: "What of that? For the sufferings which we have to undergo in this phase of our career I count not worth a thought in view of that dazzling splendour which will one day break through the clouds and dawn *upon us*" (my italics). Schlier (1977, 257f.): "Dabei erläutert der Apostel hier wie überall nicht, was mit der δόξα gemeint ist. Er deutet nur an, daß sie 'über uns' oder 'auf uns herab' (εἰς ἡμᾶς) kommt, um uns in sich aufzunehmen und verklärt oder verherrlicht sein zu lassen mit Christus in Gottes Herrlichkeit". Similarly Michel (1978): "Die Herrlichkeit Gottes wird am jüngsten Tage 'in Richtung auf uns' (εἰς ἡμᾶς = *in nos*) offenbart werden". Michel comments: "Das Offenbarwerden der 'Söhne Gottes' ist wohl als eine Art Präsentation vor dem Kosmos gedacht". Simlarly Althaus (1954). These interpretations may stand as examples of the general understanding of the expression εἰς ἡμᾶς.

[36] 1960, 282. Cranfield, following Chrysostom, holds the δόξα to be the sonship of which the believers are heirs (1980, 409). Similarly most exegetes.

[37] The introduction of a section of the text by such a thesis is not unusual in the Pauline letters. Cf. 1:18; 6:1-2.

v. 18ff. Strictly speaking, the belief that the sufferings of the present time are not worthy of comparison to the coming glory does not explain or support the belief that we will inherit glory if we suffer now.[38] Paul seems to have omitted one element in the line of thought, viz. something such as: "we certainly have to suffer but you should not be discouraged because . . . " The argument builds on what was said in TE 0 (v. 17): That we will be glorified with Christ means that as His glory transcends everything so will ours when we are glorified together with Him. Still, this understanding does not totally remove the difficulty.

TE 2 (v. 19)

ἡ γὰρ ἀποκαραδοκία τῆς κτίσεως τὴν ἀποκάλυψιν τῶν υἱῶν τοῦ θεοῦ ἀπεκδέχεται

Through γάρ TE 2 (v. 19) is presented as an explanation of TE 1 (v. 18).[39] Thus, as proof of the relevance of his evaluation in TE 1 (v. 18), Paul a little surprisingly says that Creation is eagerly longing[40] for the "revelation of the sons of God". Apparently Paul develops the idea of an ἀποκάλυψις introduced in TE 1 (v. 18). It is, however, unclear how Paul conceives of this event. The thought that something is to be revealed implies that this object is hidden. Thus there are sons of God who for the present time are hidden but who will be revealed by a future event. Who are these "sons of God"? Referring to v. 14 most interpreters equate (from v. 14) the "sons of God" to the "we" of the text, i. e. the believers. Consequently they are forced to interpret the "us" (εἰς ἡμᾶς) in TE 1 (v. 18) as the object that will be revealed, which

---

[38] According to Bauer-Aland (1988, 304, *s. v.* 1, e) the thought to be supported by γάρ in Rom 8:18 is not expressed, but has to be supplied from the context. Luz (1968, 377): "Eine Begründung im strengen Sinn liegt aber nicht vor: 'Gar' ist am ehesten mit 'aber' zu übersetzen". Similarly Newman and Nida (1973, 157) propose that the γάρ should not be understood as a logical conclusion "but rather that he [Paul] is making a theological declaration in light of his own faith and hope". Cranfield (1980) writes: "The γάρ is accounted for by the fact that v. 18 explains how the sufferings and glory referred to in v. 17 stand in relation to each other". Balz (1971, 33) sees a hidden question behind v.17c which is answered in 18ff: "V.18 wendet diese Aussagen gegen einen Einwand, der zwar nicht ausgesprochen ist, aber dennoch als zweifelnde Frage die Heilshoffnung stets bedrängt: Welchen Sinn hat es, von der künftigen Herrlichkeit der Glaubenden zu reden, wo sie doch in ihrer jetzigen Existenz unter den Bedingungen dieser heillosen Welt zu leiden haben? Röm 8, 18ff. will auf diese Frage antworten". Paulsen (1974, 108) speaks of v.18 as "eine Überleitung". Similarly von der Osten-Sacken (1975, 140f.): "Als Begründung für V. 17c läßt sich V. 18 in strengem Sinne nur formal verstehen. Denn wenn er auch mit γάρ anschließt und wie V. 17c das Verhältnis von Leiden und Herrlichkeit behandelt, so trägt die Bestimmung dieses Verhältnisses jeweils einen anderen Akzent".

[39] Käsemann (1973, 221) regards vv.19-27 as a "Gegenströmung" to v.18. I agree with Wilckens (1980, 156): "von einer solchen ist im Text nichts zu erkennen". Bindemann (1983, 25-28) severely criticizes Käsemann's theory in an excursus under the headline "Projektion in der Interpretation von Texten — eine Illustration" .

[40] Paul uses a strange expression: ἡ ἀποκαραδοκία τῆς κτίσεως ἀπεκδέχεται. The construction making ἡ ἀποκαραδοκία and not ἡ κτίσις the subject seems to be aimed at intensifying the thought of longing.

is hardly the most natural reading, as has been pointed out above.[41] The hypothesis becomes still more complicated when we realize that according to TE 5–7 (vv. 23–25) the Christians still seem to long for the adoption to take place. This creates a considerable difference from the preceding verses (12–17) and nourishes the suspicion that Paul is dependent on traditional material in TE 2 (v. 19). The main interest of TE 2 is in Creation and not in the sons of God, which also holds true for the following TEs. If Paul wanted to say: "Our sufferings in this time cannot be compared to our glory in the time to come, because this glory is of such a magnitude that the entire Creation is longing to see us glorified", he would not have lingered on the circumstances of Creation as he does in TE 3ff.

But there are more questions. How are we to conceive of Creation as eagerly expecting a revelation? What is meant by Creation in this statement, and how are we to understand the longing? Paul's proposition presupposes that Creation is in possession of intelligence and emotional life.[42] Furthermore, if Paul really speaks of a revelation of the Christians, this is the only occurence of this thought in the New Testament.[43] The logical connection between a revelation of these sons and the evaluation of present and future times made in TE 1 is unclear, to say the least, for how can the idea that sons of God will be revealed explain or confirm the statement that the present time of suffering is insignificant in relation to the coming glory? Accordingly as for the line of thought, we can only state that Creation longs for a mysterious revelation of the sons of God—whoever they are—and this to Paul is related to the coming glory.

Finally, why does Paul change from τέκνα in TE 0 (v. 17) to υἱοί (cf. v. 14)? It would have seemed natural to retain τέκνα as he develops TE 0, especially as he returns to the term in TE 3c (v. 20b).

---

[41] According to this understanding the "glory" which will be revealed to us (TE 1 v.18) is interpreted by the statement that the sons will be revealed (see note 34). But Paul does not say that the sonship spoken of in the letter would be hidden. He speaks of the believers as united with Christ in baptism and as driven by the Spirit. Both characteristics rather seem to mark them as different from the rest of the world. Furthermore, in order to explain why Creation longs for this revelation, it has to be conjectured that the deliverance of Creation is dependent on the revelation of the believers. Hence the suggestion that because Creation was cursed by the Fall of Adam it will be freed by the salvation of man. Of this we never hear in any of Paul's letters.

[42] This question has been in the centre of interest for exegetes since the Early Church (see 1.3.1).

[43] Balz remarks that if this is really the meaning, this is the only text in the Bible in which believers are the object of revelation. He comments: "Selbst die Anklänge in 1 Thess 4,13ff.; 1 Kor 15,24; 2 Petr 1,11; Mk 13,27; Mt 24,31; Lk 21,28, wo es stets um das Geschick der Gemeinde selbst im Eschaton geht, bilden keine echten Parallelen. An sich hätte die Hoffnung der Schöpfung auch dem künftigen Gerichtstag (2Petr 3,13) oder der ἀποκατάστασις πάντων (Apg 3,21) gelten können, aber Paulus scheint auf eine besondere Verbindung zwischen Schöpfung und Endgemeinde Wert zu legen, wie er sie bereits in apokalyptischen Vorstellungen vorfand" (1971, 38). Followed by Kehnscherper (1979, 413).

TE 3 (v. 20f.)

²⁰τῇ γὰρ ματαιότητι ἡ κτίσις ὑπετάγη, οὐχ ἑκοῦσα ἀλλὰ διὰ τὸν ὑποτάξαντα, ἐφ' ἐλπίδι ²¹ὅτι καὶ αὐτὴ ἡ κτίσις ἐλευθερωθήσεται ἀπὸ τῆς δουλείας τῆς φθορᾶς εἰς τὴν ἐλευθερίαν τῆς δόξης τῶν τέκνων τοῦ θεοῦ Now TE 2 (v. 19) in turn is explained by a new clause introduced by γάρ. The explanation consists in an exposition of the origin of the present situation.[44] TE 3 (v. 20f.) is rather complex. The main structure is:

τῇ γὰρ ματαιότητι ἡ κτίσις ὑπετάγη . . . ἐφ ἐλπίδι ὅτι καὶ αὐτὴ ἡ κτίσις ἐλευθερωθήσεται

In this structure Paul has included several additions. One complicating factor is the insertion in the running sentence of οὐχ ἑκοῦσα ἀλλὰ διὰ τὸν ὑποτάξαντα. The thought of the liberation of Creation is also supplemented. Furthermore, the relationship of ἐπ' ἐλπίδι to the rest of the sentence is far from evident: does it belong to ὑπετάγη or to τὸν ὑποτάξαντα or to what?[45] I divide TE 3 into three parts.

TE 3a (v. 20a)

τῇ γὰρ ματαιότητι ἡ κτίσις ὑπετάγη

The present situation came about through an event in past time. This is obvious from Paul's choice of the aorist tense in ὑπετάγη. On that occasion Creation was subdued to something. What is to be understood by the term ματαιότης is not immediately clear.[46] It is a central term in the Wisdom literature, where it means meaninglessness, futility.[47] Because Paul says that Creation was subjected to ματαιότης but will be freed from φθορά, exegetes have concluded that the two words have the same significance, i. e. that they both mean destruction.[48] That ματαιότης and φθορά actually refer to the

---

[44] Schwantes forcefully reduces the importance of TE 3 (v. 20 f.): "Man darf nun beide Verse nicht in der Weise hochschätzen, als wolle Paulus mit ihnen über die *Zukunft der Welt berichten.* Für den Zusammenhang sind sie nicht mehr als nur eine Glosse zu V. 19. . . . Paulus benutzt nun die These von der notvollen Situation des Kosmos (V. 22) als Folie für die Darstellung entsprechend menschlicher Situation (V. 23)" (1963, 50). He even calls vv.20f. a "Parenthese" (*op. cit.,* 49f.).

[45] The difference becomes important as soon as it is realized that the subject of ὑπετάγη is not necessarily identical with τὸν ὑποτάξαντα. Thus ἐφ' ἐλπίδι is taken together with ὑπετάγη by Sanday and Headlam (1962), Michel (1978), Cranfield (1980), Schlier (1977), and Paulsen (1974, 114), but with τὸν ὑποτάξαντα by Biedermann, who says:"Es is undenkbar, Satan oder der Mensch habe ihr die Hoffnung auf Befreiung gegeben. Darum bleibt nur die dritte Möglichkeit: Gott selber ist der ὑποτάξας" (1940, 74).

[46] According to Zahn (1910, 401) it must be understood as a state of weakness, and according to Lagrange (1950, 207) as a disorder.

[47] ματαιότης is not often used in profane Greek texts but rather frequently in the LXX. Bauernfeind comments: "R 8, 20 ist gültiger Kommentar zu Qoh" (1942a, 529).

[48] Biedermann (1940, 73). Most interpreters tend to believe that the two words must have the same meaning. This is not a necessary conclusion: "Die ματαιότης ist nicht mit der φθορά v.21 identisch" (Delling 1969, 41 note 5).

same background is indisputable. However, the first term alludes to the event whereby the present situation came about and the second to the present state of affairs from which Creation will be freed. The terms may thus be understood as two aspects of the same event. When speaking of the power to which Creation was subjected (TE 3a v.20a) this is seen as meaninglessness. When speaking of the power from which Creation will be freed (TE 3c v. 20c—21) this is seen as destruction.

Today it is generally assumed by exegetes that Paul has the Fall of Adam in mind. However, there are considerable differences between the story of the Fall and our TE.[49]

TE 3b (v. 20b)

οὐχ ἑκοῦσα ἀλλὰ διὰ τὸν ὑποτάξαντα

The circumstances of the event designated in TE 3a (v. 20a) by the word ὑπετάγη are more closely defined. Two facts are stated: First, Creation was subjected οὐχ ἑκοῦσα. This expression may be understood in one of two ways: "not willingly", or "without its own action".[50] Second, it was brought about διὰ τὸν ὑποτάξαντα. The expression is difficult to interpret because it is unclear whom Paul has in mind. If he thought of God as subduing Creation why did he not say so? As TE 3a (v. 20a) now stands the agent of the ὑπετάγη does not seem to be the person mentioned as ὁ ὑποτάξας. We need further information on the background in order to be able to interpret the rôle of this statement within the line of thought.

TE 3c (vv. 20c—21)

ἐφ' ἑλπίδι, ὅτι καὶ αὐτὴ ἡ κτίσις ἐλευθερωθήσεται ἀπὸ τῆς δουλείας τῆς φθορᾶς εἰς τὴν ἐλευθερίαν τῆς δόξης τῶν τέκνων τοῦ θεοῦ.

TE 3c makes the text overloaded and heavy. It seems to offer an explanation of TE 3a (v. 20a) which has said that Creation was subject to ματαιότης. Now this is qualified—it happened ἐφ' ἑλπίδι.[51] The ὅτι clause defines the content of the expression ἐφ' ἑλπίδι.[52]

---

[49] Paul does not speak of a curse but of subjection. Furthermore, the snake, Adam and Eve were not subjected to futility or destruction. In order to fit the story of the Fall to Paul's text one must interpret the punishments, which were imposed on Creation (Gen 3) as futility and destruction.

[50] E. g: "Der Mench vollbrachte die Sünde mit eigenem Entschluß, dagegen erlitt die Natur die Unterwerfung unter die Nichtigkeit ohne eigene Willenstat" (Hauck, 1935, 467); "(aber) nicht freiwillig = sie unterwarf sich nicht freiwillig" (Bauer-Aland 1988, 499, s. v.); "is naturally understood as meaning 'not through its own fault' " (Cranfield 1980).

[51] The softening of the π to an φ followed by spiritus asper in ἐφ' ἑλπίδι is attested also in papyri and inscriptions in this specific expression. "But in the case of ἐλπίς, ἰδεῖν, ἴδιος, ὀλίγος, ἐφιορκεῖν alone, where aspiration in the NT is frequenty and strongly attested , aspiration is supported by other MS tradition, by inscriptions and papyri (seldom pre-Christian . . .). The basis of the phenomenon in any case is to be sought in analogies" (Blass-Debrunner 1967, § 14). In quotations of Paul's text I shall follow this spelling.

[52] The ἐπ' ἑλπίδι usually is connected to the word ὑπετάγη. From his opinion that the

106

Explaining TE 1 (v. 19) Paul spoke of Creation as longing because it is subjected to meaninglessness. In TE 3c (vv. 20c—21) he adds another fact: There is a hope of deliverance.[53] This information is rather difficult to comprehend.[54] The hope is explicated in the ὅτι clause on the one hand as a deliverance from something (ἀπὸ τῆς δουλείας τῆς φθορᾶς) and on the other as a deliverance to something (εἰς τὴν ἐλευθερίαν τῆς δόξης τῶν τέκνων τοῦ θεοῦ).[55] Thus δουλείας τῆς φθορᾶς seems to be contrasted to ἐλευθερίαν τῆς δόξης.[56]

Paul again returns to the opposition between the present and the future time in vv. 12f., and in v. 17 (TE 0) connects it to the theme of δόξα as well as in TE 1 (v. 18). Sufferings in the present lead to glory in the future. In TE 3c (vv. 20c—21) the theme has undergone a change: this time interest is focused on Creation *itself* (αὐτὴ ἡ κτίσις) in contrast to the children of God. The future glory, which belongs to the children of God, is described as the hope of all Creation.[57] If the "sons of God" in TE 2 (v. 19) are the Christians, then at this point again Paul changes his expression back to "children of God", last mentioned in TE 0 (v. 17).

ὑποτάξας must be Adam Cranfield concludes that "Hope for the Creation was included within the hope for man" (1980, 414), a thought which is not expressed in Paul's text. The meaning of the dat. of ἐπ᾽ ἐλπίδι is not to describe a hope present in the subordinator but rather a hope given to the subordinated Creation.

[53] ἐπί with the dative is explained by Bauer-Aland as locative in the meaning "aufgrund v.d. Grund, auf dem e. Zustand, e. Handlung od. Folge beruht" (1988, 581. II. γ) and translate the expression "auf Grund der Hoffnung" (*op. cit.* 510, *s. v.* ἐλπίς 1). Similarly Blass-Debrunner translates "on the basis of hope" (1967, § 235, 2).

[54] Usually the expression ἐπ᾽ ἐλπίδι is connected to the verb ὑπετάγη. But, as we have seen, it is uncertain who is the subject of this verb and how it is related to ὁ ὑποτάξας. Most scholars understands the subject of ὑπετάγη to be God, especially since only God has the authority to promise hope to Creation (thus e. g. Schlatter 1935; Gaugler 1945; Gieraths 1950, 119; Sanday and Headlam 1962; Cranfield 1980). Zahn, who thinks that Adam is the subject of ὑπετάγη explains his position: "Gesagt ist nur, daß dabei Hoffnung vorhanden war und, da der abnorme Zustand der Kreatur seitdem wesentlich unverändert fortdauert, noch immer Hoffnung besteht, wie auch wir uns ausdrücken, ohne an ein bestimmtes Subjekt des Hoffens zu denken" (1910, 403). Schläger, (1930, 357), who thinks that ὁ ὑποτάξας is Satan does not comment on ἐπ᾽ ἐλπίδι (1930, 357). According to von der Osten-Sacken Paul is probably quoting a traditional text which he corrects by inserting the expression ἐπ᾽ ἐλπίδι and the conjunction διότι (1975, 88). Similarly Paulsen (1974, 117). Käsemann thinks that the ἐπ᾽ ἐλπίδι expresses Paul's interpretation of ἀποκαραδοκία τῆς κτίσεως (1973). Christians understand the longing and groaning of Creation as a token of hope. The words thus should be Paul's own. But Paul usually writes ἐπ᾽ ἐπλίδι (Rom 4:18; 5:2; 1Cor 9:10, here twice). It seems more likely that the unusual form of the expression depends on influence from some traditional material. (Cf. Blass-Debrunner note 51.)

[55] τῆς δόξης could be taken as *subjective gen*, expressing that freedom belongs to the glory. If so the main thought is that Creation will share the glory which belongs to the children; *qualitative*, expressing that the freedom of the children of God is glorious. The consequence in regard to Creation would be very close to the foregoing.

[56] Cranfield (1980, 416) takes δόξης to τῶν τέκνων τοῦ θεοῦ and interprets: " . . . a liberty which results from, is the necessary accompaniment of, the (revelation of the) glory of the children of God".

[57] von der Osten-Sacken declared that this is the only place in the undisputed Pauline letters where the verb ἐλευθεροῦν is used in future tense and the liberation is spoken of as a future gift (1975, 83).

Paul also retains the theme of glory (δόξα), but uses the word δόξα in a rather unusual way. δόξα normally would not be contrasted to φθορά.[58] Therefore it has been proposed that the word has undergone a change of meaning in this verse.[59] All this means that we need more information concerning the background of Paul's deliberations.[60]

Looking back on TE 3a—3c (v. 20f.) we sum up the information, inserting the TEs in the line of thought. TE 3 is presented as evidence supporting TE 2 (v. 19), which in turn should confirm TE 1 (v. 18), an evaluation of the coming glory as incomparably greater than the present sufferings. The explanation of why it can be said that Creation is longing for the sons of God to be revealed (TE 2, v. 19) consists in the belief that the present situation of suffering was once brought about in a manner which gave hope to Creation. At this point we do not know what is meant by Creation nor how it can be longing. Creation was enslaved against its will, as the result of another's action. Who is meant is debated and no certainty can be reached. Hope seems to have been explicitly granted to Creation itself, that one day it will share the very freedom that belongs to the children of God.

TE 4 (v. 22)

οἴδαμεν γὰρ ὅτι πᾶσα ἡ κτίσις συστενάζει καὶ συνωδίνει ἄχρι τοῦ νῦν
In this TE the expression οἴδαμεν . . . ὅτι marks a new turn of the text. By the plural in οἴδαμεν Paul refers to something on which the readers are expected to agree. This indicates that the material is derived from a traditional background.[61] TE 4 (v. 22) provides an explanation of the previous verse (γάρ).[62] However, it is difficult to define what is explained.[63] It seems most

---

[58] Cf., however, 1Cor 15:42b —43a: ἐν φθορᾷ / ἐν ἀφθαρσίᾳ par. ἐν ἀτιμίᾳ / ἐν δόξῃ.

[59] von der Osten-Sacken concludes that the word δόξα consequently should mean imperishableness ("Unvergänglichkeit") rather than "glory". This sense of the word, von der Osten-Sacken admits, is without parallel in Pauline writings (1975, 84).

[60] The uncertainty of the significance of this text is reflected in the interpretation of the words ματαιότης and φθορά. As we have seen, von der Osten-Sacken changes the usual meaning of φθορά, others alter that of ματαιότης (e.g. "idolatry" according to Schläger 1930; Hommel 1984, 139; "religiösen oder sittlichen Irrtum" according to Gieraths 1950, 129; "perversity" according to Fahy 1956 "St. Paul", 179), or make the two words have the same meaning (e.g. Zahn 1910; Lietzmann 1933). Balz sees δουλεία τῆς φθορᾶς as an interpretation of the ματαιότης of v. 20 (1971, 50).

[61] According to Michel Paul uses the term οἴδαμεν γάρ (or δέ) to allude to traditional material common to Paul and his readers in Rom 2:2; 3:19; 7:14; 8:22, 28 (1978, 268, note 13). That traditional material is used in 8:22 is assumed also by Paulsen (1974, 119) and Wilckens (1980). Balz is less sure thinking that Paul refers both to experience and to theological teaching because in apocalyptic texts he finds "nur gewisse Anklänge" of this thought (1971, 52). Differently Käsemann, who referring to Schlier (Schlier 1965, 605f.) says: "22 resümiert mit einleitendem, vom Glauben gesagtem οἴδαμεν" (1973, 226).

[62] I take the γάρ to be used in the ordinary way and thus explaining something. Against Balz who says: "Mit dem für den ganzen Zusammenhang typischen γάρ scheint Paulus zunächst eine Begründung einzuleiten, aber es folgt so etwas wie ein Fazit, das das leitende Motiv des 'Stöhnens' formuliert" (1971, 52). According to Wilckens (1980, 147): "In V. 22 setzt er mit 'Wir wissen

probable that the reference is to TE 3a (v. 20a).[64] Thus both Paul and his readers know that Creation is groaning and this common knowledge explains the subjection to ματαιότης. The ματαιότης is the cause of Creation's groaning and birthpangs.

The problem regarding the term κτίσις recurs. The actions ascribed to Creation are very unusual, to say the least. As we have seen at least six possibilities have been brought forward through the ages.[65] To me it seems natural to assume that Paul speaks of the total Creation outside the believers because the believers are conjoined in TE 5a (v. 23). The thought of the totality of Creation is doubly emphasized: a) Paul mentions the subject as πᾶσα ἡ κτίσις, and b) he uses the prefixed συν together with the verbs.[66] The common groaning and birthpangs have lasted, Paul says, ἄχρι τοῦ νῦν.[67] Paul seems to express the thought that Creation's oppression has reached a decisive or critical moment.

But there are more questions. How should groaning and suffering birthpangs on the part of Creation be understood? How are we to conceive of the combination of the verbs στενάζειν and ὠδίνειν?

Thus in TE 4 (v. 22) Paul refers to a conception of Creation which he has in common with the recipients of the letter. This conception is used as evidence of what he has said in the previous TEs about Creation's subjection. It seems clear that also the ideas behind those TEs (i. e. TEs 2–3, vv. 19–21) are shared by the recipients of the letter.

TE 5 (v. 23)

οὐ μόνον δέ, ἀλλὰ καὶ αὐτοὶ τὴν ἀπαρχὴν τοῦ πνεύματος ἔχοντες, ἡμεῖς καὶ αὐτοὶ ἐν ἑαυτοῖς στενάζομεν υἱοθεσίαν ἀπεκδεχόμενοι, τὴν ἀπολύτρωσιν τοῦ σώματος ἡμῶν.

The chain of thoughts on the situation of Creation is interrupted by the expression οὐ μόνον δέ, and something is added[68] to the preceding TEs. In fact Paul returns to the exposition of the state of the believers (vv. 1–17).

TE 5 (v. 23) is complicated by two expansions of the sentence. Paul has

---

nämlich' zu einer zweiten Ausführung an, die bis V. 23 reicht". Schwantes (1963, 50): "Nach diesem erläuternden Exkurs schließt nun, sachlich gesehen, V. 22 direkt an V. 19 an".

[63] Schwantes thinks that v. 22 explains v. 19. According to him v. 20f. is a gloss (1963, 47, 50). von der Osten-Sacken finds v. 22 to introduce empirical verifications of what is said in vv. 19–21 (TE 1–3) (1975, 98). Paulsen sees the verse as strangely isolated in the continuity of thoughts and speaks of it as "eine isolierte Sentenz" (1974, 118f.) .

[64] While it cannot reasonably relate to TE 0, TE 1, or TE 2, it can be connected to TE 3.

[65] See 1.3.1. and 1.3.2.4.1.

[66] There seems to be a consensus among interpreters concerning Bauer-Aland's translation of συνωδίνειν: "Zusammen in Wehen liegen od. auch allg. gemeinsam Schmerz empfinden" (1988, 1583. s. v.).

[67] In Pauline writings the expression indicates the timespan between the earthly life of Jesus and the parousia (Stählin 1942, 1116).

[68] Bauer-Aland: "οὐ μ. δέ, ἀλλὰ καί noch nicht . . . sondern auch, dazu auch (Ellipse m. Ergänzung des unmittelbaren Vorhergehenden", (1988, 1068, μόνος 2 c).

added τὴν ἀπαρχὴν τοῦ πνεύματος ἔχοντες to the αὐτοί, and τὴν ἀπολύτρωσιν τοῦ σώματος ἡμῶν to υἱοθεσίαν. In point of language, the manner in which the "we ourselves" is introduced is somewhat awkward: οὐ μόνον δέ, ἀλλὰ καὶ αὐτοὶ ... ἡμεῖς καὶ αὐτοὶ ἐν ἑαυτοῖς. TE 5 will be discussed in sections.

TE 5a (v. 23a)

οὐ μόνον δέ, ἀλλὰ καὶ αὐτοὶ ... ἡμεῖς καὶ αὐτοὶ ἐν ἑαυτοῖς στενάζομεν υἱοθεσίαν ἀπεκδεχόμενοι.

The interest again reverts to the believers. Nevertheless their groaning seems to be secondary in relation to that of Creation. Creation is not groaning alone but we ourselves groan too. When returning to the situation of the believers Paul also takes up again the themes of πνεῦμα and υἱοθεσία. The theme of longing (ἀπεκδέχεσθαι), which has been followed through this section of the text, is retained.

The overloaded expression ἀλλὰ καὶ αὐτοὶ ... ἡμεῖς καὶ αὐτοὶ ἐν ἑαυτοῖς may be due to a need to emphasize the thought of the believers as longing.[69] Paul has added the attributive τὴν ἀπαρχὴν τοῦ πνεύματος ἔχοντες and thereby separated the subject too far from the predicate. He therefore repeats the ἡμεῖς. The ἐν ἑαυτοῖς could be interpreted in three ways: a) inwardly,[70] b) inside the Christian fellowship, i. e. in the Church,[71] c) in respect to ourselves, in contrast to Creation. Since in TE 5c (v. 23c) Paul says that we long for the redemption of the body he does not seem to speak of the Church. Thus the second alternative falls. The similarity to 2Cor 4:16–5:5 has sometimes caused interpreters to choose the first alternative.[72] However, in 2Cor Paul speaks from an wholly different viewpoint, that of his own sufferings and even death. In the present text Paul develops an apocalyptic perspective on the coming glory. Thus even the first alternative must be rejected. The expression οὐ μόνον δέ, ἀλλὰ καί serves, as we have seen, to introduce something new as opposed to the foregoing. This fits the last alternative, which has to be chosen.[73]

The concept of υἱοθεσία is reintroduced. Last time it occurred in v. 14f. Up to Chapter 8 the main stream of thought has been concentrated on the righteousness revealed in Christ, which is seen as a present reality accessible through the power of the Spirit. In regard to meaning the υἱοθεσία of TE 5a (v. 23a) stands opposed to v. 14f., as it is no longer regarded as a present reality.[74] However, this tension between present and future has been silently

---

[69] "The αὐτοὶ ... καὶ αὐτοί is extremely emphatic" (Cranfield 1980).

[70] E. g. Althaus (1954), Dodd (1963), Bruce (1971).

[71] E. g. Käsemann (1973).

[72] E. g. Nygren (1947).

[73] So Vögtle (1970, 200), Balz (1971, 57).

[74] The problem is old, as can be seen in the manuscripts, where already P⁴⁶, like D G and

present in the text since Chapter 6[75] and belongs to genuine Pauline theology.

Thus the theme of longing naturally enters the discussion. Paul has said that the believers, suffering together with Christ, will be glorified together with Him. Then he devoted a section to explaining the Creation's longing for the sons of God to be revealed (ἀποκαραδοκία, ἀπεκδέχεσθαι, v. 19, συστενάζειν, συνωδίνειν, v. 22). It is natural that also the believers should long for the glorification which they are promised and for which they hope.

TE 5b (v. 23a)

τὴν ἀπαρχὴν τοῦ πνεύματος ἔχοντες

These words further define the believers, i. e. Paul himself together with the readers. Paul takes up again the theme of the Spirit. A new life is possible, he has said earlier, because the believers live in the Spirit (vv. 1–17, especially v. 14), which implies sonship to God with Christ and (a hope of) inheritance with Him. All this is now gathered in the idea of having the first fruit of the Spirit. By the expression "first fruit" of the Spirit[76] Paul may mean that we have only tasted the beginning of what Spirit means, or that we only possess the first fruit as a promise of the fullness which will be realized later, or possibly both. Thus this TE in fact seems to contradict the statements of the preceding context, which implies that the believer is already living a spiritual life. Actually the tension is not unlike that discussed under TE 5a (v. 23a).

TE 5c (v. 23b)

υἱοθεσίαν . . . τὴν ἀπολύτρωσιν τοῦ σώματος ἡμῶν

The said υἱοθεσία is further defined as the freeing of our bodies.[77] Apparently Paul here refers back to v. 10 where he speaks of the present condition of Christian life. The concept σῶμα is used by Paul to designate man as related to this world.[78] The concept per se is not negative but as worldly the

---

some others, omits the word υἱοθεσία. Schläger takes the word to be a later addition (1930, 360), so also Benoit (1961,41), Wilcke (1967, 65 note 239). Paulsen names this an "exegetische Verlegenheitslösung" (1974, 131).

[75] In baptism the believers were buried (aorist) together with Christ (συνετάφημεν αὐτῷ, 6:4). Thus they are united (perfect) with Christ in a death like his (σύμφυτοι γεγόναμεν τῷ ὁμοιώματι τοῦ θανάτου αὐτοῦ), but they will (future) be resurrected together with him (τῆς ἀναστάσεως ἐσόμεθα 6:5). Similarly in 8:13 Paul says that "if by the Spirit you kill the deeds of the body you will live" (ζήσεσθε).

[76] The gen. τοῦ πνεύματος could be interpreted differently. Cranfield (1980) mentions a) partitive, b) appositive and c) possessive genitive as possibilities. Käsemann (1973) takes it as epexegetical.

[77] Fahy says "The words ἀπολύτρωσις τοῦ σώματος mean release from the body in death" (1956 "St. Paul", 180). Similarly Lietzmann (1933). This is denied by most exegetes, since Paul never otherwise speaks of being freed from the body. The thought has to be understood from what Paul says in 1Cor 15:54; Phil 3:21; 1Thes 4:16f.

[78] Käsemann has expressed this as follows: "Will man das ontologisch definieren, ist festzustellen, Leiblichkeit sei das Wesen des Menschen in seiner Notwendigkeit, am Kreatürlichen

body can be seen as weak and associated to what is characteristic of this present world, death and destruction. Thus, through their assocation with Creation the believers long for the adoption which means that their bodies are freed. Thus there is a certain concept of ἀπεκδέχεσθαι: Creation longs for the sons of God to be revealed, and we, the believers, long for our bodies to be freed.

TE 6 (v. 24a)
τῇ γὰρ ἐλπίδι ἐσώθημεν

TE 6 explains TE 5 (v. 23) (γάρ). The dative is not instrumental[79] but modal.[80]

The construction well defines Paul's idea of salvation. It is a reality which has been brought about. Behind the statement of the aorist we must recall Paul's exposition of God's act in Christ in which the believers are incorporated through baptism. Yet, this salvation is realized in hope. In fact, this thought was also present in Chapter 6: we are already dead together with Christ but in the future we shall be resurrected together with Him. This thought was reiterated in 8:11. The same idea also lies behind 8:17: in the future the believers will be glorified together with Christ. Salvation cannot be perfected in this life, because by our bodies (TE 5c v. 23b) we are bound to the present fallen world. Thus the theme of hope, earlier discussed in relation to Creation (TE 3c v. 20c—21.), is applied to the believers.

The statement of TE 5a (v. 23a) is thus supported from the basic understanding of salvation as an "already but not yet".

TE 7 (v. 24b)
ἐλπὶς δὲ βλεπομένη οὐκ ἔστιν ἐλπίς· ὃ γὰρ βλέπει τίς ἐλπίζει;

Paul gives a logical argument to TE 6 (v. 24a). Things seen can no longer be understood as hope. The opposite would be a contradiction in terms. This is a clear rhetorical argument to which Paul adds a rhetorical question with the same meaning: "Who can hope for that which is a present reality?" The answer has to be "Nobody". Thus Paul doubly underlines the conception of the present state of the believers as one of expectation.

TE 8 (v. 25)
εἰ δὲ ὃ οὐ βλέπομεν ἐλπίζομεν, δι' ὑπομονῆς ἀπεκδεχόμεθα

TE 8 has the form of a conditional clause of reality. Hope of what is not seen means persistent hope. By the term ἀπεκδεχόμεθα Paul closes the circle which was begun in TE 5a (v. 23a). The eschatological aspect of salvation, or the υἱοθεσία, is brought into strong relief.

---

zu partizipieren, und in seiner Fähigkeit zur Kommunikation im weitesten Sinne, nämlich seiner Bezogenheit auf eine ihm jeweils vorgegebene Welt" (1969 "Anthropologie", 43).

[79] Lietzmann (1933), equivalent to the ἐπ' ἐλπίδι of TE 3c, v.20.

[80] Sanday and Headlam (1962, 209f.), Luz (1968, 375), Cranfield (1980).

TE 9 (v. 26a)

Ὡσαύτως δὲ καὶ τὸ πνεῦμα συναντιλαμβάνεται τῇ ἀσθενείᾳ ἡμῶν

The expression ὡσαύτως δὲ καί marks a new section of the text.[81] It is difficult to determine what is the reference of the ὡσαύτως.[82] To this question I shall return.

In this section of the text the interest is centred on the concept of the Spirit as intercessor which is a new aspect. Paul has stressed the believers' groaning despite their possession of the Spirit. The groaning seems to signify participation in the groaning of Creation. He calls this participation ἀσθένεια, a term which in Paul's theology marks man's dependence[83] on the surrounding world.[84] This aspect of weakness is present in the TEs 5–8 (vv. 23–25). The believers are weak, therefore their salvation still remains a hope, a hope which means that they long for the liberation of their bodies.

Into this situation the Spirit enters as an aid (συναντιλαμβάνεται). The prefixed συν can be understood as intensifying the verb.[85] However, the prefix may express something more, viz. the association of the Spirit with the believer.[86]

TE 10 (v. 26bc)

τὸ γὰρ τί προσευξώμεθα καθὸ δεῖ οὐκ οἴδαμεν ἀλλὰ αὐτὸ τὸ πνεῦμα ὑπερεντυγχάνει στεναγμοῖς ἀλαλήτοις

TE 10 explains TE 9 (v. 26a) (γάρ). It contains two parts which presumably correspond to the two elements of TE 9 (v. 26a). The first element of TE 9,

---

[81] Fuchs (1949, 111): "8,26-27 ist nur lose angehängt"; Käsemann (1973, 229): "Der dritte Unterteil in 26-27 . . . hat keine neutestamentlichen Parallelen und wirkt selbst bei Paulus wie ein Fremdkörper . . . ".

[82] Following Zahn's structure several scholars connect ὡσαύτως to πᾶσα ἡ κτίσις TE 4 (v.22) and ἡμεῖς of TE 5a (v.23). So Lietzmann (1933), Althaus (1954), Balz, who speaks of "abschließender Gedanke" (1971, 69), Paulsen (1974, 122), Cranfield (1980). Others connect it only to TE 5a (v. 23): Sanday and Headlam (1962), Michel (1978), von der Osten-Sacken, who says: "Nach dem jetzigen Zusammenhang ist ωσαυτως auf V. 24f. bezogen" (1975, 93). This solution, however, disregards the fact that the στεναγμός of the Spirit is different in kind from the στεναγμός of the believers. This is pointed out by Paulsen (1974, 122).

[83] In Paul's anthropology man is part of, and therefore dependent on, Creation. Schniewind writes: "Es steht also die Schwäche der Menchenart—denn das bedeutet σάρξ—im Gegensatz zum Geist, der die Gegenwart Gottes ist" (1952, 83f.; cf. Käsemann above note 78). Therefore man is weak. He cannot separate himself from his surrounding world. Salvation means incorporation in Christ (Rom 6:7-11). But this life still means weakness, as long as man is in the world. He does not do what he wants (Rom 7:14-20). His life together with Christ is a life in hope of the redemption of the body (Rom 8:23).

[84] When Paul says in 5:6 that Christ died for us while we still were sinners, he does not mean that thereby we were taken out of the world. The term "flesh" (σάρξ) signifies the "worldliness" of our existence and is therefore marked by weakness (6:19). The flesh weakens the Law (8:3). In fact the problem in regard to food, which seems to be one of the problems in the Roman Church, is understood by Paul as a sign of weakness (Rom 14:21; 15:1; compare for instance 1Cor 8:7, 9-11; 9:22).

[85] Cranfield (1980), Sanday and Headlam (1962).

[86] Bauer-Aland translates "take part with" (" . . . mithelfe, beistehen") (1988, 1565 s. v.). This at least seems to apply in the other of the two occurrences in the NT, Lk 10:40.

speaking of our weakness (ἀσθένεια), by the expression οὐκ οἴδαμεν, and the second, referring to the help of the Spirit (συναντιλαμβάνεσθαι), in interpreted by the word ὑπερεντυγχάνει. Thus the crux of the explanation lies in the contrast between our helplessness and the support offered by the Spirit. The two parts of TE 10 will be treated separately.

TE 10a (v. 26b)

τὸ γὰρ τί προσευξώμεθα καθὸ δεῖ οὐκ οἴδαμεν

As already said, TE 10a is presumably directed towards the expression τῇ ἀσθενείᾳ ἡμῶν. Our weakness is caused by our participation with Creation and is expressed by our ignorance of how to pray καθὸ δεῖ. It is strange that, although we possess the Spirit as ἀπαρχή, we do not know what to, or how to pray.[87] What Paul may have meant by this statement is unclear, since otherwise he never seems to doubt that we know these things.[88]

TE 10b (v. 26c)

ἀλλὰ αὐτὸ τὸ πνεῦμα ὑπερεντυγχάνει στεναγμοῖς ἀλαλήτοις

Apparently this TE contrasts the prayer of the Spirit to our inability to pray aright (ἀλλά). Because of our inability the Spirit intercedes on our behalf. The expression στεναγμοῖς ἀλαλήτοις describes the manner in which the Spirit prays. It is difficult to comprehend the exact meaning of this statement, since nowhere else in the Pauline letters, or the rest of the New Testament, do we hear of the Spirit groaning.[89] The only possible explanation seems to be hidden in the connection to TE 9 (v. 26a) where Paul uses a prefixed συν. It is possible that Paul wanted to express the thought that the Spirit joins the believers in their weakness. Thus Paul explains in TE 10a (v. 26b) that this sharing in the situation of the believer consists in prayer.[90]

---

[87] Michel (1978) thinks that the expression καθὸ δεῖ is equivalent to κατὰ θεόν in v. 27.

[88] Käsemann writes: "Der wichtigste Satz lautet, für das Urchristentum völlig unerhört, wir wüßten nicht, was zu beten sich gebührt. Überall wird fleißig gebetet, und das Vaterunser darf als allgemein bekannt und, in liturgischen Formularen überliefert, als fest im Gottesdienst verankert gelten. Vielfache Formen der Bitte, Fürbitte, des Dankes, der Lobpreisung, hymnischer Anbetung und glossolalischen Gebetes wiederlegen die Meinung, an dieser Stelle habe es für die erste Kirche ein Problem gegeben" (1973, 229f.). Similarly Paulsen: "Vor allem sind die paulinischen Aussagen, sofern sie von der Unmöglichkeit menschlichen Betens sprechen, innerhalb des Urchristentums vollkommen singulär; Vergleichbares läßt sich ihnen nicht an die Seite stellen" (1974, 123). In his commentary Käsemann briefly reviews the many ways in which exegetes have tried to solve the problem (1973, 229).

[89] This difficulty is well illustrated by J. A. T. Robinson who transfers the groaning from the prayer of the Spirit to our own prayer translating: " . . . through our inarticulate groans the Spirit himself is pleading for us . . . " and comments "Previous English versions attribute the groans or sighs to the Spirit, which is not easily intelligible" (1979, 103f.).

[90] When the believer is groaning, being fettered in this world, the Spirit sustains him in prayer. That this thought in fact was already common in Jewish belief is denied by Sanday and Headlam: "The Jews had a strong belief in the value of the intercessory prayer of their great saints, . . . but they have nothing like the teaching of these verses" (1962, 214). That Paul so believed is denied by Cranfield who says "It is surely much more probable that the reference is to groanings imperceptible to the Christians themselves" (1980 423).

Which idea underlies the information that the Spirit intercedes by groaning without words (στεναγμοῖς ἀλαλήτοις) is difficult to comprehend. The most likely meaning is that the Spirit associates Itself to the groaning (στενάζομεν, v. 23) of the believers.

TE 11 (v. 27a)

ὁ δὲ ἐραυνῶν τὰς καρδίας οἶδεν τί τὸ φρόνημα τοῦ πνεύματος

TE 11 adds a further feature to the picture of the interceding Spirit. The information given in TE 10b (v. 26c) of the way the Spirit is praying has appeared to make the prayer primarily an expression of help and comfort through participation in the groaning. Now Paul says that God understands the mind of the praying Spirit.[91] (The One who knows the hearts is a designation of God.[92]) Thus Paul seems to make a rather unusual distinction between the Spirit and God Himself:[93] if the Spirit prays, it would not usually be necessary to say that God knows the mind of the Spirit, and similarly that prayers of the Spirit accord with the will of God.

The contrast to v. 14, where Paul speaks of the believers as driven by the Spirit, should not be overlooked. In vv. 1–17 Paul has only referred to a Spirit Which creates a victorious life in the believers.[94] In fact we are again left only with guesses about what Paul meant unless we can find the proper background of the words.

TE 12 (v. 27b)

ὅτι κατὰ θεὸν ἐντυγχάνει ὑπὲρ ἁγίων

This TE seems to connect to οἶδεν in TE 11 (v. 26c). The sentence rephrases the τί τὸ φρόνημα τοῦ πνεύματος, which it interprets. It explains the φρόνημα of the prayer of the Spirit as in accordance with the will of God. Thus the word φρόνημα seems to mean something like "intention". The intention of the Spirit is to intercede according to the will of God. The difference between God and the Spirit is not removed.

---

[91] According to Schniewind φρόνημα means " 'die Sinnesart' des Geistes, das, 'worauf der Geist bedacht ist'; es meint keineswegs nur die 'Sprache', die 'Meinung' des Geistes" (1952, 83). The denied possibilities are proposed by Jülicher resp. Lietzmann (1933).

[92] 1Kgs 8:39; Ps 26:2; 44:21; 139:1, 2, 23; Prov 15:11; Jer 17:10; Luk 16:15; Acts 1:24; 15:8; Rev 2:23.

[93] This problem is observed by Sanday and Headlam who write: "This verse and the next go to show that St. Paul regarded the action of the Holy Spirit as personal, and as distinct from the action of the Father. The language of the Creeds aims at taking account of these expressions, which agree fully with the triple formula of 2 Cor. xiii.14; Matt. xxviii.19" (1962, 214). The authors, however, do not regard the wide difference between this formula and the Church's later credal expressions of the Holy Trinity.

[94] Käsemann offered an original solution to this problem by proposing that Paul speaks of the glossolalia which he corrects in this text (1969, "Schrei"). His interpretation has found a wide acceptance among commentators.

3.2 The Flood Tradition as Background of Rom 8:18–27

The majority of today's exegetes are agreed that in Rom 8:18–27 Paul uses Jewish apocalyptic material. It is my contention that this apocalyptic material comes from what I have termed the Flood tradition. In what follows I shall therefore examine possible relations between Paul's text and this traditional material. I shall first consider those thought elements of Paul's text in which the Flood tradition presents itself as an obvious solution to the questions concerning the background and which have not found any other explanation. Then I shall consider those parts of Paul's text which have been interpreted from some other background than the Flood tradition, but where I believe that they could be regarded as being equally at home there. Thirdly I shall discuss the parts of the text which cannot be connected to the Flood tradition.

3.2.1 Thought Elements Only Paralleled in the Flood Tradition

TE 9–12 (vv. 26f.)
The TEs 9–12 depict the Spirit as intercessor in a way which has no parallel in the rest of the New Testament.

(TE 9 v. 26a) Ὡσαύτως δὲ καὶ τὸ πνεῦμα συναντιλαμβάνεται τῇ ἀσθενείᾳ ἡμῶν·
(TE 10a v. 26b) τὸ γὰρ τί προσευξώμεθα καθὸ δεῖ οὐκ οἴδαμεν,
(TE 10b v. 26c) ἀλλὰ αὐτὸ τὸ πνεῦμα ὑπερεντυγχάνει στεναγμοῖς ἀλαλήτοις·
(TE 11 v. 27a) ὁ δὲ ἐραυνῶν τὰς καρδίας οἶδεν τί τὸ φρόνημα τοῦ πνεύματος,
(TE 12 v. 27b) ὅτι κατὰ θεὸν ἐντυγχάνει ὑπὲρ ἁγίων.

That these TEs are close to some material of what in this dissertation is called the Flood tradition has long been realized by some exegetes.[95] It seems clear to me, that they have indicated the only possible background of the TEs in Paul's text, which are under discussion. I shall comment on each of the TEs individually.

TE 9 (v. 26a)
Ὡσαύτως δὲ καὶ τὸ πνεῦμα συναντιλαμβάνεται τῇ ἀσθενείᾳ ἡμῶν
Paul speaks of the believers' weakness, ἀσθένεια, which is in a sense a sharing of Creation's present situation. In the Flood tradition a similar weakness is encountered: men suffer together with Creation in that they are destroyed through deception by the teaching of the forbidden knowledge (1En 8:1–4; 9:6) and through bloodshed caused by the giants (1En 7:3–5; 9:9). Thus the people are helpless in the face of the evil on earth (1En 9:10). The helplessness of the righteous Noah is similarly depicted in 1En 65:3–5. Noah seeing the

---

[95] See 1.3.2.4.5.

destruction on earth cries: "Tell me what this thing is which is being done upon the earth, for the earth is struggling in this manner and is being shaken; perhaps I will perish with her in the impact". Moreover he is said to have tried to save the world by preaching repentance before the Flood but without result.[96]

Paul says that the Spirit takes part in, or shares in,[97] our weakness. As was already said, this picture of the Spirit is found in no other passage in the NT but is close to the action of the angels in the Flood tradition, in which their care for the tortured Creation is vividly depicted. Watching from heaven what happens on earth, they say to each other: "The spirits and the souls of the people groan and entreat saying (στενάζουσιν ἐντυγχάνοντα καὶ λέγοντα): 'bring our cause before the Highest and our destruction before the Majesty of glory, before the One who by his majesty is Lord over all' " (1En 9:3)[98] and they intercede before the Lord on the earth's behalf.[99]

Paul uses the motif of the interceding angels but changes it, letting the Spirit support, or take part in, the weakness of the believers and bring their groaning before God.[100]

TE 10a (v. 26b)

τὸ γὰρ τί προσευξώμεθα καθὸ δεῖ οὐκ οἴδαμεν

What is expressed in TE 10a bears some similarities to the situation recounted in the Flood tradition. The καθὸ δεῖ can be said to represent the thought that the earth is unable to pronounce its prayer before God, but groans and entreats the angels to plead her cause before Him: "And then the earth brought accusation against the oppressors" (1En 7:6).[101] Michael, Uriel, Raphael, and Gabriel looking down from heaven say: "A crying voice comes from the

---

[96] SibOr 1:147-198; Jos *Ant* I,74; 2Pet 2:5; 1Clem 7:6. The motif of Noah preaching repentance is rather common in Jewish literature. See Ginzberg (1942 V, 174 note 19) and Lewis (1968, 102).

[97] συνατιλαμβάνεσθαι. Cf. Ex 18:22; Luk 10:40 .

[98] 1En 9:3 (Sync): Τὰ πνεύματα καὶ αἱ ψυχαὶ τῶν ἀνθρώπων στενάζουσιν ἐντυγχάνοντα καὶ λέγοντα ὅτι Εἰσαγάγετε τὴν κρίσιν ἡμῶν πρὸς τὸν ὕψιστον, καὶ τὴν ἀπώλειαν ἡμῶν ἐνώπιον τῆς δόξης τῆς μεγαλωσύνης, ἐνώπιον τοῦ κυρίου τῶν κυρίων πάντων τῇ μεγαλωσύνῃ. The second Sync. MS reads: Τὰ πνεύματα καὶ αἱ ψυχαὶ τῶν ἀνθρώπων ἐντυγχάνουσι στενάζοντα καὶ λέγοντα . . . Thus both the Sync. MSS use the words ἐντυγχάνειν and στενάζειν. Cod. Pan. only has ἐντυγχάνειν.

[99] This commitment by the angels is pictured also outside the Flood tradition. Thus 2Bar 67:2 says that the angels mourn when interceding for Zion (Cf. also Tob12:15). In the NT cf. Mt 18:10; Rev 8:3.

[100] Besides this passage Paul in Rom 8:34 speaks of Christ as interceding for the believers. In Lk Christ intercedes during his earthly life, Lk 22:32; 23:34. Closer to the picture of the interceding angels are the passages in John speaking of the Paraclete (Jn 14:16, 26; 15:26; 16:7; 1Jn 2:1).

[101] τότε ἡ γῆ ἐνέτυχεν κατὰ τῶν ἀνόμων. Similarly in 1En 8:4 (Sync.): "Thus a cry went up to heaven when the people was destroyed" (τῶν οὖν ἀνθρώπων ἀπολλυμένων ἡ βοὴ εἰς οὐρανοὺς ἀνέβη. Cf. 1En 87:1.

earth unto the gates of heaven" (1En 9:2).[102] In their intercession the angels say to the Lord: "And now, behold the souls of the people who have died cry and pray until the gates of heaven, and their groaning rose but they cannot escape from before the lawless things on earth" (1En 9:10).[103] The prayers do not reach God directly, even if they attain the "gates of heaven". Only when they are brought before God by his angels do they seem to be heard by Him.

Paul applies this motif to the present situation of the believers. Because of the connection to the rest of Creation they are weak and groan together with it. They are in fact unable to pray as they should.[104] Thus prayer is possible only with the aid of the Spirit. Paul's perspective is close to that of the Flood tradition.

In regard to the motif of prayer still another parallel may be noted: similarly to the traditional depiction of a groaning and a prayer of the entire Creation Paul speaks of a groaning from the Creation in its totality (συστενάζειν, συνωδίνειν). To the continuation of this TE I shall return.[105]

TE 11 (v. 27a)

ὁ δὲ ἐραυνῶν τὰς καρδίας οἶδεν τί τὸ φρόνημα τοῦ πνεύματος

The strange statement of TE 11, that God knows the mind (τὸ φρόνημα) of the Spirit,[106] becomes more understandable once the background of the text, i. e. the Flood tradition, is comprehended. The main point in the use of the tradition in the Enochic literature is the encouragement of an oppressed and despairing people. The present time is marked by oppression and suffering. Thus the old question of God's silence lies behind the text of 1En 6–11. Why does He allow evil to prevail? The angels express the anguish of this question in their prayer:

---

[102] φωνὴ βοώντων ἐπὶ τῆς γῆς μέχρι πυλῶν τοῦ οὐρανοῦ. The Ethiopic version reads: "The earth, (from) her empty (foundation), has brought the cry of their voice unto the gates of heaven".

[103] καὶ νῦν ἰδοὺ βοῶσιν αἱ ψυχαὶ τῶν τετελευτηκότων καὶ ἐντυγχάνουσιν μέχρι τῶν πυλῶν τοῦ οὐρανοῦ, καὶ ἀνέβη ὁ στεναγμὸς αὐτῶν καὶ οὐ δύναται ἐξελθεῖν ἀπὸ προσώπου τῶν ἐπὶ τῆς γῆς γινομένων ἀνομημάτων.

[104] Thus the καθὸ δεῖ does not mean "pray in the right manner", or to pray "in sufficient amount", and it should not be interpreted as equivalent to κατὰ θεόν of TE 12 (v. 27). (For these interpretations see 3.1.2 TE 10a.) Käsemann (1969 "Schrei", 219-221; 1973, 229) seems to be right in saying that it is an extraordinary thought that Christians do not know how to pray. Cranfield (1980) contradicts Käsemann, but presents no evidence supporting his statement that the idea of the text is common in the NT, except the general thought that everything in the Christian life is marked by weakness and thus dependent on the grace of God.

[105] To make the thought complete I would now have continued by discussing TE 10b which I believe expresses motifs from the Flood tradition. However, as TE 10b has been explained from another background, it will be treated under 3.2.2.

[106] Cranfield tries to solve the problem but seems to make it still more intrusive when he writes: "Implicit in its [the designation used for God] use here is the thought that, since God searches the secrets of man's hearts, He must *a fortiori* be supposed to know the unspoken desires of His own Spirit . . . " (1980, 424). Cranfield refers to 1Cor 2:10f.

You made everything and possess all power, and everything is visible and uncovered (ἀκάλυπτα) before you, and you see everything which Azael has done, who taught all unjustice on earth and made known (ἐδήλωσεν) the eternal mysteries which are in heaven . . . and the women gave birth to giants by whom the whole world (ἡ γῆ) has been filled with blood and injustice (1 En 9:5f., 9).[107]

The answer is that despite the present silence God knows everything and finally will put an end to evil.[108] The prayer of the angels thus at first would seem superfluous. However, it makes God's knowledge evident and declares that He carefully follows what is taking place on earth and will certainly act.

TE 12 (v. 27b)

ὅτι κατὰ θεὸν ἐντυγχάνει ὑπὲρ ἁγίων

Intercession before God is not an unusual thought in Jewish literature.[109] The belief in angels as intercessors before God is present in the OT[110] but it is widely developed in the intertestamental literature.[111] Such intercession accords with the Divine will as part of the heavenly worship which is performed continuously before the throne of God.[112] The angels sing and praise the Lord, and pray for those who dwell upon the earth. In the Book of Similitudes the author says that he sees the four archangels standing before the throne of God among the thousands of angels:

The first voice was blessing the name of the Lord of the Spirits. The second voice I heard blessing the Elect One and the elect ones who are clinging unto the Lord of the

---

[107] See also 2.1.2.2.3. According to the Greek manuscripts the prayer ends: "but you do not tell us what is necessary for them to do about it". The Ethiopic text reads: "(but) you do not tell us what is proper for us that we may do regarding it".

[108] This motif is traceable in several texts recounting the Flood tradition. In a variant representation of the tradition Enoch prays: "There is no such thing as non-existence before him. (Even) before the world was created he knows what is forever and what will be from generation to generation. Those who do not slumber, but stand before your glory, did bless you" (1En 39:11f.). "Typical of the theology of the period is the stress upon the Most High's foreknowledge" (Hanson 1977, 200). On this point Hanson quotes Jub 1:4, 26; 1QH 1:7-9, 19-20, 23-24, 28; 15:13-14, 17, 22; CD 2:7-10; 1QpHab 7:13-14; 1QS 3:15-17 (op. cit. 200, note 14).

[109] The Jewish literature mentions several intercessors before God: Abraham (Gen 18:20-33; 20:7), Moses, (Ex 5:22f.; 8:8-13; 32:11-14; Lev 27:5; Num 14:13-20; Deut 9:25-29; TMos 11:17), Samuel (1Sam 7:5.8f.; 12:19, Jer 15:1), Enoch (1En 83:10; 84:1-6), in a certain sense also the prophets (Amos 7:1-6; Jer 5:28; 13:9-22; 14:7-9; 2Bar 85:1f.). 2Bar 85:1f. also mentions holy men as intercessors.

[110] Zech 3:1ff., possibly also in Job 16:19-22; 19:25-27; 33:23ff.

[111] 1En 39:5 (possibly related to the Flood tradition); 40:6; 47:2; 99:3; 104:1; TLev 3:5; 5:5ff.; TDan 6:2; TAdam 2:1-12; ApSedr 14:1ff. Sometimes one angel is said to intercede: 1En 40:9; 89:76 (Michael); 49:6 (Gabriel). (For Rabbinic material see Str-B 1 (1922) 153, 891, 672, 973, 983f.; II (1926) 569f.). Cf. Tob 12:15; 1QH 6:13; TLev 3:5; 5:6-7; TDan6:2; TAd 2:1.

[112] "Closely related to this function of 'ministering' is that of intercession for men. This belief is to be found, of course, even in the Old Testament itself (cf. Zech. 1.12; Job 5.1; 33.23); but in the apocalyptic books it finds much greater prominence, particularly in the Book of Enoch. In 1 Enoch 15.2, for example, God says to the Watchers, 'You should intercede for men, and not men for you', as if this duty of intercession was something naturally expected of them (cf. 12.6; 14.7)" (Russell, 1976, 242).

Spirits. And the third voice I heard interceding and praying on behalf of those who dwell upon the earth and supplicating in the name of the Lord of the Spirits. And the fourth voice I heard expelling the demons and forbidding them from coming to the Lord of the Spirits in order to accuse those who dwell upon the earth (1En 40:4–7).

When the seer asks the names of the four praying figures he is told that they are the archangels, Michael, Raphael, Gabriel and Phanuel, " . . . these are his four angels: they are of the Lord of the Spirits" (*op. cit.* 40:10).[113] The thought of praying and interceding angels is also to be found in the New Testament.[114]

In the Flood tradition the prayer of the angels plays a most significant role. It shows, on the one hand, the helplessness of Creation in the face of oppression but, on the other, God's control of the situation. According to the Flood tradition, the angels pray for men, and when the angels pray God acts. Paul has used the traditional motif to strengthen the idea that the believers, in their weakness as part of Creation, are the object of the activity of the Spirit.

Paul employs the motif of the interceding angels but changes it, letting the Spirit support, or take part in, the weakness of the believers and bring their groaning before God.

TE 2 (v. 19)

ἡ γὰρ ἀποκαραδοκία τῆς κτίσεως τὴν ἀποκάλυψιν τῶν υἱῶν τοῦ θεοῦ ἀπεκδέχεται

The picture of Creation drawn here has no parallel in the rest of the New Testament. In fact this TE supplies two remarkable pieces of information. First: Creation is pictured as intelligent, and second: certain sons of God will be revealed at a future event which is eagerly desired by Creation. At the same time we must observe that Creation is pictured as groaning, unable to express itself in clear words.

The problem of what Paul meant by the word κτίσις is tied to the fact that he ascribes consciousness to Creation. The Flood tradition shows a Creation which is conscious of its situation. Here really the *earth itself accuses* the outlaws: τότε ἡ γῆ ἐνέτυχεν κατὰ τῶν ἀνόμων (1En 7:6).

Usually exegetes assume that the expression οἱ υἱοὶ τοῦ θεοῦ means "the children of God" i. e. the believers. However, some comments must be made in regard to this explanation: a) In no other place in the New Testament do we hear of a revelation of the believers.[115] b) The revelation of the sons of

---

[113] The archangels are sometimes mentioned as four and sometimes as seven. See further Bietenhard 1951, 108.

[114] Cf. above ch. 1, note 136.

[115] Bultmann (1973, 49) finds Rom 8:17–19 to be close to 1Jn 3:2: ἀγαπητοί, νῦν τέκνα θεοῦ ἐσμεν, καὶ οὔπω ἐφανερώθη τί ἐσόμεθα. οἴδαμεν ὅτι ἐὰν φανερωθῇ, ὅμοιοι αὐτῷ ἐσόμεθα, ὅτι ὀψόμεθα αὐτὸν καθώς ἐστιν. However, there is a significant difference in regard to the object which will be disclosed (the author uses the word φανεροῦν not ἀποκαλύπτειν, a fact of smaller significance but still to be noted). While Paul says that "the sons of God" will be revealed 1Jh

120

God is a revelation to the Creation. Usually revelation seems to be directed to the believers or at least to people. c) In Rom 8:18–27 we find no information which identifies the sons as believers. In addition, most exegetes agree that the background of vv. 18–27 is different from the background of the context. Hence it is at least doubtful whether, it is right without further ado to use v. 13f. for the identification of the sons of God in TE 2. d) According to the text the believers long for the υἱοθεσία which they consequently do not yet possess, at least not in full. It should be borne into mind that the term "sonship" is not used in a strict sense in this text, but has different shades of meaning in different verses. The problem causes us to take seriously the insight that the two verses refer to different backgrounds.

I propose that in TE 2 (v. 19) Paul refers to the angels of the Last Judgment, who will arrive to free the earth from oppression.[116] Creation "waits with eager longing" for these angels, whom Paul calls "sons of God", to be revealed. The apocalyptic idea of revelations of secret things recurs in different parts of the letter. God's righteousness has been revealed in Christ (Rom 1:17), the wrath of God is revealed (Rom 1:18), and on the day of wrath, which means final judgment on the sinners, God's righteous judgment will be revealed (Rom 2:5). In this scheme it would not be unnatural to speak of the revelation, i. e. the advent of the angels for the final Judgment.

This thought fits ideas which Paul expresses in other letters. When Christ comes the archangel will blow his trumpet and gather all people for the judgment (1Thes 4:15f., cf. 1Thes 3:13). According to 2Thes 1:7[117] Jesus will be revealed with His angels in power and glory: ἐν τῇ ἀποκαλύψει τοῦ κυρίου

3:2 says that "what we will be" is not yet disclosed. The author of 1Jh knows that we will be transformed at the parousia of Jesus so that we will be like Jesus. This is close to Paul who says that we do not yet know the form of the transformed body (Phil 3:21; cf. Col 3:4; 1Cor 15:35-41). The expression "for we shall see him as he is" is close to 2Cor 3:18.: ἡμεῖς δὲ πάντες ἀνακεκαλυμμένῳ προσώπῳ τὴν δόξαν κυρίου κατοπτριζόμενοι τὴν αὐτὴν εἰκόνα μεταμορφούμεθα ἀπὸ δόξης εἰς δόξαν καθάπερ ἀπὸ κυρίου πνεύματος. Thus the thought material of 1Joh 3:2 is very close to what Paul says in some other texts but not to what is said in Rom 8:19.

A second text which sounds similar to Paul's words in TE 2 (v. 19) is found in Col 3:4: ὅταν ὁ Χριστὸς φανερωθῇ ἡ ζωὴ ὑμῶν, τότε καὶ ὑμεῖς σὺν αὐτῷ φανερωθήσεσθε ἐν δόξῃ. However, the author here speaks of *the life in Christ* which at present is hidden but which will be revealed at the parousia of Christ. He does not think of a revelation to the world but rather of the perfection of Christian existence. The words are part of a parenesis. The believer shall now look for the things that are above, not for what is on earth. The passage is close to other Pauline texts such as Rom 6:1-11; Gal 2:19-20; Phil 3:10f. but not to Rom 8:19.

[116] Fuchs (1949, 108) seems to hint at this idea when saying: "Die υἱοὶ τοῦ θεοῦ sind vielleicht ursprünglich die zahlreichen Gestalten der Erlöser, nach deren Offenbarung die κτίσις immer wieder 'ausspäht'. Bei Paulus sind es natürlich die Kinder Gottes . . . ". Fitzmyer (1989) refers to the covenant at the Flood: "It recalls Jahweh's promise to Noah of the covenant to be made 'between myself and you and every living creature (Gn. 9:12-13; Cf. Ps. 135)".

[117] 2Thes most probably was not written by Paul (Koester II 1982, 241-246). However, the author used genuinely Pauline thoughts and language. I consider this verse to represent the same motif as is found in 1Thes 3:13 and 4:16.

Ἰησοῦ ἀπ' οὐρανοῦ μετ' ἀγγέλων δυνάμεως αὐτοῦ. As we have seen,[118] Rom 8:18-27 testifies to Paul's understanding of the present world as on the verge of the final events of its history (τοῦ νῦν καιροῦ TE 1, v. 18; ἄχρι τοῦ νῦν TE 4, v. 22). It is clear from 1Thes 4:13-18 that Paul expected the parousia of Christ in a very near future. This belief is reflected also in Rom 13:11f.: "Besides this you know what hour it is, how it is full time now for you to wake from sleep. For salvation is nearer to us now than when we first believed; the night is far gone, the day is at hand".

Thus the sons of God will be "revealed". The use of the term ἀποκάλυψις for the appearance of the angels (the sons of God) is in line with ordinary language in speaking of the events at the end of days in Jewish apocalyptic texts.[119] Thus the Messiah will be "revealed" at that time according to 4Ezra 7:28: "For my son the Messiah shall be revealed (*revelabitur*) with those who are with him, and those who remain shall rejoice four hundred years".[120] Similarly 2Bar 39:7: "And it will happen when the time of its fulfillment is approaching in which it will fall, that at that time the dominion of my Anointed One which is like the fountain and the vine, will be revealed". 1En 38:1ff. speaks of different revelations at the end of time: "When the congregation of the righteous shall appear, sinners shall be judged for their sins" (v. 1). The expression "the congregation of the righteous" might mean the believers; "when the Righteous One shall appear before the face of the righteous" (v. 2). "When the secrets of the righteous One are revealed . . . " (v. 3). According to 1En 52:9; 62:7; 69:27 the Son of Man will be revealed. Often this revelation at the end of time is a revelation of judgment.[121] The introductory chapter of 1En is particularly interesting in this context. 1En 1:4 says: "God . . . will appear (φανήσεται) in the strength of His might from heaven" and more explicitly:

Because he comes with his myriads and his holy ones in order to make judgment upon all and to destroy all the ungodly and to censure all flesh on account of all their wicked deeds that they have done and the ungodly and hard words, [and all their slander] which the sinners have spoken about him (1En 1:9).[122]

---

[118] See above TE 1 (v.18).

[119] Lietzmann holds the story of Adam to be the proper background of the text but still assumes a connection to apocalyptic texts: "Es ist eine eigenartige Wendung des alten apokalyptischen Gedankens, daß im messianischen Zeitalter ein 'neuer Himmel und eine neue Erde' sein wird: Js 65:17; 66:12; Henoch 91:16, 17; Jubiläen 1:29; 4 Ezra 7:57 u. ö. Auch Act 3:21; Apoc 21:1 vgl. Mt 19:28" (1933, 84f.).

[120] Cf. 4Ezra 13:32. According to the idea of the author of 4Ezra 13:26 the Son of Man when he comes will "deliver his [i. e. God's] Creation". Also in Luk 17:30 it is said that the Son of Man will be revealed.

[121] The idea that the angels will appear and summon all to the Judgment is widespread: 1En 55:3; 91:14ff.; 100:4; WissSol 2:214-220; 2:241-251 (a Christian interpolation).

[122] ὅτι ἔρχεται σὺν ταῖς μυριάσιν αὐτοῦ καὶ τοῖς ἁγίοις αὐτοῦ, ποιῆσαι κρίσιν κατὰ πάντων, καὶ ἀπολέσει πάντας τοὺς ἀσεβεῖς, καὶ ἐλέγξει πᾶσαν σάρκα περὶ πάντων ἔργων τῆς ἀσεβείας αὐτῶν ὧν ἠσέβησαν καὶ σκληρῶν ὧν ἐλάλησαν λόγων, ⟨καὶ περὶ πάντων ὧν κατελάλησαν⟩ κατ' αὐτοῦ ἁμαρτωλοὶ ἀσεβεῖς. The mention of the "myriads of holy" is still readable in 4QEn°.

Thus in 1En the coming revelation of God and His angels plays a significant role.[123] God will come together with His angels to execute judgment on all.[124] However, the righteous apparently shall not fear. On the contrary, for them relief is at hand.[125] The motif of judgment is used in the Book of the Watchers as encouragement and comfort. In fact the book is entitled "The blessing of Enoch with which he blessed the elect righteous who will be present on the day of calamity to remove the enemies and [on which] the righteous will be saved".[126] The author says furthermore that on that day the righteous will be freed and all evil will disappear.[127] The similarities between the function of the judgment motif in 1En and that of the coming of the sons of God in Rom 8 are conspicuous.

Paul shared the apocalyptic ideas with other New Testament writers. So the passage from 1En 1:9 (cited above) is directly quoted in Jude v. 14f.[128] The picture of the Lord arriving "with his holy myriads"[129] is close to Mt 25:30f.: "When the Son of Man comes in his glory, and all the angels with him, then he will sit on his glorious throne".[130] 1Pt 1:5ff. also speaks of an eschatological revelation in similar terms: salvation will be revealed (v. 5), and Christ will be revealed (v. 7).

Now it has to be admitted that the expression "sons of God" cannot be found as a designation of the archangels in the texts representing the Flood tradition. Yet, in the Flood tradition the fallen angels and the good archangels have the same background, both being sons of God (cf. Gen 6:2).[131] This

---

[123] For the angels' several functions at the judgment see Volz 1934, 276f.

[124] In Dan 12:1ff. the Archangel Michael will arise (יַעֲמֹד; LXX: παρελεύσεται; Theodotion: ἀναστήσεται) and introduce ". . .a time of trouble, such as never has been since there was a nation till that time". The author seems to refer to the beginning of the last crisis. "Also beginnt mit dem Auftreten Michaels das eschatologische Drama, er gibt das Zeichen zum Anfang . . . " (Volz 1934, 200).

[125] Cf. 1En 1:4-9; 38:1ff.; 62:8-16.

[126] λόγος εὐλογίας Ἐνώχ, καθὼς εὐλόγησεν ἐκλεκτοὺς δικαίους οἵτινες ἔσονται εἰς ἡμέραν ἀνάγκης ἐξᾶραι πάντας τοὺς ἐχθρούς, καὶ σωθήσονται δίκαιοι (1En 1:1).

[127] "Destroy injustice from the face of the earth. And every iniquitous deed will end, and the plant of righteousness and truth will appear forever and he will plant joy. And then all the righteous ones will escape; and become the living ones until they multiply and become tens of hundreds; and all the days of their youth and the years of their retirement they will complete in peace" (1En 10:16f.). The cleansing of the earth from evil reappears in 10:20, 22. 1En 62 describes the judgment of the oppressors. They will be delivered "to the angels for punishment" (v. 11), but "The righteous and elect ones shall be saved on that day; and from thenceforth they shall never see the faces of the sinners and the oppressors" (v13).

[128] Jude v. 14f.: Ἰδοὺ ἦλθεν κύριος ἐν ἁγίαις μυριάσιν αὐτοῦ ποιῆσαι κρίσιν κατὰ πάντων καὶ ἐλέγξαι πᾶσαν ψυχὴν περὶ πάντων τῶν ἔργων ἀσεβείας αὐτῶν ὧν ἠσέβησαν καὶ περὶ πάντων τῶν σκληρῶν ὧν ἐλάλησαν κατ' αὐτοῦ ἁμαρτωλοὶ ἀσεβεῖς.

[129] This passage from 1En is preserved also in 4QEnᵃ. The expression "holy" here denotes the good angels in contrast to the evil ones (Milik 1976, 144).

[130] Cf. the synoptic parallels Mt 16: 27 / Mk 8:37 / Lk 9:26 and Mt 24:30f./ Mk 13:26f. / Lk 21:27; and further 1En 91:15:—17.

[131] Originally the sons of God were subordinated divine beings at the throne of Jahwe (Ps 29:1; 82:6; 89:7; Job 1:6; 2:1; 38:7; Deut 32:8). Thus the reader of the Holy Scriptures, which

conception appears in 1En 6:2 where the evil angels are named " . . . the angels, the children of heaven". That good angels could be described as sons of God also in Paul's time can be demonstrated from the Qumran texts (e.g. 1QS IV,22; XI,8; 1QH III,22).[132]

Thus Paul appears to use the motif of the archangels who come for judgment according to the Flood tradition. 1En 7 (quoted above) spoke of Creation as being conscious of the situation: it not only groaned but also accused the oppressors before God. So God sent the archangels to execute judgment on the oppressors and to restore Creation (1En 10:7). Paul uses this motif when saying that the sons of God will be revealed. This is God's answer to Creation's groans and despair.

3.2.2 Thought Elements which Cannot Exclusively be Referred to the Flood Tradition

TE 4 (v. 22)

οἴδαμεν γὰρ ὅτι πᾶσα ἡ κτίσις συστενάζει καὶ συνωδίνει ἄχρι τοῦ νῦν

In TE 4 Paul refers to a motif which the recipients of the letter know from tradition (οἴδαμεν). Several statements are made in regard to this motif: a) Creation is groaning and in travail, b) the situation pictured has been prevalent "until now" (ἄχρι τοῦ νῦν), and c) the situation is shared by Creation in its totality.

The νῦν in the expression ἄχρι τοῦ νῦν denotes the end of a certain period and thus marks the borderline between past and future[133] (e. g. not apocalyptically Phil 1:5; apocalyptically Mt 24:21). In our text the νῦν recalls the time designated in TE 1 (v. 18) (τοῦ νῦν καιροῦ),[134] which is the present of sufferings as opposed to the future of glory. It thus reflects the apocalyptic perspective of the text.[135] The readers are placed in the decisive final period of history. The perspective is similar to that of 1 Enoch. The introductory chapter of 1En says that it is a blessing directed to "the elect and righteous

---

we call the Old Testament, found the name "sons of heaven" (υἱοὶ οὐρανοῦ) used for the angels in 1En 6:2. In the Enochian literature both groups of angels, the archangels who fell and the remaining faithful archangels, are supposed to have had the same rank. The fallen angels as well as the faithful ones are called Watchers, stars, angels, and holy ones in the different writings.

[132] In Qumran the sons of God were supposed to fight together with the Qumran people in the final battle against Belial. One should not too hastily deny the influence on Paul of ideas held in the Qumran community. Fitzmyer has demonstrated that in 1Cor 11:10 Paul says that angels are present in the community, an idea which is well known from the Qumran writings. "No one knows *how* the theological ideas of the Qumran sect influenced Paul. That they *did* so is beyond doubt" (Fitzmyer 1957-58, 201). 1QH XI,19ff. is also cited by Zeller as parallel material for the groaning mentioned in Rom 8:22 (1985, 162).

[133] Stählin 1942, 1103f.

[134] The ἄχρι τὸ νῦν repeats the τοῦ νῦν καιροῦ of TE 1 (v18). See note 63.

[135] Vögtle (1970, 198), Michel (1978), Balz (1971,52). Against this Cranfield (1980).

who would be present on the day of tribulation" (1:1). "I thought not at this present generation, but speak for a distant one", Enoch says (v. 2).[136] By identifying the people to whom the blessing is directed as "the elect and righteous", by mentioning the people who will be put to death, when God comes for judgment, as "the ungodly", and further by using Old Testament language in depicting the Theophany the author impels the readers to recognize themselves as those who will be saved on this day of Judgment.[137]

Furthermore we noted that Paul speaks of the totality of Creation. He uses both the adjective πᾶς and the prefix συν in συστενάζειν and συνωδίνειν.[138] This talk of Creation as a whole comes close to the Flood tradition where the entire created world is laid under the destructive forces of the Watchers and the giants.[139] The all-encompassing sufferings thus involve the four kinds of inhabitants in the world. The giants devoured all the crops and then mankind, "and they began to sin against the birds, against the wild animals, against the reptiles, and against the fishes, and to eat each other's flesh and they drank the blood. Then the earth brought accusations against the lawless ones" (1En 7:5f.).[140] However, in other passages human beings are the subject of the crying. This happens in 1En 8:4, "The cry of the people who perished rose to heaven"[141] and similarly in the angels' prayer, 1En 9:3, 10.[142] Still the cry represents the anguish of the whole of Creation.[143] The version represented by the Dream Visions turns the description around. There the cattle, which symbolize the inhabitants of the world, are violated by the fallen stars, the fallen angels. One would have expected the cattle to complain but in fact the author says: " . . . the earth began to cry aloud" (1En 87:1). The author thus uses the word "the earth" to designate its inhabitants.

The solidarity of men and the rest of Creation is also seen in the fact that

---

[136] καὶ οὐκ εἰς τὴν νῦν γενεὰν διενοούμην, ἀλλὰ ἐπὶ πόρρω οὖσαν ἐγὼ λαλῶ (1En 1:2).

[137] Hartman (1979, 121–145) makes a detailed analysis of how the author applied the tradition to his readers. "In short, once the author has established a typological relationship between the Genesis stories and *his own time*, and once his own circumstances and world view lead him to identify the angels and giants as evil, he can employ the ancient myth as aetiology of evil in *his own time*, and he can find in the Noah story a promise of the divine resolution of *his* problem" (Nickelsburg 1977, 396. Italics mine).

[138] This understanding of the prefix is common among exegetes today.

[139] This emphasis on the totality of all inhabitants of the earth should not be a surprise since in the original story in Gen 6–9 the whole Creation is involved. The covenant made by God is not only with Noah and his family but with Creation in all its parts (Gen 9:8–17).

[140] καὶ ἤρξαντο ἁμαρτάνειν ἐν τοῖς πετεινοῖς καὶ τοῖς θηρίοις καὶ ἑρπετοῖς καὶ τοῖς ἰχθύσιν καὶ ἀλλήλων τὰς σάρκας κατεσθίειν, καὶ τὸ αἷμα ἔπιον. τότε ἡ γῆ ἐνέτυχεν κατὰ τῶν ἀνόμων.

[141] τῶν οὖν ἀνθρώπων ἀπολλυμένων ἡ βοὴ εἰς οὐρανοὺς ἀνέβη. Similarly in both the Panopolitan and the Syncellus manuscripts.

[142] For the text of 1En 9:4–11 see ch.2 at note 45. The Greek text of v. 3 is quoted above in note 98.

[143] A strange similarity seems to be at hand in 1QH III, 32f. This passage is also cited as a background by some exegetes. Thus e. g. von der Osten-Sachen (1975, 101).

to the author of 1 Enoch all parts of Creation have the same obligation to obey the Law of God. Sun, moon and stars, the seas, the seasons of the year, the trees and so on, "do not divert from their appointed order" (2:1). The sinners, however, have transgressed the laws. The same is said of the fallen Watchers.

We encounter the same wide view when the paradisaical new world after the Flood is described in 1En 10:7f.:

And the earth will be healed which the angels destroyed, and make visible the healing of the earth so that its wound will be healed, in order that not all sons of man will be destroyed by the whole mystery which the watchers ordered and taught their sons, so that the entire earth was made desolate through the works of Azael's teaching. And write on his account all the sins.[144]

In the following verses the author describes the new plantation on the earth, which will be done "in righteousness", and its abundant fruitfulness (1En 10:17–19).[145]

Lastly, in this TE Paul also speaks of a world which groans and lies in birth-pangs. The thought of the earth crying is rarely found in texts outside Rom 8,[146] but has an important place in the Flood tradition. Syncellus' version of 1En 9:3 may bring to mind the wording of the text of Romans:[147] "The spirits and the souls of the people groan and entreat saying (στενάζουσιν ἐντυγχάνοντα καὶ λέγοντα): 'bring our cause before the Highest and our destruction before the Majesty of glory, before the One who by his majesty is Lord over all". That the earth cries, as in 1En 7:5 and 87:1 (see above), is of course natural since the angels and the giants destroy not only men but the entire Creation.

To the συστενάζειν Paul has coupled συνωδίνειν. The verb ὠδίνειν does not belong to the ordinary language of the extant texts which contain the Flood tradition. It designates the pain of childbirth, and therefore presents

---

[144] καὶ ἰαθήσεται ἡ γῆ, ἣν ἠφάνισαν οἱ ἄγγελοι, καὶ τὴν ἴασιν τῆς γῆς δήλωσον, ἵνα ἰάσωνται τὴν πληγήν, ἵνα μὴ ἀπόλωνται πάντες οἱ υἱοὶ τῶν ἀνθρώπων ἐν τῷ μυστηρίῳ ὅλῳ ᾧ ἐπέταξαν οἱ ἐγρήγοροι καὶ ἐδίδαξαν τοὺς υἱοὺς αὐτῶν, καὶ ἠρημώθη πᾶσα ἡ γῆ ἀφανισθεῖσα ἐν τοῖς ἔργοις τῆς διδασκελίας Ἀζαήλ· καὶ ἐπ' αὐτῷ γράψον τὰς ἁμαρτίας πάσας.

[145] Cf. 2Bar 74:1-4.

[146] There are a few texts in the Old Testament which speak of earth as groaning. One of them, Isa 24:4, says that "The earth mourns and withers, the world languishes and withers; the heavens languish together with the earth". It has been suggested by Hanson (1977, 212f.) that the same myth of a "rebellion in heaven" lies behind both the story of the Flood and Isa 24: 21-23. Although the version of the myth underlying Isa 24 may be different, it is possible that the text builds on the same mythological material. A cry from the earth is mentioned in the VisEzra 14. But in this case it is a request for punishment of sinful men because they have worked impiety on earth.

[147] The verbs στενάζειν and ἐντυγχάνειν recur, also in the variant Syncellus' text in 1En 9:3 (ἐντυγχάνουσι στενάζοντα) and 9:10 (...τὰ πνεύματα τῶν ψυχῶν τῶν ἀποθανόντων ἀνθρώπων ἐντυγχάνουσιν, καὶ μέχρι τῶν πυλῶν τοῦ οὐρανοῦ ἀνέβη ὁ στεναγμὸς αὐτῶν).

itself as a natural expression to authors who want to describe distress or fear.[148] It is natural that it was also used in the descriptions of the judgment as in 1En 62:4: "Then pain shall come upon them as on a woman in travail with birth pangs—when she is giving birth (the child) enters the mouth of the womb and she suffers from childbearing". The word is also used in other apocalyptic texts, often as a term for the suffering preceding the end (e. g. the birthpangs of the Messiah).[149]

TE 10b (v. 26c)
ἀλλὰ αὐτὸ τὸ πνεῦμα ὑπερεντυγχάνει στεναγμοῖς ἀλαλήτοις
Possibly TE 10b contains a conception of the heavenly world which we find in Paul's Corinthian correspondence. In the third heaven he had heard ineffable words (ἄρρητα ῥήματα) which human ears were not allowed to hear (2Cor 12:4). The language of angels is different from the language of men (1Cor 13:1; 2Cor 12:4).[150] However, the most natural explanation of the TE seems to be that the Spirit thus expresses the groaning of Creation before God.[151] The dative of στεναγμοῖς ἀλαλήτοις is modal.[152]

Paul has used the rare word συναντιλαμβάνεσθαι to describe how the Spirit assumes the burden of the groaning believer. This is in line with the many passages which speak of the interceding angels.[153] "Do you think that

---

[148] In Acts 2:24 Peter speaks of the resurrection of Jesus as an act of God λύσας τὰς ὠδῖνας τοῦ θανάτου.

[149] Different backgrounds have been proposed for the word ὠδίνειν. Michel mentions the parallels drawn by Wendland to the hermetic literature (1972, 182), further to "Gedanken der hellenistischen Apokalyptik" and finally says: "Verwandt sind die Klagen der getöteten Menschenseelen, aber auch das Seufzen der gerichteten himmlischen Wächter in der äthHen-Apokalyptik (9,3ff.; 12,4). In 4Ezr finden wir eine doppelte Klage: das Weib Zion klagt über den Verlust des Sohnes, die Erde über das Verderben ihrer Kinder" (1978, 269, note17). To some scholars the background seems Messianic. Schlier (1977) writes: "Wahrscheinlich denkt Paulus dabei an die ὠδῖνες (Mk 13,18; Mt 24,8; vgl. 1Thess 5,3; Apg 2,24; Apk 12,2), die Wehen, unter denen die messianische Zeit nach alt.-prophetischer und apokalyptischer Auffassung geboren wird". Similarly Käsemann (1973, 226), Bruce (1971). Paul used the word ὠδίν in 1Thes 5:3 in a different meaning, i. e. not of the entire world including the believers but only of the ungodly people as caught in "travail" at the coming of the final judgment. Some exegetes quote 1QH III, 7ff. as evidence of the Jewish background of the word. Thus e. g. Käsemann (1973), Paulsen (1974, 119 note 62), Black (1984). Zeller refers to 1QH III, 32f. (1985). Lohse thinks that 1QH III, 7ff. is apocalyptic but denies that it speaks of the Messiah (1971, 292, notes 10-13). Zeller (1985, 160) also refers to 1QH IX, 35 and 1 QS IV, 20ff.; XI 7f.; 1 QH III, 21f.; IV 23; XI, 10ff. as background of Rom 8:14.

[150] Käsemann, 1973, understands the passage in Rom as a Pauline correction of the enthusiasts in the Church. Lietzmann thinks that ". . .die Pneumalehre des Paulus tatsächlich mit Vorstellungen operiert, welche der hellenistischen Mystik entstammen, und daß Paulus sich vielfach auch in der Ausdrucksweise eng an diese Vorbilder anschließt. . . . Gemeinsam ist dem Apostel mit der hell. Mystik die Grundvorstellung, daß in dem Wiedergeborenen die Gottheit als πνεῦμα Wohnung genommen hat und in ihm wirkt" (1933, 87).

[151] So Michel, 1978.

[152] Cranfield interprets the word as "not spoken", saying: "The Spirit's groanings are not spoken, because they do not need to be, since God knows the Spirit's intention without its being expressed" (1980).

[153] See note 109-111.

there is no mourning among the angels before the Mighty One, that Zion is delivered up in this way?'', says the author of 2Bar 67:2. By these words he articulates the belief that the angels share the anguish of the people, suffering as they do. Paul expresses himself in a similar way when he says that the Spirit groans just like the believers and the Creation.[154] The Spirit thus brings before God the groaning of the believers. Thus still keeping to the motif from the Flood tradition Paul develops TE 9 further. When the believers do not know how to pray καθὸ δεῖ the Spirit intercedes for them with στεναγμοῖς ἀλαλήτοις.

In the Flood tradition the angels stress that God knows: "You know everything before it happens and you see these things and you allow them, but you do not tell us what they should do about it" (1En 9:11).[155] Thus even the archangels themselves do not know what to do, but they bring the cause of Creation before God according to Creation's own prayer. In Paul's use of the traditional motif this becomes a groaning on the part of the Spirit which thereby expresses the anguish of Creation.

TE 1 (v. 18)

Λογίζομαι γὰρ ὅτι οὐκ ἄξια τὰ παθήματα τοῦ νῦν καιροῦ πρὸς τὴν μέλλουσαν δόξαν ἀποκαλυφθῆναι εἰς ἡμᾶς

The word καιρός designates "the decisive moment".[156] It is used in Gen 6:13 as a remarkable translation of קץ.[157] The contrast between a present characterized by sufferings and a future characterized by glory makes the apocalyptic colour of the text evident. The present time thus stands out as the decisive turning point in history.

This way of contrasting the present time of suffering to the future time of blessing and glory is used in 1 Enoch, as in other apocalyptic texts, to communicate hope and encouragement to oppressed readers. The author places himself in the beginning of history in the guise of Enoch and from there forecasts the history to come. From the perspective of this putative author the

---

[154] "By using the device of interceding angels, the author has the opportunity to interpolate into his narrative a lengthy prayer which represents, in the logic of the story, the sentiments of those for whom the angels are interceding" (Nickelsburg 1977, 387).

[155] Καὶ σὺ πάντα οἶδας πρὸ τοῦ αὐτὰ γενέσθαι, καὶ σὺ ὁρᾷς ταῦτα καὶ ἐᾷς αὐτούς, καὶ οὐδὲ ἡμῖν λέγεις τί δεῖ ποιεῖν αὐτοὺς περὶ τούτων. Cf. 1En 39:5; 40:1-10.

[156] Even if it is difficult to know the original meaning of the word " . . . doch stellt sich an Hand der sprachlichen Entwicklungslinie als Grundbedeutung heraus *das Entscheidende, der wesentliche Punkt*, und zwar erstens örtlich, zweitens sachlich und drittens zeitlich verstanden" (Delling 1938, 456). In the NT as in the LXX the word primarily means "der (schicksalhaft) entscheidende Zeitpunkt" (*op. cit.* 461). This way of using the word νῦν is typical of Paul. Stählin (1942, 1108): "Für Paulus ist eine Wendung charakteristisch, die er fast immer auf die Periode zwischen den Aeonen bezogen gebraucht: ὁ νῦν καιρός". It is so used in Rom 11:5 where Paul discusses the divine plan of salvation: In the present time, ἐν τῷ νῦν καιρῷ, there is a remnant left of the real Israel.

[157] Cf. Ezek 7:12; 22:3 where καιρός translates עת.

course of history is presented as secret knowledge which is transmitted through visions and dream.[158] He helps his readers, his contemporaries, to evaluate their own distress and to trust in God with regard to their own future when the sinners on earth will be judged and the new world with superabundant blessings will be erected.

Paul follows this apocalyptic program. He designates the present time as one of suffering and the future as a time of incomparable glory which will be revealed to the believers. However, the letter does not give the impression of being written to a suffering community. Paul rather uses the apocalyptic perspective to express the universal scope of the thought of righteousness by faith. The entire Creation will attain the glory which belongs to the children of God.

TE 3a (v. 20)

τῇ γὰρ ματαιότητι ἡ κτίσις ὑπετάγη

The root μαται- conveys the basic meaning "worthless", "meaningless". Unlike the concept κενός it signifies not only emptiness but a violation of the rule.[159] In the LXX the group of words formed from this stem are used primarily to describe objects which are opposed to God and to which man attaches himself so as to become ungodly. This is also the way the group of words is used in the NT.[160] Balz concludes that these words belongs to the language of mission of the Early Church.[161]

The aorist tense of the verb ὑπετάγη tells us that Paul conceives of the subjection as an individual event whereby Creation was subjected to ματαιότης. Thus ματαιότης does not belong to the natural state of human life, as it does according to the Wisdom literature.[162] As we have already seen above, the term φθορά of TE 3c (v. 21) has been assumed to convey the same meaning as ματαιότης. This, however, is hardly convincing.[163] The terms rather define different aspects of the event to which they refer. Creation was once subjected to ματαιότης but is now enslaved under φθορά. One should rather

---

[158] . . . Ἐνώχ· (ἄνθρωπος δίκαιός ἐστιν, [ᾧ] ὅρασις ἐκ θεοῦ αὐτῷ ἀνεῳγμένη ἦν, ἔχων τὴν ὅρασιν τοῦ ἁγίου καὶ τοῦ οὐρανοῦ·) 1En 1:2a.

[159] Bauernfeind (1942, 528). Futile, worthless, may be for instance thoughts, Ps 93:11; beauty, Prov 31:30, salvation which comes from man, Ps 59:13, Isa 30:7.

[160] μάτην, Mt 15:9; Mk 7:7; ματαιοῦσθαι, Rom 1:21; μάταιος, Acts 14:15; 1Cor 3:20; Tit 3:9; James 1:26; 1Pet 1:18; ματαιότης, Rom 8:20; Eph 4:17; 2Pet 2:18.

[161] 1971, 39.

[162] Words derived from the root μαται- are especially frequent in the Wisdom literature (Prov 13 times and Eccl 37 times). Here it describes the human life as meaningless, i. e. something which belongs to life from the beginning. To this meaning Paul's use in TE 3a (vs 20) stands in marked contrast. For different translations of ματαιότης see chapter 2 note 59.

[163] Michel differentiates the words, saying: " . . . φθορά ist also noch etwas anderes als ματαιότης" (1978, 268). He translates μάταιος by "Der Begriff bezeichnet die Vergeblichkeit, die Inhaltsleere und die Nichtigkeit, vielleicht auch die Verkehrtheit und die Unordnung der Welt" (op. cit. , 267). Similarly Schlier (1977, 261).

draw the conclusion that the subjection to ματαιότης caused the φθορά.

It is possible that by the term ματαιότης Paul signifies the forbidden knowledge taught by the angels.[164] The motif in the Flood tradition serves to describe the sinful way of life which is said to result from the depraving teaching of the angels.[165] Although the author of 1En dwells on the violence of the giants, the motif of the Watchers' teaching is far more important to him because he can thereby describe all the ungodly behaviour of his surrounding gentile world.[166] 1 Enoch reflects how the surrounding world frightened the author by its different culture and religion. This is expressed by his use of the motif of the teaching of the fallen angels. According to 1En 7:1 the watchers taught the use of drugs (φαρμακεία), charms (ἐπαοιδαί), cutting of roots (ῥιζοτομία),and use of plants (βοτάναι). The description of the teaching is repeated in 1En 8:1–4:[167] Azael taught the people warfare, how to work metals, decorations and cosmetic, jewelry and coloring of cloth. Furthermore they taught the use of charms and astrology. To the author this knowledge is against God's will: it is rejected by heaven[168] and sinful.[169] Noah alone had not learnt the secret teaching of the angels and therefore remained righteous ("... the Lord of the Spirits knows that you are pure and kindhearted; you detest the secret things", 1En 65:11f.). The change caused by the customs and the habits of the oppressive powers are understood as a deformation of the world and will lead to destruction: "In those days, Noah saw the earth that she had become deformed and that her destruction was at hand" (1En 65:1). To the author of the Book of the Watchers (1En 1–36) as well as to the author of the Book of Similitudes (1En 37–71) the teaching of the angels thus was a more important motif than the destruction through the giants, because by the motif of the teaching he was able to describe the sur-

---

[164] It appears that the LXX translators used ματαιότης to refer to rebel angels, rulers of stars, and pagan gods: e. g. 1Kings 16:2, 13; Isa 2:20; 30:15; Jer 8:19; Hos 5:11b. Bauernfeind (1942, 527): "Das Besondere des Begriffes ματαιότης in der LXX liegt vielmehr—schon rein lexikalisch—darin, daß er uns immer wieder in der jenseitigen Sphäre begegnet: μάταια heißen in erster Linie eben die Götter der ἔθνη, also die Götter, die im Griechentum so oder so Garanten des dem μάταιον Entnommen sind". Bultmann felt that Gnostic mythology lay behind the term (1968, 174).

[165] 1En 7:1; 8:1-4; 64:1; 65:6-11; 69:4-15.

[166] In Bar 3:26-28 the giants are depicted as both violent and stupid.

[167] See text and translation at ch. 2 note 41. The two descriptions of the teaching may be due to the compilatory character of the text (Nickelsburg 1977). Very instructive about the relation to the surrounding foreign world is the following text: "An order has been issued from the court of the Lord against those who dwell upon the earth, that their doom has arrived because they have acquired the knowledge of all the secrets of the angels, all the oppressive deeds of the Satans, as well as all their most occult powers, all the powers of those who practice sorcery, all the powers of (those who mix) many colors, all the powers of those who make molten images; how silver is produced from the dust of the earth, and how bronze is made upon the earth—for lead and tin are produced from the earth like silver ... " (1 En 65:6-7). Cf. also 1En 57:4; 69:4-15, 28.

[168] 1En 16:3.

[169] 1En 13:2.

rounding world and the oppressors as godless and cursed by God.[170] Therefore in the Enochic writings the destruction is more often directly connected to the teaching of the fallen angels than to the giants. This is explicitly stated in 1En 10:7 where the angels are ordered to heal the earth so that "not all the sons of men will be destroyed through the mystery which the watchers told and taught to the sons of men".[171]

In Rom 1:21 Paul describes the general sinfulness of this world in terms which recall the Flood tradition, and uses the word ἐματαιώθησαν.[172] God subjected the world to ματαιότης because it refused to give praise and thanks to Him. Instead the created beings wanted to be equal to their creator. This situation could well fit the Flood tradition,[173] which can support an assumption that the Flood tradition also is involved in TE 3a.

TE 3b (v. 20b)

οὐχ ἑκοῦσα ἀλλὰ διὰ τὸν ὑποτάξαντα

TE 3b expands the meaning of the passive voice of ὑπετάγη in TE 3a. Creation did not contribute to the subjection, which was caused by a particular person, ὁ ὑποτάξας.

Several explanations have been proposed as regard the question of who is meant by ὑποτάξας, but most exegetes assume that Paul is referring to the story of the Fall of Adam. However, the idea expressed in Paul's text seems to be as at home in the Flood tradition as in Gen 3.[174] According to the Flood tradition it was not because of any action or any will on the part of Creation that the oppression came about. The earth was subdued by the Watchers through their teaching of sinful knowledge, and their giving birth to the giants. So the earth was perverted and destroyed. With the expression διὰ τὸν ὑποτάξαντα Paul may thus designate the leading angel who caused the oppression on earth.

If so, Paul was not then alone in his view. According to TNaph 3:5 the Watchers abandoned their natural order and rendered the previously colonized and fruitful earth uninhabitable:

Ὁμοίως δὲ καὶ οἱ Ἐγγρήγορες ἐνήλλαξαν τάξιν φύσεως αὐτῶν, οὓς καὶ κατηράσατο Κύριος ἐπὶ τοῦ κατακλυσμοῦ, δι' αὐτοὺς ἀπὸ κατοικησίας καὶ καρπῶν τάξας τὴν γῆν ἀοίκητον.

---

[170] In the other parts of 1En this interest is less explicit.

[171] For the text see note 144.

[172] Schlier (1977) differentiates ματαιότης from φθορά, referring back to the meaning of ματαιότης in Rom 1:21. The importance of this reference was also noted by Gieraths (1950, 114). ματαιότης is found only in Eph 5:17; and 2Pet 2:18 in the N T, and μάταιος only in Acts 14:15; 1Cor 3:20; 15:17; Ti 3:9; Jas 1:26 and 1Pet 1:18.

[173] Rom 1:21 is the only occurrence of the verb ματαιοῦν in the NT.

[174] Zahn has tried (see 1.3.2.4.3) to prove that Paul has Gen 3:17 in mind by referring to Gen 8:21. This verse represents a similarlity in thought to that of Gen 3:17 in sofar as they both speak of a curse (ἐπικατάρατος, καταράσθαι) which was forced on Creation because of man. Zahn connected this idea to that in Rom 8:21 because the syntactical construction in Gen 8:21 is similar to that in Rom 8:21.

By the expression δι' αὐτούς, which refers to the fallen Watchers,[175] the author signifies the cause of the Flood and the destruction it brought.[176] The fact that TNaph mentions angels in plural whereas Paul only speaks of one person as causing the subjection does not radically change the picture. As has been pointed out in chapter 2, there were different versions of the Flood tradition. Even in 1 Enoch, which surely speaks of two leaders who command multitudes of lower angels, it can be said: "And to him [Azael] ascribe all the sin" (1En 10:8).[177]

It is often assumed that by the expression οὐχ ἑκοῦσα Paul alludes to the idea that Creation, according to Gen 3, was laid under the curse, which ensued not from its own sin but that of Adam. But the Flood story fits Paul's text as least as well. I even suggest that the idea that the earth is accursed, as in the story of the Fall of Adam, corresponds to Paul's expression less than does the Flood tradition,[178] since Paul says that Creation is "subjected to meaninglessness", not that it is "cursed".

TE 3c (v. 21)
ἐφ' ἐλπίδι ὅτι καὶ αὐτὴ ἡ κτίσις ἐλευθερωθήσεται ἀπὸ τῆς δουλείας τῆς φθορᾶς εἰς τὴν ἐλευθερίαν τῆς δόξης τῶν τέκνων τοῦ θεοῦ
The result of the subjection mentioned in TE 3a is an enslavement under φθορά.[179] Creation was subdued to ματαιότης but will be freed from φθορά. 1En 106:15–18 uses the word φθορά in a version of the story of the Flood.[180]

---

[175] The author speaks of the angels in plural, not thinking especially of the leader. The plural seems to be more in line with the picture from the Book of the Watchers.

[176] It is probably sheer coincidence that the author of TNaph uses διά with acc to indicate the cause of the destruction in the same way as Paul writes διὰ τὸν ὑποτάξαντα.

[177] Similarly Sync. ". . . because of the deeds and teaching of Azael". Nickelsburg points to 1En 86-88, where one star first falls from heaven and is then followed by many more stars, as evidence of a version of the myth which was different from that of the Book of the Watchers. In 1En 86ff. one angel is responsible for the fall (Nickelsburg 1977, 398 note 65).

[178] As already noted (ch. 1 at not 149), many of the interpreters quote 4Ezra 7:11: ". . .and when Adam transgressed my statutes, what had been made was judged. And so the entrances of this world were made narrow and sorrowful and toilsome; they are few and evil, full of dangers and involved in great hardships" (translation by Metzger in Charlesworth 1983). It should not be denied that this text shows similarities to the thoughts in both Rom 1:18ff. and Rom 8:18ff. Still I believe the similarities between the Flood tradition and Paul's thoughts in Rom to be more striking.

[179] φθορά is used in the NT in Rom 8:21; 1Cor 15:42, 50; Gal 6:8; Col 2:22; 2Pet 1:4; 2:12, 19. φθείρω is used 1Cor 3:17; 15:33; 2Cor 7:2; 11:3; Eph 4:22; 2Pet 2:12; Jude 10; Rev 19:2. φθαρτός is used in Rom 1:23; 1Cor 9:25; 15:53f.; 1Pet 2:18; 2Pet 2:16.18.

[180] καὶ ἔσται ὀργῆ μεγάλη ἐπὶ τῆς γῆς καὶ κατακλυσμός, καὶ ἔσται ἀπώλεια μεγάλη ἐπὶ ἐνιαυτὸν ἕνα· καὶ τόδε τὸ παιδίον τὸ γεννηθὲν καταλειφθήσεται, καὶ τρία αὐτοῦ τέκνα σωθήσεται ἀποθανόντων τῶν ἐπὶ τῆς γῆς· καὶ πραϋνεῖ τὴν γῆν ἀπὸ τῆς οὔσης ἐν αὐτῇ φθορᾶς. καὶ νῦν λέγε Λάμεχ ὅτι τέκνον σού ἐστιν δικαίως καὶ ὁσίως, [καὶ] κάλεσον αὐτοῦ τὸ ὄνομα [Νῶε]· αὐτὸς γὰρ ἔσται ὑμῶν κατάλειμμα ἐφ' οὗ ἂν καταπαύσητε καὶ οἱ υἱοὶ αὐτοῦ ἀπὸ τῆς φθορᾶς τῆς γῆς καὶ ἀπὸ πάντων τῶν ἁμαρτωλῶν καὶ ἀπὸ πασῶν τῶν συντελειῶν ἐπὶ τῆς γῆς. The background of the text is that Lamech, because of the strange appearance of his son, suspects him to be begotten by one of the Watchers, who, according to the story, had united themselves to the women. In the answer to this problem we hear of Noah's mission.

It seems that this text describes the situation after the Flood.[181] V. 15 speaks of the Flood which will persist for one year and v. 17 says "and make the earth calm from the destruction that is on her". However, the original Hebrew text seems to have been different. Here the word "destruction" seems to denote the situation before the Flood, the destruction caused by the angels and the giants. One copy of the Qumran fragments, by Milik designated 4QEn[c], has preserved these verses (Milik 1976, 209f.). The word חבל in v. 17, which corresponds to φθορά in the Greek texts, is still legible in the manuscript. Milik translates it "corruption" and it seems to signify not the Flood itself but the corruption before the Flood. This reading of v. 17 seems to be confirmed by the Ethiopian text saying: "and the earth shall be washed clean from all the corruption". The idea of a φθορά thus belongs to the traditional material recounting the Flood story.

There is more evidence from the Old Testament to support what has already been said. Words developed from the root φθερ- (and φθαρ-) are used in the LXX to describe the situation before the Flood, i. e. the corruption and depravation of moral and religion. Thus φθείρειν translates the Hebrew שחת in Gen 6. In v. 11 it describes the perversion of the way of life before the Flood; likewise twice in v. 12b.[182]

In Gen 6:13 and 17 καταφθείρειν refers to the Flood , i. e. death. Biggs, in a commentary on 2Pet 2:19, which is very close to Rom 8:21, rightly says: "The two senses of corruption and of destruction are not easy to keep apart".[183] I conclude from this evidence that when Paul speaks of a deliverance from slavery under φθορά he uses a traditional idea from the Flood tradition designating the perversion and destruction of the present world.

TE 3c further mentions hope in a double way. Creation will be freed from δουλεία τῆς φθορᾶς and will reach ἐλευθερίαν τῆς δόξης. The statement sounds like an echo of the Flood tradition, predicting the freedom and glory of Creation in the new world which will follow the final Judgment. The evil angels will be bound and kept under the earth until the Day of Judgment. The earth, it is said, will be healed (see 1En 10:7, transl. at note 144).

Since the Flood tradition includes and develops Gen 6–9 it is not surprising

---

[181] Milik comments: "[καὶ] πραΰνεῖ τὴν γῆν ἀπὸ τῆς οὔσης ἐν [αὐτ]ῇ φθορᾶς abridges quite extensively the original formulation. Since we have here a new development, which describes the situation after the flood, we would expect [τότε] rather than [καί]. Further, the transitive πραΰνεῖ τὴν γῆν is not at all satisfactory; it is the earth, etc., which rests after a critical period, e.g. [עא]ר ותנוח in En[g] I ii 16 (probably a more detailed text of En 91:10; see 91:5ff. on the state of violence on the earth)" (Milik 1976, 213). (In my opinion the expression πραΰνεῖ refers to Noah's offering and the covenant. The offering was pleasing to God who "smelled the pleasing odour". Cf. Jub 6:2, Noah "made atonement for the land").

[182] והנה נשחתה כי-השחית כל-בשר את-דרכו על-הארץ, cf. καὶ ἦν κατεφθαρμένη, ὅτι κατέφθειρεν πᾶσα σάρξ τὴν ὁδὸν αὐτοῦ.

[183] Biggs 1961, 286.

that Creation has a central rôle in the idea of the new world, which will appear after the Judgment. At the same time it is evident that this world is closely connected to the idea of a righteous mankind. These two ideas are fundamental to the Flood tradition, particularly as presented in the Enochic literature. This may be exemplified by the following text:

Destroy all the spirits of adultery and the sons of the Watchers because they did unjustice against men. And destroy all injustice from the earth and make an end to all wicked deeds and let the plant of righteousness and truth appear for ever. It will be planted with joy. And now will all the righteous ones escape; ... And then the whole earth will be worked in righteousness, a tree will be planted on her, and will be filled with blessing. And all the trees on the earth will rejoice. They will be planted, and they will be planting vines, and if they plant a vine they will produce wine in thousandfold. And one measure of seed will yield a hundred measures, and one measure of olives will yield ten measures of pressed oil. And you cleanse the earth from all injustice, and from all sin, and from all impiety, and all defilement which is being done on earth; remove them from the earth. And all the nations shall worship and bless and prostrate themselves to me. And the earth shall be cleansed from all pollution, and from all uncleanness, and from all wrath, and from all scourge; and it shall not happen again that I shall send (these) upon the earth from generation to generation and forever (1En 10:15–22).

To my mind Paul uses the Flood tradition when writing that Creation itself has the hope of being liberated from the slavery under destruction and to arrive at the glorious freedom which belongs to the children of God.

3.2.3 Thought Elements which are not Paralleled in the Flood Tradition

In the middle of our text there is a series of TEs which do not seem to echo the Flood tradition. It is not feasible to refer them to any other special religiohistorical background either, but they are in line with Paul's own theology as expressed in other letters.

TE 5a (v. 23)
οὐ μόνον δέ, ἀλλὰ καὶ αὐτοὶ ... ἡμεῖς καὶ αὐτοὶ ἐν ἑαυτοῖς στενάζομεν υἱοθεσίαν ἀπεκδεχόμενοι.
Paul also mentions that the believers are groaning in the present situation in 2Cor 4:16–5:5 which is reminiscent of Rom 8:23–25.

Here indeed we groan (στενάζομεν), and long to put on our heavenly dwelling, so that by putting it on we may not be found naked. For while we are still in this tent, we sigh with anxiety (στενάζομεν βαρούμενοι); not that we would be unclothed, but that we would be further clothed, so that what is mortal may be swallowed up by life. He who has prepared us for this very thing is God, who has given us the Spirit as a guarantee (τὸν ἀρραβῶνα τοῦ πνεύματος) (2Cor 5:2–5).

Paul refers to these ideas as common knowledge (2Cor 5:1 οἴδαμεν).[184] That the groaning takes place within the believers is also expressed in a similar way in 2Cor 1:9: ἀλλὰ αὐτοὶ ἐν ἑαυτοῖς τὸ ἀπόκριμα τοῦ θανάτου ἐσχήκαμεν.[185]

TE 5b (v. 23)

τὴν ἀπαρχὴν τοῦ πνεύματος ἔχοντες

The word ἀπαρχή is used in other passages with a different connotation. Paul uses it of Christ in 1Cor 15:20, 23,[186] of the first believers in 1Cor 16:15[187] and of a sacred first lump of dough in Rom 11:16.

But Paul employs the term ἀρραβῶν which has a similar meaning to that of ἀπαρχή in Rom 8. The Spirit is given by God as a guarantee, ἀρραβῶν, of this coming heavenly world.[188] Rom 8:23 thus represents Pauline language and articulates thoughts which are at home in Paul's theology and apparently also in wider circles in the Early Church.

TE 5c (v. 23)

υἱοθεσίαν ... τὴν ἀπολύτρωσιν τοῦ σώματος ἡμῶν

This TE is fully in line with the Pauline conception of man. The term σῶμα in Pauline thought stands as an expression of man's relation to this world.[189] The full sonship means to Paul that the body is freed. This is what he expects will happen at the parousia of Christ: "But our commonwealth is in heaven, and from it we await a Saviour, the Lord Jesus Christ, who will change our lowly body to be like his glorious body, by the power which enables him even to subject all things to himself" (Phil 3:20f).[190] Christ will return, the trumpet of the archangel will sound, the dead will be resurrected and the living believers will be changed and taken up and they will all live with him for ever (1Thes 4:15–18).

---

[184] The groaning of the people of God in distress in this world is an old motif. According to Ex 2:23 the cry (ἡ βοή) of the sons of Israel rose to heaven when they were oppressed in Egypt and God listened to their groaning (τὸν στεναγμὸν αὐτῶν). The Psalmist groans in prayer, Ps 6:7; a close parallel is found in Isa 24:3–7: ³φθορᾷ φθαρήσεται ἡ γῆ, καὶ προνομῇ προνομευθήσεται ἡ γῆ· τὸ γὰρ στόμα κυρίου ἐλάλησεν ταῦτα. ⁴ἐπένθησεν ἡ γῆ, καὶ ἐφθάρη ἡ οἰκουμένη, ἐπένθησαν οἱ ὑψηλοὶ τῆς γῆς. ⁵ἡ δὲ γῆ ἠνόμησεν διὰ τοὺς κατοικοῦντας αὐτήν, διότι παρέβησαν τὸν νόμον καὶ ἤλλαξαν τὰ προστάγματα, διαθήκην αἰώνιον. ⁶διὰ τοῦτο ἀρὰ ἔδεται τὴν γῆν, ὅτι ἡμάρτοσαν οἱ κατοικοῦντες αὐτήν· διὰ τοῦτο πτωχοὶ ἔσονται οἱ ἐνοικοῦντες ἐν τῇ γῇ, καὶ καταλειφθήσονται ἄνθρωποι ὀλίγοι. πενθήσει θῖνος, ⁷πενθήσει ἄμπελος, στενάξουσιν πάντες οἱ εὐφραινόμενοι τὴν ψυχήν. This text, however, seems to recount the myth which lies behind the Flood tradition as well.

[185] "...we felt that we had received the sentence of death..."

[186] Χριστὸς ἐγήγερται ἐκ νεκρῶν ἀπαρχὴ τῶν κεκοιμημένων.

[187] Cf. Rom 16:5; 2Thes 2:13; Jas 1:18; Rev 14:4.

[188] 2Cor 1:22; 5:5. Cf. Eph 1:14.

[189] Beside the article quoted in note 78 the concept of man is studied especially by Käsemann 1933 and by J. A. T. Robinson 1977.

[190] Cf. 1Cor 15:23.

TE 6 (24a) τῇ γὰρ ἐλπίδι ἐσώθημεν·

TE 7 (24b) ἐλπὶς δὲ βλεπομένη οὐκ ἔστιν ἐλπίς· ὃ γὰρ βλέπει τίς ἐλπίζει;

TE 8 (25) εἰ δὲ ὃ οὐ βλέπομεν ἐλπίζομεν, δι' ὑπομονῆς ἀπεκδεχόμεθα

TEs 6–8 presents a perception of hope which we recognize from other Pauline texts. Although salvation is a present reality it must still be regarded as fulfilled only in the future world. This thought of hope has already been presented in Romans. Abraham, righteous through faith, continued to hope in a situation where hope was impossible (Rom 4:18). Hope thus proves faith. To Paul righteousness through faith necessarily contains hope. This may be expressed as "being proud" (καυχᾶσθαι) of the hope of the glory of God (Rom 5:2).

In Paul's conception of righteousness through faith salvation is both a present reality and a hope for the future. Because of the death and resurrection of Christ salvation is already a reality for those who put their trust into him, something which is realized through baptism (Rom 6:3–11). But at the same time salvation becomes reality through hope because the believer is not yet translated into the perfect world of righteousness. He shares the conditions of the sinful world until the parousia of Christ.

3.3 Conclusions

In this chapter I have compared the thought elements in Rom 8:18–27 with motifs found in the Flood tradition, going from clear to weaker relations.

In regard to vocabulary no distinct dependence can be established. Only a few of the words which seem unusual to Paul can be found in the extent texts which recount the Flood tradition. This fact, however, is of minor interest, since it has been shown that the use of the tradition was very free; and moreover, Paul may have drawn on a version of the tradition which has been lost.

More important is the question of similarities in regard to the motifs presented in the two texts. It has been demonstrated that all of the unusual ideas in Paul's text can be paralleled in the Flood tradition and given a good context there. Thus the following motifs in Rom 8:18–27 have more or less close parallels in the Flood tradition:

Sons of God will be revealed
Creation is subjected to meaninglessness and destruction
Creation longs for the sons of God to appear and is groaning
Creation will participate in the freedom which belongs to the children of God
The righteous are weak and do not know how to pray
The Spirit shares the weakness of the righteous

The Spirit intercedes for the righteous

The motif of hope, which is common in the Pauline letters, is certainly at home also in the Flood tradition, as is similarly the admonition to keep hope alive.

The Flood tradition gives an unambiguous meaning to the controversial word κτίσς, which signifies the entire created world. Similarly it helps to define the ὁ ὑποτάξας, who subjeced Creation to meaninglessness and destruction. ὁ ὑποτάξας is the evil angel(s) who brought evil in the world. The implicit event when evil came into the world was the Fall of the angels. This was against the will (οὐχ ἑκοῦσα) of the entire Creation.

It is of a certain interest to note that each of the three groanings mentioned in Paul's text, of Creation, of the righteous, and of the Spirit, all find a counterpart in the Flood tradition. But still more conspicuous is the fact that all these motifs, which are otherwise foreign to Paul, are to be found within the Flood tradition.

4 Concluding Remarks

At the outset of this study I expressed my opinion that the understanding of Rom 8:18ff. depends on the religio-historical background of the motifs involved in the text, consequently, as long as the background is not made clear, the text will remain enigmatic. Most modern scholars are agreed that the background of Rom 8:18–27 is apocalyptic. However, they do not relate the apocalyptic motifs of the text to any coherent tradition.[1] Apocalyptics in general is too wide a definition to solve the problems inherent in this text, so that its background has remained vague. In this study I believe I have explained the different motifs from one coherent background, viz. that of the Flood tradition.[2] I shall now summarize the results reached.

4.1 Motifs and Thoughts in Rom 8:18–27

Reading Rom 8:18–27 against the background of the Flood tradition solves several problems with thoughts and motifs in Rom 8:18–27. Admittedly, Paul's allusions are not made in words which can be proved to be dependent on any known specific text which represents the Flood tradition. However, the vagueness of the allusions should not surprise us, since, as I have shown, the use of the Flood tradition could be very free, and as a matter of fact we have come across similar uses thereof. All of the motifs in Rom 8:18ff., which otherwise are foreign to the NT, are paralleled in the same traditional material; indeed most of them are even found in a single document, i. e. the Book of the Watchers, 1En 1–36, more precisely Chapters 6–11 thereof. The Flood

---

[1] See quotation from Bindemann under 1.3.3.

[2] Keck, discussing Paul's apocalyptic thought-world, says: "The problem of Paul and apocalyptic would be more soluble if one could show that Paul had read an apocalypse (especially one we too can read), or if the presence in Paul's letters of ideas emphasized also in certain apocalypses (such as God's wrath) proved that his thought was apocalyptic, or if, conversely, the absence from Paul's letters of ideas common in apocalypses (e.g. portrayal of saved and the damned) proved that Paul's thought was not apocalyptic. Unfortunately, these requirements cannot be met. One must not repeat Albert Schweitzer's error, who in the name of reclaiming Paul as a coherent thinker constructed an eschatological scenario from various apocalypses and then claimed that Paul modified it by introducing a special resurrection for believers who had died before the parousia . . . We have no evidence that apocalypses influenced Paul's thought directly . . ." (1984, 231). In a way Rom 8:18–27 provides an example of apocalytic material used by Paul which we can read although we do not have access to the exact version of the tradition which Paul used.

tradition thus supplies a coherent background against which Paul's text can be read. This being so, I think it is more probable that Paul alludes to that tradition than is dependent on several writings representing disparate material.

The following motifs and thoughts have been shown to be paralleled in the Flood tradition.

a) To all exegetes working with Rom 8:18ff the concept of Creation is problematic. The problem is that some statements which are made in the text seem to be in disharmony with the usual concept of Creation, and, furthermore, sometimes in conflict with Paul's theology in general.[3] However, they all fit well into the story presented in the Flood tradition. From the background of the tradition it seems probable that by the word κτίσις Paul in this text denotes the sub-human Creation.[4] First, the Flood tradition explains the present situation of Creation as being enslaved under meaninglessness and destruction. According to the tradition Creation was, and still is, subjected to futility through the teaching of the fallen Watcher(s) (1En 6–8; 10:8), and was destroyed by the giants (1En 7:3–7). Second, the Flood tradition explains the groaning of Creation: it was groaning, and in the apocalyptic perspective still is, because of the oppression caused by the fallen angels and the giants (1En 8:4; 9:3, 10). Third, the strange consciousness on the part of Creation is in harmony with the Flood tradition, whereby the earth accused the Watchers and the giants (1En 9:3; 87:1). Fourth, the promise of deliverance from oppression was given through God's command that at the final judgment the evildoers will be destroyed and the earth will regain its original blessedness (1En 10:7–11:2). In the apocalyptical perspective the final destruction is still to come. The oppressed Creation thus can be pictured as longing for the final judgment, i. e. its deliverance.[5]

b) The motif of the Spirit as groaning and interceding on behalf of the believers (vv 26–27) is paralleled in the Flood tradition by the element of the

---

[3] The thought that Creation is longing for such a specific event as the revelation of the sons of God demands a capacity of thinking. However, according to TE 5a (v. 23) the Christians cannot be meant, and if Paul thought of non-Christian humanity this amounts to nothing less than salvation outside Christian faith, which is hardly Pauline. If humanity is not meant at all, the only rational beings would be the angels, but again, salvation of the angels is an idea foreign to Pauline theology. Thus we are left with the strange thought of a rational sub-human Creation, which is in conflict with the usual conception of Creation.

[4] Six different lines of interpretation have been suggested: universal, cosmic-angelological, cosmic, anthropological, angelological, and cosmic-anthropological (see 1.3.1.1—5, and 1.3.2.4.1 d).

[5] From the background of the Flood tradition it may even be possible to read the strange syntactical structure of Rom 8:19–21 in a new way. Paul, starting to speak about the longing Creation, inserted the words τῇ γὰρ ματαιότητι ἡ κτίσις ὑπετάγη, οὐχ ἑκοῦσα ἀλλὰ διὰ τὸν ὑποτάξαναντα (v. 20) as a parenthesis explaining the background of the statement made. Thus the ἐφ' ἐλπίδι should be taken together with the ἀπεκδέχεται of v. 19 expressing the hope of the longing Creation. The ἐφ' ἐλπίδι thus is inspired by the traditional material.

archangels who intercede on behalf of the suffering, crying and praying Creation (1En 9). The picture of praying angels was a common motif in Jewish and Christian theology, but Paul expresses some thoughts which are more precisely paralleled in the Flood tradition. First: according to Paul the believers do not know how to pray aright. In the Flood tradition we encounter the motif that Creation is not able to express its situation in such a way as to reach God directly. Second: the believers reach God by their prayer through intercession by the Spirit. Similarly Creation reaches God with its prayer only through intercession by the angels. The transition from angels to the Spirit is not far-fetched. Angels were often called spirits.[6] Thus for instance in Heb 1:3–9 the author in a quotation from Ps 2 works with the double concept of angels and spirits, viz., Paul actually only exchanges the spirits for *the* Spirit mentioned in the preceding context (Rom 8:14–16). Third: Paul speaks of a groaning of the believers *and* of the Spirit. In the Flood tradition the angels express the groaning of Creation before God: καὶ νῦν ἰδοῦ βοῶσιν αἱ ψυχαὶ τῶν τετελευτηκότων καὶ ἐντυγχάνουσιν μέχρι τῶν πυλῶν οὐρανοῦ, καὶ ἀνέβη ὁ στεναγμὸς αὐτῶν καὶ οὐ δύναται ἐξελθεῖν ἀπὸ προσώπου τῶν ἐπὶ τῆς γῆς γινομένων ἀνομημάτων (1En 9:10). Paul expresses the same idea: the Spirit brings the groaning before God, but the Apostle articulates it differently. In the Flood tradition the angels tell God that Creation groans whereas with Paul the Spirit groans when interceding before God. Thus Paul adds a new perspective to the earlier exposition of the Spirit. In the present time of weakness the believers groan, but the Spirit intercedes for them, bringing even their groaning before God as an intercession.

c) The Flood tradition also explains the strange figure mentioned as ὁ ὑποτάξας. Paul thinks not of God, nor of Satan, nor of Adam (man)[7] but speaks of the leading angel (Azael? cf. 1En 9:6; 10:4,8) who caused sin to penetrate the entire world.[8] Because of this angel the earth was subjected to meaninglessness and destruction without its own action or without its own will (οὐχ ἑκοῦσα).

d) The sons of God, who will be "revealed", are paralleled by the archangels who will "reveal" themselves on the last day to summon all mankind to the judgment.[9] Thus in this verse Paul primarily thinks not of the Christians but of the angels.[10]

---

[6] "Diese Bezeichnung ist in der apokalyptischen Literatur geläufig" Schweizer (1959, 373). Cf. 1En 15:4, 6f.; 61:12; 69:22; 75:5; 106:17; Jub 1:25; 2:2; 15:31f.; 2En 12:1f.; 16:7; TLev 4:1; 4Ezra 6:41. According to Schweizer the name of God as the Lord of the Spirits ("Herr der Geister") in the Similtudes in 1En should be understood from this perception of angels (*loc. cit.* note 214).

[7] For these interpretations see 1.3.2.4.3.

[8] Close to this are Pallis and Schläger who interpret ὁ ὑποτάξας as Satan (see ch. 1 note 128).

[9] The connection between the sons of God and the archangels of 1En 10 is seen by Eareckson (1977, 110ff.). Unfortunately Eareckson presupposes the common idea that Gen 3 has to be the background of Rom 8:18ff. and is therefore forced to say that "we", the Christians, are these "heralds of the triumphant Christ in his kingdom" (*op. cit.*, 112).

[10] The text is ambiguous at this point. As Paul in v. 14 names the Christians sons of God he

e) That Creation will reach the freedom which belongs to the children of God is in harmony with the Flood tradition, in which the entire Creation, sub-human as well as human, reaches its original freedom and glory together with the righteous Noah. In Gen 8:21–9:17 the Covenant is explicitly made with both Noah and the rest of the world. The picture is transformed in 1En into an eschatological promise of a new world (1En 10:7–11:2). This emphasis on the entire Creation, and not only the chosen people, makes a decisive difference between this Covenant and other covenants mentioned in the OT. As a matter of fact Creation in this tradition is bound to the fate of the righteous.

Some of the motifs and thoughts in Rom 8:18ff. are not paralleled in the Flood tradition. However, these motifs are genuinely Pauline and speak of the hope and longing of the believers (vv. 23–25). This section is inserted into the traditional material via the words οὐ μόνον δέ, αλλὰ καὶ αὐτοί (v. 23).

4.2 The Structure of Rom 8:18ff.

The structure of the text becomes clearer when it is read against the background of the Flood tradition. A natural delimitation would be vv. 18 — 30.[11] The latter termination should be set after v. 30, since v. 31 begins with a rhetorical question which announces the conclusion of Chapters 1–8. V. 28 leaves the theme of suffering and glory and returns to the thought of the certainty of salvation for the believers. The cohesion of the reasoning in vv. 17–30 is visible in that vv. 28–30 return to the introductory thought of v. 17:

v. 15ff. ἐλάβετε πνεῦμα υἰοθεσίας ... ὅτι ἐσμὲν τέκνα θεοῦ
v. 29   εἰς τὸ εἶναι αὐτὸν πρωτότοκον ἐν πολλοῖς ἀδελφοῖς

v. 17   τέκνα — κληρονόμοι θεοῦ — συγκληρονόμοι Χριστοῦ — συμπάσχομεν
v. 29   συμμόρφους τῆς εἰκόνος τοῦ υἱοῦ αὐτοῦ

v. 17   συνδοξασθῶμεν
v. 30   ἐδόξασεν

may include them among these final figures who will be revealed on the last day. In 1Cor 6:1–3 Paul posits that the Christians will be together with Christ on the last day, judging the world and even the angels. Thus the ambiguity in regard to the sons of God in Rom 8 may be intentional. However, this does not really diminish the probability of a dependence on the Flood tradition.

[11] Thus Schlatter (1935), Bruce (1971), Balz (1971, 93), Käsemann (1973), von der Osten-Sacken (1975, 139), Cranfield (1980).

We should first notice that the traditional material of the text is limited to vv. 20–22 (the suffering of Creation) and 26–27 (the intercession of the Spirit). Paul has expanded the former section by mentioning of the suffering of the believers, vv. 23–25; they suffer because they are part of the present world, i.e. Creation. The first half of the text thus speaks of present suffering. The next section deals with the intercession of the Spirit, and the last returns to the theme of v. 17—salvation is sure because it depends on God's action.

This helps us to see the similarity between Paul's text and the Flood tradition in regard to thought-pattern. In the Flood tradition evil is introduced into the world through the fall of the angels and increases until the entire Creation is about to be destroyed. At the groaning and prayer of Creation the angels intercede before God. The intercession of the angels thus marks the turning-point of the story. The second part speaks of the future judgment and the establishment of a new world. Similarly, having stated the thesis in v. 18, Paul speaks first of Creation's suffering in the present time, but with the perspective of longing for the coming deliverance from evil. To this Paul adds a section on the suffering believers. The motif of the praying Spirit constitutes the turning-point of the text. In the second part Paul leaves the traditional material and speaks of the certainty of the coming glory. In Paul's thought the change of the situation is bound to God's act in Christ. This act therefore plays an important rôle in the beginning and the end of the text.

The text thus assumes the following structure: v. 17 has a double function as a transition from the preceding context but supplying at the same time the foundation for the whole section: union with Christ's suffering is necessary for a future glory together with Him. This statement can also be understood in another way: union with Christ in suffering guarantees a union with Him in His glory.[12] On this basis v. 18 forms a thesis: the sufferings of the present time cannot be compared to the glory to come. This thesis is then demonstrated in three steps: First the present situation is described: a) vv. 19–22 (introduced by γάρ) depict the longing and hope of the sub-human Creation, and b) vv. 23–25 (introduced by οὐ μόνον δέ . . . ἀλλὰ καί, and not directly dependent on the Flood tradition)[13] the longing and hope of the believers. The second step: in this present suffering the Spirit intercedes for the believers (vv. 26–27). This section is the turning-point of the text. Thirdly: the certainty of deliverance is illustrated in vv. 28–30 which conclude the passage. In this last section Paul returns to the thought presented at the beginning of the text.[14]

The text thus can be outlined as follows:

---

[12] The construction of the two clauses beginning with εἴπερ . . . ἵνα sharpens the thought that the foundation of the coming glory is the incorporation into Christ's sufferings.

[13] Within this structure the comment in v. 20 τῇ γὰρ ματαιότητι ἡ κτίσις ὑπετάγη, οὐχ ἑκοῦσα ἀλλὰ διὰ τὸν ὑποτάξαντα functions as a parenthetic explanation of the present situation of Creation implied in v. 20. In v. 26 Paul begins with an ὡσαύτως, which has puzzled the commentators. In the light of the usage of the Flood tradition I suggest the following explanation: vv. 23–25 do not build on the Flood tradition, and his leaving of this background may be faintly

- Transition from the preceding and basis for the thesis (v. 17)
- Thesis: The present suffering is nothing as compared with the future glory (v. 18)
- A. The present suffering (vv. 19–25)
    - a. Testimony from Creation (vv. 19–22)
    - b. Testimony from the believers (vv. 23–25)
- B. The turning-point at the Spirit's intercession (vv. 26–27)
- C. The coming glory (vv. 28–30)

Paul's aim, to speak of the future glory which encompasses the entire world, is evident in the beginning of the text, v. 17, and again in its ending, vv. 29–30.

4.3 The Relation of Rom 8:18–27 to its Context

My investigation supports the view that the text fits well into the major thought-structure of the entire letter.[15] A brief retrospect on the line of thought of the letter may suffice to illustrate my opinion. In 1:16f Paul presents the theme which he will discuss; righteousness from God which is "first for the Jew and then for the Gentile" because it is given to men through faith alone. The discussion starts in 1:18: "The wrath of God is revealed from heaven against all ungodliness". Both Jew and Gentile are fallen in sin and "there will be tribulation and distress for every human being who does evil, the Jew first and also the Greek. For God shows no partiality" (2:9f). Consequently God "will justify the circumcised on the ground of their faith and the uncircumcised through their faith" (3:30). Up to 7:25 Paul discusses how God in Christ saves from the powers of sin and death, a so to speak "negative" description of the new righteousness. But this salvation could not help man because living in the flesh he is weak and cannot lead a righteous life in his own power. Paul therefore turns to the positive side of the new righteousness and spends Chapter 8 on the power of the holy Spirit. Positively the new righteousness is thus described as a life in holy Spirit (8:2–17). The Spirit

---

heard in οὐ μόνον δέ, ἀλλὰ καὶ αὐτοί. The return to the Flood tradition via ὡσαύτως could then imply something like "as the tradition speaks of the suffering Creation so, similarly, it speaks of a spiritual intercession".

[14] The structuring in three "concentric circles" according to the three mentioned groaning figures thus seems to be artificial (the expression was invented by Zahn, see 1.3.2.3). The main interest of the text in fact falls on the eschatological glory rather than on the present groaning, and thus the key-word is glory (δόξα) rather than groaning.

[15] Thus Paulsen (1974, 179ff.). Bindemann notes the fact that many exegetes tend to lose sight of the context when they comment on Rom 8:18ff: "Ein großer Teil der Untersuchungen zum Text leidet darunter, daß der Text weitgehend vom Kontext isoliert wird" (1983, 16).

makes possible a righteous life outside, although not against the law. In this world the believer, being flesh, is still part of the world, but he is saved in hope and will share perfect life with Christ at the eschaton.

In 8:17 Paul makes a transition to the eschatological perspective of the new righteousness. The perspective is that of the Flood tradition, in which the entire Creation is longing for deliverance and finally also is renewed together with the righteous.[16] The longing is explained by some allusions to the origin of the present situation. But in the present time of suffering the Spirit is also at work interceding for the believers. This eschatological section is concluded in vv. 28–30. In Christ the believers know that God works for good with them. The text is followed by the triumphant statement, expressed in hymnic language, that salvation is sure and no power will be able to separate the believers from God's love in Christ (8:31–39). Rom 8:31–39 is the logical conclusion to the line of thought begun in 1:18ff.[17]

The exposition of righteousness, as available on the same terms to both Jew and Gentile, is thus finished by an eschatological outlook which opens up an universal perspective of this new righteousness. As sin is universal, so is salvation in Christ. Paul can then move to next great section in the letter, the direct discussion of the relations between Jews and Gentiles (9–11). This section is followed by the paraenetic conclusion of the letter (12–15) and, finally, the salutations (16). Rom 8:18–27 thus plays an important part in the section of the letter which serves as the fundation of Paul's argument in favour of the unity of mankind in chapters 9–11.

4.4 The Message of Rom 8:18–30

The message to the readers is signaled in the termination of the text. These verses contain three important thoughts: a) the believers are already God's children and thus brethren of Christ; b) they will be formed in His likeness, and c) they will share the eschatological glory together with Christ. The expected glory is granted to the believer because of his incorporation into Christ (v. 17). This statement functions as a basis of the thesis in v. 18. Similarly,

---

[16] The universal perspective made the Flood tradition an alternative to that Jewish thinking, which was centered to Covenants with the Jewish people. God showed his concern for the entire Creation through Noah. This vision was already intrinsic in the earliest Flood stories (see Ch. 2 note 34) and is also essential to the Enocic version. Hartman wrote: "Another remarkable thing in this second half of our passage [1En 10:16-11:2] is that it deals with all mankind and all nations rather than with righteous Jews only" (1983, 19).

[17] Eareckson: "Only here is the great damage of the fall in 1:18ff, with its cosmic dimensions, given an adequate response" (1977, 162). This perspective is in harmony with Paul's conception of Christ as cosmocrator (cf. Rom 8: 31-39; 11:36; 1Cor 25; Phil 2:11).

the concluding words in v. 29f. declare that the said glory is granted by God and accords with His plan. Thus the beginning and the end of the passage emphasize that the expected glory is granted only through God's action and through Christ. There is no possibility of gaining it by one's own action. These verses thus are in perfect harmony with the letter as a whole, speaking of Jews and Gentiles as one in Christ. The eschatological perspective of the Flood tradition also fits in: not a single people, but the entire world is involved in God's plans for the future, in which the righteous life will be perfected.

Finally this message could be applied more closely to what seems to have been the concrete situation in Rome. In a way the eschatological reality was already present to the believers, Jewish and Gentile Christians alike. Both had received the first fruit of the Spirit, so being God's sons (although also longing for the definite adoption). Both groups, not only the Jews, were elected—the classical honor of Israel!—called, justified, and expecting the glory. But this common divine sonship through the Spirit also implied a "with Christ", which meant sufferings, e.g. such as expulsion from Rome through an imperial decree. The indwelling Spirit should, however, also positively form their common life (vv. 12–14): a falling back into Gentile ways would mean living according to the flesh (v. 12f.; cf., e.g. 12:2; 13:13), but so would also an unjustified boasting on the part of the Gentile Christians vis-à-vis the Jews (11:18), or offensive behaviour toward fellow Christians with scruples about food and drink (Chapter 14). Indeed, sharing the eschatological now and the eschatological hope, both developed in 8:18–30, Jewish and Gentile Christians in Rome had every reason to "be in harmony with one another in accord with Christ" (15:5).[18]

---

[18] The message of Rom 8:18ff. thus is not comfort in suffering, although it might so be in situations of suffering, nor is Paul concentrating on Christian hope as a part of his theological dogma. He is not even speaking of solidarity between man and Creation as part of an ecological or political debate. It may be legitimate to use the text in discussion of such questions, but it is important to make clear that they lie far beyond Paul's horizon.

Bibliography

The English Bible is quoted from the Revised Standard Version.

Abbreviations

Abbreviation of Biblical books and Ancient authors are made according to Charlesworth, J. L., ed., *The Old Testament Pseudepigrapha* I. London (1983) xlv–l.

DivTom	Divus Thomas (Piacenza).
ExWNT	Exegetisches Wörterbuch zum Neuen Testament.
IKZ	Internationale Kirchliche Zeitschrift.
IrThQ	Irish Theological Quarterly.
JDT	Jahresbücher für deutsche Theologie.
LingBibl	Linguistica Biblica.
NThT	Nieuw Theologische Tijdschrift.
TüZT	Tübinger Zeitschrift für Theologie.

Other abbreviations of periodicals etc. according to the JBL system (see Journal of Biblical Literature 95, 1976, 331–346).

Texts and Translations

Biblia Hebraica Stuttgartensia. Eds. Kittel, R., Elliger, K., Rudolph, W. Stuttgart 1983.
Septuaginta. Ed. Rahlfs, A. Stuttgart 1971.
The Old Testament in Greek according to the Septuagint. I–III. Ed. Swete, H. B. Cambridge 1909–1912.
Targum Onkelos I–II. Ed. Berliner, A. Berlin, Frankfurt, London 1884.
Pseudo-Jonathan (Thargum Jonathan ben Usiel zum Pentateuch) nach der Londoner Handschrift. Ed. Ginsburger, M. Hildersheim, New York 1971.
Targum Neophyti I. Ed. Díez Macho, A. Madrid, Barcelona 1968.
The Bible in Aramaic based on Old Manuscripts and Printed Texts, I. The Pentateuch. Ed. Sperber, A. Leiden 1959.
Targum Jonathan ben Uziel on the Pentateuch. Ed. Rieder, D. Jerusalem 1974.
Novum Testamentum Graece. Eds. Nestle, E., Aland, K. Stuttgart [26]1979.
Synopsis Quattor Evangeliorum. Ed. Aland, K. Stuttgart [7]1971.

The Apocrypha and Pseudepigrapha of the Old Testament in English, I–II. Ed. Charles, R. H. Oxford 1913.
Die Apokryphen und Pseudepigraphen des Alten Testaments. Ed. Kautzsch, E. Tübingen 1962.

De Gammeltestamentlige Pseudepigrapher I–II. Hammershaimb, E., Munck, J., Noack, B., Seidelin, P. København 1953–1976.

The Old Testament Pseudepigrapha, I–II. Ed. Charlesworth, J. H. London 1983–1985.

The Books of Enoch Aramaic Fragments of Qumrân Cave 4. Ed. J. T. Milik. Oxford 1976.

Vita Adae et Evae. Ed. Meyer, W. (Abhandlungen der philosophisch-philologischen Classe der Könglich Bayerischen Akademie der Wissenschaften 49). München 1978, 187–244.

Apocalypse syriaque de Baruch. Ed. Bogaert (SC 144, 145). Paris 1969.

Apocalypsis Baruchi Graece. (PVTG 2) ed. Picard, J.-C. Leiden 1977.

Apocalypsis Henochi Graeci, Ed. Black, M. (PVTG 3). Leiden 1970.

The Ethiopic Book of Enoch. A new edition in the light of the Aramaic Dead Sea fragments, I–II. Knibb, M. A. Oxford 1978.

The Book of Enoch or 1 Enoch. A New English Edition with Commentary and Textual Notes. Black, M (SVTP). Leiden 1985.

Visio Beati Esdrae. Ed. Wahl, O. (PVTG 4). Leiden 1977.

Das Buch der Jubiläen. Ed. Rönsch H. Leipzig 1874.

Das Buch der Jubiläen. Ed. Berger, K., (Jud. Schr. aus Hell. Zeit II, Lieferung 3). Gerd Mohn 1981.

The Assumption of Moses. Ed. Charles, R. H. London 1897.

Pseudo-Philo Les antiquités Bibliques. I—II. Harrington, D. J., Cazeaux, J. (SC) Paris 1976.

Apocalypsis Sedrach. Ed. Wahl, O. (PVTG 4). Leiden 1977.

Testamenta XII Patriarcharum . . . Ed. De Jonge, M. (PVTG). Leiden 1964.

Die Texte aus Qumran. Ed. Lohse, E. Darmstadt 1971.

The Genesis Apocryphon of Qumran Cave I. Ed. Fitzmyer, J. (BibOr 18). Rome 1966.

The Dead Sea Scriptures in English Translation with Introduction and Notes. Gaster, Th. H. (Anchor Books). New York ²1964.

Die Texte vom Toten Meer. Hebräisch und Deutsch. Ed. Maier, J. München, Basel 1960.

The Dead Sea Scrolls in English. Vermes, G. Worcester ³1987.

Josephus, *De bello Judaico. Der Jüdische Krieg*. Ed. Michel, O., Bauernfeind, O. Darmstadt 1959–69.

— *Antiquitates Judaicae*. Ed. Thackeray, H. St. J. (LCL). London, Cambridge, Mass. 1978.

Philo of Alexandria, *De Gigantibus*. Ed. Colson, F. H. and Withaker, G. H. (LCL). London, Cambridge Mass. 1958.

— *De vita Mosis*. Ed. Colson, F. H.(LCL). London, Cambrigde Mass. 1959.

— *Praemiis et Poenis*. Ed. Colson, F. H. (LCL). London, Cambridge Mass. 1960.

— *Quaestiones et solutiones in Genesin et Exodum*. Suppl. I. Ed. Marcus, R. (LCL). London, Cambridge Mass. 1961.

Midrash Rabba Translated into English. 8 Eds. Freedman, H., Simon, M. London ³1961.

Mekilta de Rabbi Ishmael. Ed. Lauterbach, J. S. Philadelphia 1949.

Mekilta Jischamel. Bet ha-Midrash. Sammlung kleiner Midrashim. Ed. von Jellinek, A. 1967.

Sifre zu Numeri übersetzt und Erklärt. Kuhn, K. G. Stuttgart 1951.

Sanhedrin . . . Eds. Shacter, J., Freedman, H. (in The Babylonian Talmud, ed. Epstein, I.). London 1935.

Shabbath . . . Ed. Freedman, H. (in The Babylonian Talmud, ed. Epstein, I.). London 1938.

Yebamot . . . Ed. Slotki, I. W. (in The Babylonian Talmud, ed. Epstein, I.). London 1936.

New Testament Apocrypha I–II. Eds. Hennecke, E., Schneemelcher, W. Tübingen 1959–1964.

Die Apostolischen Väter I. Ed. K. Bihlmeyer (SAQ). Tübingen ³1970.

Augustine, *De diversis quaestionibus octoginta tribus. De octo dulcitii quaestionibus.* Ed. Mutzenbecher, A. (CChr XLIV A). Turnholti 1975.

— *De catechizandis rudibus.* Ed. Migne, J.—P. (PL 40). Paris 1845.

Athenagoras, *Legatio* and *De Resurrectione*, (Oxford Early Christian Texts). Ed. Schoedel, W. R. Oxford 1972.

Tertullian, *De monogamia.* Ed. Bulhart, V. (CSEL 76) Vindobonae 1957.

Clemens Alexandrinus, *Stromata* II–III. Ed. Stählin, O.(GCS). Leipzig 1906–1909.

— *Protrepticus und Paedagogus.* Ed. Stählin, O. (GCS). Berlin ³1972.

Die Pseudoclementinen. I Homilien 1969; II Rekognitionen. Ed. Rehm, B. (GCS) Berlin 1965.

The Clementine Homilies. Ed. Roberts, A. and Donaldson, J. (ANF 8). Grand Rapids 1951.

Irenaeus, *Contra Haereses.* Ed. Sagnard, F. (SC 34). Paris 1952.

Justinus, *Apologia.* Justinus des Philosophers und Märtyrers Apologien I–II. Ed. Pfättisch, J. M. Münster 1912.

Minucius Felix *Octavius.* Ed. Halm, C. (CSEL 2). Vindobonae 1867.

Origenes, *Gegen Celsus (Contra Celcum).* Ed. Koerschau, P. (GCS). Leipzig 1899.

Paulus Orosius, *Historiae adversum paganos.* Ed. Zangmeister, C. (CSEL 5). Vindobonae 1882.

Apocryphon Johannis. The Coptic Text of the Apocryphon Johannis in the Nag Hammadi Codex II. Ed. Giversen, S. (Acta Theologia Dana 5). Copenhagen 1963.

The Hypostasis of the Archons. The Coptic Text with Translation and Commentary. Bullard, R. A. Berlin 1970.

Die Ezra-Apokalypse (IV Ezra). I. Ed Violet, B. (GCS 18) Leipzig 1910.

Die Oracula Sibyllina. Ed. Geffcken, J. (GCS). Leipzig 1902.

Sibyllinische Weissagungen. Ed. Kurfess A.-M. München 1951.

Visio sancti Pauli. Ed. Silverstein Th. (Studies and Documents IV). London 1935, 219–229.

Dio Cassius, *Roman History* V–VII. Ed. Foster, H. B. and Cary, E. (LCL). London, Cambridge Mass. 1969–1981.

Suetonius, *De vita Caesarum. V, Divus Claudius.* Ed. Rolfe, J. C. (LCL). London, Cambridge Mass. 1965.

Literature

Achtemeier, P. J., 1985. *Romans, Interpretation: A Biblical Commentary for Teaching and Preaching.* Atlanta.

— 1987. *The Quest for Unity in the New Testament Church.* Philadelphia.

Aland, K., 1971. *Synopsis* . . . See Texts and Translations.

Alethaeus, Th. 1714. *Gründliche Erleuterung der dunckelen Oerter und Steine des*

Anstosses A. und N. Testaments, 1-12. Versuch. Leipzig.

Allen, D. C., 1949. The Legend of Noah. Illinois.

Allen, W. C., [7]1957. A Critical and Exegetical Commentary on the Gospel According to S. Matthew. (ICC) Edinburgh.

Alexander, P. S., 1972. 'The Targumim and Early Exegeisis of "Sons of God" in Gen 6', JJS 23, 60-71.

Althaus, P., 1954. Der Brief an die Römer. (NTD 6) Göttingen.

Anderson, B. W., 1978. 'From Analysis to Synthesis: The Interpretation of Genesis 1-11', JBL 97, 23-39.

Attridge, H. W., 1989. The Epistle to the Hebrews. Philadelphia.

Balz, H., 1971. Heilsvertrauen und Welterfahrung. Strukturen der paulinischen Eschatologie nach Römer 8, 18-39. (BEvT 59) München.

— 1980. 'ἀποκαραδοκία', EWNT I, 318f.

Bamberger, B., 1952. Fallen Angels. New York.

Bardenhewer, O., 1926. Der Römerbrief des heiligen Paulus. Freiburg.

Barker, M., 1987. The Older Testament. London.

Barrett, C. K., 1957. A Commentary on the Epistle to the Romans. (Black's NT Commentaries) New York.

Barth, K., 1985. Der Römerbrief. (Karl Barth Gesamtausgabe II) Zürich.

Bauer, W., and Aland, K. 1988. Griechisch-deutsches Wörterbuch zu den Schriften des Neuen Testaments und der frühchristlichen Literatur. Ed. Aland, K. and Aland, B. Berlin, New York.

Baur, F. C., 1836. 'Ueber Zweck und Veranlassung des Römerbriefs und die damit zusammenhängenden Verhältnisse der römischen Gemeinde. Ein historisch-kritische Untersuchung', TüZT 2, 59-178.

Bauernfeind, O., 1942. 'μάταιος etc', TWNT 4, 525-530.

— 1942. 'νικάω etc', TWNT 4, 941-945.

— 1969. 'τυγχάνω etc', TWNT 8, 238-245.

Beare, F. W., 1962. 'Romans, Letter to the', IDB 4, 112-122.

Beasley-Murray, G. R., 1981. The Book of Revelation. (New Century Bible Commentary) London.

Beck, J.T., 1884. Erklärung des Briefes Pauli an die Römer. Gütersloh.

Behm, J., 1933. 'ἀρραβών', TWNT 1, 474.

— 1954. 'παράκλητος', TWNT 5, 798-812.

Beker, J. C., 1970. 'Erwägungen zur apokalyptischen Tradition in der paulinischen Theologie', EvT, 30, 593-609.

— 1982. Paul's Apocalyptic Gospel The Coming Triumph of God. Philadelphia.

— [2]1984. Paul the Apostle The Triumph of God in Life and Thought. Philadelphia.

— 1986. 'The Faithfulness of God and the Priority of Israel in Paul's Letter to the Romans', HTR 79, 10-16.

Benoit, P., 1961. ' "Nous gémissons, attendent la délivrance de notre corps." (Rom VIII, 23)', Exégèse et Théologie II, 41-52, Paris.

Berger, K., 1981. Das Buch der Jubiläen. See Texts and Translations.

Bertram, G., 1935. 'ἔργον etc', TWNT 2, 631-653.

— 1958. 'ἀποκαραδοκία', ZNW 49, 264-270.

— 1964. 'στενός etc', TWNT 7, 604-608.

— 1964. 'συνεργος etc', TWNT 7, 869-875.

— 1969. 'ὕψος etc', TWNT 8, 600-619.

— 1973. 'ὠδίν, ωδίνειν', TWNT 9, 668-675.

Best, E., 1967. The Letter of Paul to the Romans. Cambridge.

Biedermann, H., 1940. Die Erlösung der Schöpfung beim Apostel Paulus. (Classiciacum 8) Würzburg.

Bietenhard, H., 1951. *Die himmlische Welt im Urchristentum und Spätjudentum.* Tübingen.

Biggs, C., 1961. *A Critical and Exegetical Commentary on the Epistles of St. Peter and St. Jude.* (ICC) Edinburgh.

Billerbeck, P., 1922. See Strack, H. L.

Bindemann, W., 1983. *Die Hoffnung der Schöpfung Römer 8:18–27 und die Frage einer Theologie der Befreiung von Mensch und Natur.* (Neukirchener Studienbücher 14) Neukirchen—Vluyn.

Bisping, A., 1870. *Erklärung des Briefes an die Römer.* (Exegetisches Handbuch zum NT V,1) Münster.

Black, M., 1970. *Apocalypsis Henochi* . . . See Texts and Translations.

— [3]1984. *Romans.* (New Century Bible Series) London.

— 1985. *The Book of Enoch* . . . See Texts and Translations.

Blass, F., Debrunner, A., [3]1967. *A Greek Grammar of the New Testament and Other Early Christian Literature.* Trans. Funk, R. W. Chicago.

Bloch, R., 1957. 'Midrach', *Dict. de la Bib. Suppl.* 6, 1263–1281.

Boers, H., 1982. 'The Problem of Jews and Gentiles in the Macro-structure of Romans', *SEÅ* 47, 184–196.

Bornkamm, G., [2]1969. *Paulus.* Stuttgart.

— 1977. 'The Letter of the Romans As Paul's Last Will and Testament', in Donfried, K. P., ed., *The Romans Debate.*, 17–31. Originally published as 'Der Römerbreif als Testament des Paulus', in *Geschichte und Glaube* II. München 1971, 120–139.

Bousset, W., 1906. *Die Religion des Judentums im neutestamentlichen Zeitalter.* Berlin.

Boyd, R. F., 1954. 'The Work of the Holy Spirit in Prayer. An Exposition of Romans 8, 26–27', *Int* 8, 35–42.

Bruce, F. F., [6]1971. *The Epistle of Paul to the Romans. An Introduction and a Commentary.* (The Tyndale NT Commentaries) London.

Brunner, E., 1938. *Der Römerbrief.* (Bibelhilfe für die Gemeinde, Ntl. Reihe, Bd. 6) Leipzig.

Budde, 1883. *Die Biblische Urgeschichte* (Gen. 1–12,5). Bonn.

Bultmann, R., 1935. 'ἐλπίς', *TWNT*, 2, 515–531.

— 1967. 'Glossen im Römerbrief', *Exegetica*, 278–284, Tübingen.

— [2]1968. "History" = *The History of Synoptic Tradition.* Oxford.

— [5]1968. "Theology" = *Theology of the New Testament* I. London.

— 1973. *The Johannine Epistles.* (Hermeneia), Philadelphia.

Caduff, G. A., 1986. *Antike Sintflutsagen.* (Hypomnemata, Untersuchungen zur Antike und zu ihrem Nachleben 82) Göttingen.

Campbell, W. S., 1981. 'The Romans Debate', *JSNT* 10, 19–28.

Charles, R. H., 1912. *The Book of Noah.* Oxford.

— 1913. *The Apocrypha* . . . I–II. See Texts and Translations.

— 1959. *A Critical and Exegetical Commentary on The Revelation of St. John*, II. (ICC) Edinburgh.

Clifford, R. J., and Murphy, R. E., 1989. 'Genesis', *The New Jerome Biblical Commentary*, 8–43.

Closen, G. E., 1937. *Die Sünde der 'Söhne Gottes'* (Gen VI,1–4). Rom.

Collins, J., 1978. 'Methodological Issues in the Study of 1En: Reflections on the Articles of P. D. Hanson and G. W. Mickelsburg', in Achtemeier, P. J., ed., *SBL 1978 Seminar Papers*, 1, Missoula, 315–322.

Conzelmann, H., 1975. *1 Corinthians. A Commentary on the First Epistle to the Corinthians.* (Hermeneia) Philadelphia.

Cooke, G., 1964. 'The Sons of (the) God(s)', *ZAW* 76, 22–47.

Cornley, R., 1896. *Commentarius in S. Pauli Apostoli epistulam ad Romanos*. (Cursus Scripturae Sacrae, II, I) Paris.

Cranfield, C. E. B., 1963. 'I Peter', *Peake's Commentary on the Bible*, London, Edinburgh, Paris, Melburne, Johannesburg, Toronto and New York, 1026-1030.

— 1966. 'Romans 8,28', *SJTh* 19 (1966), 204-215.

— ⁴1980. *A Critical and Exegetical Commentay on the Epistle to the Romans*. I. (ICC) Edinburg.

Dalton, W. J., 1988. 'The Background and Meaning of the Biblical Flood Narrative', *Austral.Cath.Rec.* 34 (1957), 292-304; and 35 (1958), 23-39.

— 1965. *Christ's Proclamation to the Spirits*. Rome.

Davies, W. D., 1965. *Paul and Rabbinic Judaism. Some Rabbinic Elements in Pauline Theology*. London.

Decok, P. B., 1983. 'Holy Ones, sons of God, and the transcendent future of the righteous in 1 Enoch and the New Testament', *Neot*, 70-82.

Delling, G., 1933. 'ἀποκαραδοκία', *TWNT* I, 392.

— 1933. 'ἄρχω etc', *TWNT* I, 476-488.

— 1935. 'ἡμέρα', *TWNT* II, 945-956.

— 1938. 'καιρός etc', *TWNT* III, 456-465.

— 1942. 'λαμβάνω etc', *TWNT* IV, 5-16.

— 1959. 'πλήρης etc', *TWNT* VI, 283-309.

— 1969. 'τάσσω etc', *TWNT* VIII, 27-49.

— 1977. 'Die "Söhne (Kinder) Gottes" im Neuen Testament', in *Die Kirche des Anfangs*. Festschrift für Heinz Schürmann. Schnackenburg, E., & Wanke, J., Eds. Leipzig, 615-631.

Denton, D. R., 1982. ''Αποκαραδοκία', *ZNW* 73, 138-140.

Dexinger, F., 1966. *Sturz der Göttersöhne oder Engel vor der Sintflut? Versuch eines Neuverständnisses von Genesis 6,2-4 unter Berücksichtigung der religionsgeschichtlichen Methode*. (Wiener Beiträge zur Theologie XIII) Wien.

Dietzel, A., 1957. 'Beten im Geist', *TZ* 13, 12-32.

Dimant, D., 1978. '1 Enoch 6-11: A Methodological Perspective', in *SBL Seminar Papers 1978*, I, ed. Achtemeier, P. J., Missoula, 323-340.

Dodd, C. H., ⁴1963. *The Epistle of Paul to the Romans*. London.

Donfried, K. P., ed. 1977. "Debate". = *The Romans Debate*. Minneapolis.

— 1977. "Notice" = 'A Short Notice on Romans 16' in Donfried K. P., *The Romans debate*, 50-60. Originally published in *ST* 25 (1971), 61-73.

— 1977. "False" = 'False Presuppositions in the Study of Romans', in Donfried, K. P., ed. *The Romans Debate*, 120-148. Originally published in *CBQ* 36 (1974), 356-358.

Dulau, P., 1934. ' "Omnis creatura ingemiscit" (Rom. VIII, 22)', *DivTom* 37, 386-392.

— 1935. ' "Omnis creatura ingemiscit" (Rom. VIII, 19-23)', *DivTom* 38, 430-31.

Dundes, A., ed. 1988. *The Flood Myth*. Berkeley, Los Angeles, London.

Dunn, J. D. G., 1988. 'Paul's Epistle to the Romans: An Analysis of Structure and Argument', *Aufstieg und Niedergang der Römischen Welt*. Bd. 25.4. Ed. Haase, W., 2842-2890.

Eareckson, V. O. III, 1977. *The Glory to be Revealed Hereafter: The Interpretation of Romans 8:18-25 and its Place in Pauline Theology*. Diss. Princeton, Princeton New Jersey.

Eissfeldt, O., 1966. *The Old Testament. An Introduction*. Oxford.

Fahy, T., 1956. "St. Paul" = 'St. Paul: Romans 8:16-25', *IrThQ* XXIII, 178-181.

— 1956. "Romans" = 'Romans 8:29', *IrThQ* XXIII, 410–412.

Fitzmyer, J., 1957–58. 'A Feature of Qumran Angelology and the Angels of 1 Cor. 11:10', *NTS* 4, 48–58.

— 1966. *The Genesis Apocryphon* . . . See Texts and Translations.

— 1967. 'Romans, Epistle to', *NCE* XII, 635–639.

— 1985. *The Gospel According to Luke* (x–xxiv). New York.

— 1989. 'Romans, Epistle to the', *New Jerome Biblical Commentary*, Avon.

Foerster, W., 1933. 'ἄξιος etc', *TWNT* I, 378–380.

— 1938. 'κτίζω etc', *TWNT* III, 999–1034.

Forde, G. O., 1984. 'Romans 8:18–27', *Itp* 38, 281–285.

Frazer, G. F., 1988. 'Folklore in the Old Testament', in Dundes, A., ed., *The Flood Myth*, 113–124. Originally published in *Folklore in the Old Testament*, London 1918, 104–107; 332–338.

Friedrich, G., 1961. 'Römerbrief', *RGG* V, 1137–1143.

Fritz, V., 1882. ' "Solange die Erde steht" —Vom Sinn der jahwistischen Fluterzählung in Gen 6–8', *ZAW* 94, 588–614.

Fritzsche, K. F. A., 1839. *Pauli ad Romanos epistola*. Halle.

Frost, S. B., 1952. *Old Testament Apocalyptic. Its Origin and Growth*. London.

Frommann, K., 1863. 'Ueber die seufzende Kreatur, Röm. 8,19–23', *JDT* 8, 25–50.

Frymer-Kensky, T., 1988. 'The Atrahasis Epic and Its Significance for Our Understanding of Genesis 1–9', in Dundes, A., *The Flood Myth*, 61–73. Originally published in the Nov./Dec. issue of *Biblical Archaeology Review*, 1978.

Fuchs, E., [2]1949. *Die Freiheit des Glaubens*. (BEvT 14) München.

— 1954. *Hermeneutik*. Bad Cannstatt.

Gager, J. G., 1970. 'Functional Diversity in Paul's End-time Language', *JBL* 89, 325–337.

Gaster, Th. H., [2]1964. *The Dead Sea Scriptures* . . . See Texts and Translations.

Gaugler, E., 1945. *Der Römerbrief I. Teil: Kapitel 1–8*, Zürich.

— 1961. 'Der Geist und das Gebet der schwachen Gemeinde. Eine Auslegung von Röm. 8,26–27', *IKZ* 51, 67–94.

Gerber, U., 1966. 'Römer viii 18 als exegetisches Problem der Dogmatik', *NovT* 8, 58–81.

Gieraths, H. K., 1950. *Knechtschaft und Freiheit der Schöpfung. Eine historisch-exegetische Untersuchung zu Röm 8,19–22* (Diss. Bonn, typewritten manuscript).

Ginzberg, L., [2]1947. *The Legends of the Jews*, I, V. Philadelphia.

Giversen, S., 1963. *Apocryphon Johannis* . . . See Texts and Translations.

Godet, F., [2]1893. *Kommentar zu dem Brief an die Römer*. Hannover.

Goedt, M. de, 1972. 'The Intercession of the Spirit in Christian Prayer (Rom 8:26–27)', *Concilium*, 79, 26–38.

Gougel, M., 1935. 'Le caractère et le rôle de l'élément cosmologique dans la sotériologie paulinienne', *RHPR* 15, 335–359.

Graystone, K., 1964. 'The Doctrine of Election in Romans 8, 28–30', *SE* II, 574–583.

Griffith, G. O., 1945. 'The Apocalyptic Note in Romans', *ExpTim* 56, 153–155.

Guardini, R., 1940. *Das Harren der Schöpfung. Eine Auslegung von Röm 8:25–39*. Würzburg.

Gunkel, H., 1901. *Genesis übersetzt und erklärt*. Göttingen.

Gutjahr, P. S., 1923. *Die Brief an die Römer*. (Der Briefe des heiligen Apostels Paulus, III, 1.3) Graz und Wien.

Habel, N. C., 1988. 'The Two Flood Stories in Genesis', in Dundes, A., ed., *The Flood Myth*, 13–28. Originally published in *Literary Criticism of the Old Testament*. Philadelphia 1971.

Haering, Th., 1926. *Der Römerbrief des Apostels Paulus*. Stuttgart.

Hamilton, V. P., 1982. *Handbook on the Pentateuch*. Grand Rapids.

Hammershaimb, E., 1953-1976. *De Gammeltestamentlige* . . . See Texts and Translations.

Hanson, P. D., 1976. "Genre" = 'Apocalypse, Genre', *IDB* Suppl., 27-28;

— 1976. "Apocalypticism" = 'Apocalypticism', *IDB* Suppl., 28-34.

— 1977. 'Rebellion in Heaven, Azazel, and Euhemeristic Heroes in 1 Enoch 6-11', *JBL* 96, 195-233.

Hartman, L., 1966. *Prophecy Interpreted. The Formation of some Jewish Apocalyptic Texts and of the Eschatological Discourse Mark 13 par.* (ConB 1) Lund.

— 1977. ' "Comfort of the Scriptures"—an Early Jewish Interpretation of Noah's Salvation, 1 En. 10:16—11:2', *SEÅ* 41-42 (1976-77), 87-96.

— 1979. *Asking for a Meaning*. A Study of 1 Enoch 1-5. (ConB, NT ser. 12) Lund.

— 1983. 'An early example of Jewish exegesis: 1 Enoch 10:16-11:2', *Neot* 17, 16-27.

Hatch, E., Redpath, H. A., 1975. *A Concordance to the Septuagint and the Other Greek Versions of the Old Testament* (*including the Apocryphal Books*). Oxford.

Hauck, D. F., 1935. 'ἑκών etc', *TWNT* II, 467-468.

Heidland, H. W., 1942. 'λογίζομαι etc', *TWNT* IV, 287-295.

Heil, J. P., 1987. *Romans—Paul's Letter of Hope. A Reader-Response Commentary*. (An Bib 112) Rome.

Hellholm, D., 1989. 'Paulus fra Tarsos. Til spørsmålet om Paulus' hellenistiske utdannelse', in *Dionysos og Apollon*. Eds. Eide, T. and Hägg, T. Bergen, 259-282.

Hendel, R. S., 1987. 'Of Demigods and the Deluge: Towards an Interpretation of Genesis 6:1-4', *JBL* 106, 13-26.

Herrmann, W., 1960. 'Die Göttersöhne', *ZRGG* 11, 242-251.

Hill, E., 1961. 'The Construction of Three Passages From St. Paul', *CBQ* 23, 296-301.

Holtzmann, O., 1926. *Das Neue Testament nach dem Stuttgarter griechischen Text übersetzt und erklärt*, Giessen.

Hommel, H., 1984. 'Das Harren der Kreatur', *Sebasmata* 2 (WUNT 32), Tübingen, 127-140. Originally published in *Theologia Viatorum* 4, Berlin 1952 (1953), 108-124.

— 1989. 'Denen, die Gott lieben . . . Erwägungen zu Römer 8,28', *ZNW* 80, 126-129.

Hooke, S. H., 1963. 'Genesis', *Peake's Commentary on the Bible*. Eds. Black, M., and Rowley, H. H., London etc, 175-207.

Hoppe, Th., 1926. *Die Idee der Heilsgeschichte bei Paulus mit besonderer Berücksichtigung des Römerbriefes*. (Beiträge zur Förderung christlicher Theologie, 30,2) Gütersloh.

Huby, J., 1940. *Aux Romains*. (VS X) Paris.

Jervell, J., 1960. *Imago Dei*. (FRLANT 58) Göttingen.

— [2]1978. *Gud og hans fiender. Forsøk på å tolke Romerbrevet*. Oslo, Bergen, Tromsø.

— 1977. 'The Letter to Jerusalem' in Donfried, K. O., ed. *The Romans Debate*, 61-74. Originally published as 'Der Brief nach Jerusalem', *ST* 25 (1971), 90-108.

Jewett, R., 1982. 'Romans as an Ambassadorial Letter', *Int* 36, 5-20.

— 1987. 'Paul the Apostle', *The Encyclopedia of Religion* 11, 212-221.

Jung, L., 1924-26. 'Fallen Angels in Jewish, Christian and Mohammedan Thought. A Study in Comparative Folklore', *JQR* 15, 467-502; 16, 45-88, 171-205, 287-336.

Jülicher, A., 1917. *Der Brief an die Römer*. (Schriften des Neuen Testaments II) Göttingen.

Käsemann, E., 1933. *Leib und Leib Christi. Eine Untersuchung zur paulinischen Begrifflichkeit.* Tübingen.

— 1969. "Schrei" = 'Der Gottesdienstliche Schrei nach der Freiheit.' *Paulinische Perspektiven*, Tübingen, 211–236. Originally published in *Apophoreta*, Festschrift für E. Haenchen, Berlin 1964, 142–155.

— 1969. "Anthropologie" = 'Zur paulinischen Anthropologie', *Paulinische Perspektiven* 9–60, Tübingen.

— 1973. *An die Römer.* (HNT 8a) Tübingen.

Karris, R. J., 1977. "Occasion" = 'Romans 14:1–15:13 and the Occasion of Romans', in Donfried, K. O., ed., *The Romans Debate*, 75–99. Originally published in *CBQ* 35 (1973), 155–178.

— 1977. "Response" = 'The Occation of Romans: A Response to Prof. Donfried', in Donfried, *The Romans Debate*, 149–151

Kayser, W., [14]1969. *Das sprachliche Kunstwerk. Eine Einführung in die Literaturwissenschaft.* München.

Keck, L. E., 1984. 'Paul and Apocalyptic Theology', *Int.* 38, 229–241.

Kehnscherper, G., 1979. 'Theologische und homiletische Aspekte von Röm 8,19', *ThLZ* 104, 412–424.

Kertelge, K., 1971. *Der Brief an die Römer.* (Geistliche Schriftlesung 6) Düsseldorf.

Kettunen, M., 1979. *Der Abfassungszweck des Römerbriefes.* (Annales Academiae Scientiarum Humanarum Litterarum 18) Helsinki.

Kieffer, R., [2]1979. *Nytestamentlig teologi.* Lund.

Klein, G., 1969. 'Der Abfassungszweck des Römerbriefes' in *Rekonstruktion und Interpretation Gesammelten Aufsätze zum NT*, (BEvTh 50) 129–144.

— 1977. 'Paul's Purpose in Writing the Epistle to the Romans', in Donfried, K. O., ed. *The Romans Debate*, 32–49.

Klijn, A. F. J., 1981. 'An Analysis of the Use of the Story of the Flood in the Apocalypse of Adam', in G. Quispel, *Studies in Gnosticism and Hellenistic Religions.* Leiden.

Knatschbull, N., 1701. *Animadversiones in libros Novi Testamenti.* Frankfurt.

Knibb, M. A., 1978. *The Ethiopic Book . . .* See Texts and Translations.

Knopf, R., [3]1930. *Einführung in das Neue Testament.* Bibelkunde des Neuen Testaments . . . in Sammlung Töpelmann, Die Theologie im Abriss 2. Gießen.

Köllner, E., 1834. *Commentar zu dem Briefe des Apostels Paulus an die Römer.* Darmstadt.

Köster, J. F., 1862. 'Sendschreiben an die Herren Consistorialräthe D. Reiche in Göttingen und D. Meyer in Hannover über die seufzende Kreatur, Röm. 8,18–28', *TSK* 35, 755–764.

Koester, H., 1982. *Introduction to the New Testament*, I, II. Philadelphia.

Kraeling, E. G., 1947. 'The Significance and Origin of Gen 6:1–4', *JNES* 6, 193–208.

Kramer, W., 1963. *Christos Kyrios Gottessohn. Untersuchungen zu Gebrauch und Bedeutung der christologischen Bezeichnungen bei Paulus und den vorpaulinischen Gemeinden.* (ATANT 44) Zürich, Stuttgart.

Kuhn, K. G., 1938. 'βασιλεύς", C. מלכות שמים in der rabbinischen Literatur', *TWNT* I, 570–573.

Kühl, E., 1913. *Der Brief des Paulus an die Römer.* Leipzig.

Kümmel, G. W., [6]1987. *Introduction to the New Testament.* London.

Kuss, O., 1959. *Der Römerbrief übersetzt und erklärt* 2, Regensburg.

Kvanvig, H. S., 1988. *Roots of Apocalyptic.* (WMANT 61) Neukirchen.

Lagrange, M. J., 1950. *St. Paul. Epître aux Romains.* (Etudes Bibliques) Paris.

Lambert, W. G., 1955. 'Il n'y aura plus jamais de déluge (Genèse IX,11)', *Nouvelle revue théologique* 77, 581–601, 693–724.

— 1980. 'Babylon und Israel', *TRE* 5, 67–79.

Layton, B., 1987. 'Another Seed', *RB* 94, 608–613.

Lewis, J. P., 1968. *A Study of the Interpretation of Noah and the Flood in Jewish and Christian Literature*. Leiden.

Liddell, H. G., Scott, R., 1968. *A Greek-English Lexicon*. Oxford.

Lietzmann, D. H., ⁴1933. *An die Römer*. (HNT 8) Tübingen.

Limborch, Ph., 1711. *Commentarius in Acta Apostolorum et in epistolas ad Romanos et ad Hebraeos*. Roterodami.

Lipsius, R. A., ²1892. *Der Brief an die Römer*. (HKNT, II,2) Freiburg.

Lohse, E., 1971. *Die Texte* . . . See Texts and Translations.

Louw, J. P., Nida, E. A., Smith, R. B., Munson, K. A., 1988. *Greek-English Lexicon of the New Testament based on Semantic Domains*. I, II. New York.

Lüdemann, G., 1984. *Paul, Apostle to the Gentiles. Studies in Chronology*, Philadelphia.

Luz, U., 1968. *Das Geschichtsverständnis des Paulus*. (BEvT 49) München.

— 1969. 'Zum Aufbau von Röm. 1–8', *TZ* 25, 161–180.

MacRae, G., 1980. 'A Note on Romans 8:26–27', *HTR* 73, 227–230.

Maier, A., 1847. *Commentar über den Brief Pauli an die Römer*. Freiburg.

Maier, J., 1960. *Die Texte vom Toten Meer*. See Texts and Translations.

Manson, T. W., 1977. 'St. Paul's Letter To The Romans—And Others', in Donfried, K. O., ed., *The Romans Debate*, 1–16. Originally published in BJRL 31 (1948), 224–240.

— 1963. 'Romans', *Peake's Commentary to the Bible*, London etc, 940–953.

Marshall, I. H., ²1989. *The Gospel of Luke. A Commentary on the Greek Text*. (The New International Greek Testament Commentary) Grand Rapids.

May, J., 1980. 'Religious Symbolisations of Nature in Ethical Argumentation. A 'Pragmasemantic' Analysis of Romans 8:18–25 and a Buddhist Comparison', *LingBibl* 48, 19–48.

Meyer, H. A. W., ⁵1872. *Kritisch-exegetisches Handbuch über den Brief des Paulus an die Römer*. (MeyerK) Göttingen.

Michaelis, W., 1954. 'πάσχω etc', *TWNT* V, 903–939.

Michel, O., 1978. *Der Brief an die Römer*. (MeyerK) Göttingen.

Milik, J. T., 1976. *The Books of Enoch* . . . See Texts and Translations.

Minear, P. S., 1971. *The Obedience of Faith. The Purposes of Paul in the Epistle to the Romans*. (Studies in Biblical Theology 19) London.

Moffat, J., 1926. *A New Translation of the Bible*. London.

Molenberg, C., 1984. 'A Study of the Roles of Shemihaza and Asael in 1 Enoch 6–11', *JJS* 35, 136–146.

Morris, L., 1988. *The Epistle to the Romans*. Grand Rapids, Michigan.

Munck, J., 1959. *Paul and the Salvation of Mankind*. Richmond.

Müller, F., 1941. 'Zwei Marginalien im Brief des Paulus an die Römer', *ZNW* 40, 249–254.

Murray, J., 1959. *The Epistle to the Romans*. (NICNT VI) Grand Rapids.

Neary, M., 1981. 'The Cosmic Emphasis of Paul', *IThQ* 48, 1–26.

Newman, B. M. and Nida, E., 1973. *A Translator's Handbook on Paul's Letter to the Romans*, Stuttgart.

Nickelsburg, G. E. W., 1977. 'Apocalyptic and Myth in 1 Enoch 6–11', *JBL* 96, 383–405.

— 1981. *Jewish Literature Between the Bible and the Mishnah*. Philadelphia.

Niederwimmer, K., 1964. 'Das Gebet des Geistes, Röm, 8,26f.' *TZ* 20, 252–265.

Noth, M., 1972. *History of Pentateuchal Traditions*. Engelwood Cliffs, N.J.

Nygren, A., 1947. *Pauli brev till romarna.* (Tolkning av NT VI) Stockholm.

Obeng, E. A., 1984. The Spirit Intercession Motif in Paul', *ET* 95, 360–364.
— 1986. "Origin" = 'The Origin of the Spirit Intercession Motif in Romans 8:26', *NTS* 32, 612–632.
— 1986. "Reconciliation" = 'The Reconciliation of Rom. 8:26f to New Testament Writings and Themes', *SJT* 39, 165–174.
Olshausen, H., 1835. *Die Briefe Pauli an die Römer und Korinther.* (Biblischer Commentar über sämtliche Schriften des NT, III,1) Königsberg.
Osten-Sacken, von der, P., 1975. *Römer 8 als Beispiel paulinischer Soteriologie.* Göttingen.
Otto, G. W., 1886. *Commentar zum Römerbrief.* Glauchau.

Pallis, A., 1920. *To the Romans.* Liverpool.
Parrot, A., 1955. *The Flood and Noah's Ark.* London.
Paulsen, H., 1974. *Überlieferung und Auslegung in Römer 8.* (WMANT 43) Neukirchen.
Peake, H., 1930. *The Flood.* London.
Petersen, D. L., 1976. 'The Yahwist on the Flood', *VT* 26, 438–446.
Peterson, P. and Donaldson, J. *Clementine Homilies* . . . See Texts and Translations.
Petrausch, J. S. J., 1966. 'An Analysis of Romans viii,19–22', *IrEcclRec* 105, 314–323.
Phildius, V., 1958. *Le Soupir de la Création. Essai d'exégèse théologique de Rom. 8.18–27.* Lausanne.
Picard, J.-C., 1967. *Apocalypsis Baruchi* . . . See Texts and Translations.

Rad, von, G., 1961. *Genesis. A Commentary.* London.
— [4]1968. *Old Testament Theology* I. Edinburgh.
Reiche, J. G., 1834. *Versuch einer ausführlichen Erklärung des Briefes Pauli an die Römer.* Göttingen.
Reicke, B., 1946. *The Disobedient Spirits and Christian Baptism.* (ASNU 13) Lund.
Riesenfeld, H., 1977. 'Guds söner och de heligas församling', *SEÅ* 41–42 (1976–77), 179–188.
Robinson, J. A. T., 1977. *The Body: A Study in Pauline Theology.* Philadelphia.
— 1979. *Wrestling with Romans.* London.
Rolland, Ph., 1980. *Épitre aux Romains. Texte Grec Structuré.* Rome.
— 1988. 'L'antithèse de Rm 5–8', *Bib* 69, 396–400.
Rubinkiewicz, R., 1984. *Die Eschatologie von Hen 9–11 und das Neue Testament.* Habilitationsschrift Lublin 1980 (Österreichische Biblische Studien 6) Klosterneuburg.
Rudhart, J., 1987. 'The Flood', *The Encyclopedia of Religion* V, 353–357.
Russell, D. S., [7]1976. *The Method and Message of Jewish Apocalyptic.* (The OT Library) Philadelphia.
Russell III, W. B., 1988. 'An Alternative Suggestion for the Purpose of Romans', *BSac*, 174–184.
Rupprecht, J. M., 1851. 'Betrachtung der Stelle Röm 8,18–23, mit besonderer Rücksicht auf die erklärung von Prof. Zyro', *TSK* 24, 214–236.

Sanday, W. and Headlam, A. C., 1962. *A Critical and Exegetical Commentary on the Epistle to the Romans.* (ICC) Edinburgh.
Schields, B. E., 1981. *Creation in Romans.* (Diss. Tübingen. Typewritten manuscript) 1980.
Schlatter, A., 1935. *Gottes Gerechtigkeit. Ein Kommentar zum Römerbrief.* Stuttgart.

Schlier, H., 1935. 'ἐλεύθερος etc', *TWNT* II, 484–500.

— 1958. *Mächte und Gewalten im Neuen Testament*. (Quaest. Disp. 3) Freiburg.

— 1965. 'Das, worauf alles wartet. Eine Auslegung von Römer 8,18–30', *Interpretation der Welt*, Festschrift Guardini, ed. Kuhn, H., Kahlfeld, H., Forster, K. Würtzburg, 599–616.

— 1977. *Der Römerbrief*. (HTKNT VI) Freiburg, Basel, Wien.

Schläger, G., 1930. 'Das ängstliche Harren der Kreatur. Zur Auslegung von Römer 8,19ff.', *NThT* 19, 353–360.

Schmidt, H. W., 1962. *Der Brief des Paulus an die Römer*. (THKNT 6) Berlin.

Schmidt, K. L., 1933. 'βασιλεία etc', *TWNT* I, 573–595.

Schmithals, W., 1980. *Die Theologische Anthropologie des Paulus. Auslegung von Röm 7:17—8:39*. Stuttgart

Schneider, J., 1964. 'στενάζω etc', *TWNT* VII, 600–603.

Schniewind, J., 1952. 'Das Zeufzen des Geistes. Röm 8,26–27', *Nachgelassene Reden und Aufsätze*. Berlin, 81–103.

Schwantes, H., 1963. *Schöpfung der Endzeit, Ein Beitrag zum Verständnis der Auferweckung bei Paulus*. (Arbeiten zur Theologie I,12) Stuttgart.

Schweizer, E., 1959. 'πνεῦμα etc', *TWNT* VI, 387–453.

— 1962. *Erniedrigung und Erhöhung bei Jesus und seinen Nachfolgern*. (AThANT 28) Zürich.

— 1963. 'Röm. 1,3f und der Gegensatz von Fleisch und Geist vor und bei Paulus', *Neotestamentica*, Stuttgart, 180–189.

— 1964. 'σῶμα etc' *TWNT* VII, 1024–1091.

— 1969. 'υἱός D. Neues Testament', *TWNT* VIII, 364–395.

— 1969. 'υἱοθεσία im Judentum', *TWNT* VIII, 401–402.

Schulz, J. P., 1981. *Judaism and the Gentile Faiths. Comparative Studies in Religion*. London, Toronto.

Schulz, S., 1972. *Q, die Spruchquelle der Evangelisten*. Zürich.

Schürer, E., 1987. *The History of the Jewish People in the Age of Jesus Christ (175 B.C.—A.D. 135)* III,2. Edinburgh.

Selwyn, E.G., [7]1961. *The First Epistle of St. Peter*. London.

Sickenberger, J., [4]1932. *Die beiden Briefe des heiligen Paulus an die Korinther und sein Brief an die Römer*. (Die Heilige Schrift des Neuen Testamentes 6) Bonn.

Smend, R., 1912. *Die Erzählung des Hexateuch auf ihre Quellen untersucht*. Berlin.

Speiser, E. A., 1964. *Genesis*. Introduction, Translation, and Notes. (AB I) Garden City, New York.

Stählin, G., 1942. 'νῦν etc' *TWNT* IV, 1099–1117.

— 1954. 'ὀργή. Der Zorn des Menschen und der Zorn Gottes im NT', *TWNT* V, 419–448.

Stendahl, K., 1976. *Paul Among Jews and Gentiles, and Other Essays*. Philadelphia.

Strack, H. L. and Billerbeck, P., 1922–1928. *Kommentar zum Neuen Testament aus Talmud und Midrasch*, I–III. München.

Strack, H. L. and Stemberger, G., [7]1982. *Einleitung in Talmud und Midrasch*. München.

Stroumsa, G. A. G., 1984. *Another Seed. Studies in Gnostic Mythology*. (NHS 24) Leiden.

Stuhlmacher, P., 1985. 'Paul's understanding of the Law in the Letter to the Romans', *SEÅ* 50, 87–104.

— 1986. 'Der Abfassungszweck des Römerbriefes', *ZNW* 77, 180–193.

Thackeray, H. St. J., 1978. , Josephus *Antiquitates* . . . See Texts and Translations.

Thomassen, E., 1976. *Altets åpenbaring. En soteriologisk term i Evangelium Veritatis*. Bergen. (Typewritten manuscript.)

Toluck, A., 1856. *Commentar zum Brief an die Römer.* Halle.

VanderKam, J. C., 1978. 'Enoch Tradition in Jubilees and Other Second-century Sources', in *SBL 1978 Seminar Papers* I, 229–251. Ed. Achtemeier, P. J. Missoula.

— 1980. 'The Righteousness of Noah', in *Ideal Figures in Ancient Judaism. Profiles and Paradigms.* 13–32. Eds Collins J. J. and Nickelsburg, G. W. E. Chico, CA. Chico, CA.

Vermes, G., 1987. *The Dead Sea Scrolls* . . . See Texts and Translations.

Viard, A, 1952, 'Expectatio creaturae (Rom VIII,19–22)', *RB* 59, 337–354.

Vielhauer, Ph., 1975. *Geschichte der urchristlichen Literatur* . . . Berlin New York.

Volz, P., 1934. *Die Eschatologie der jüdischen Gemeinde.* Tübingen.

Vögtle, A., 1970. *Das Neue Testament und die Zukunft des Kosmos.* Düsseldorf.

Wedderburn, A. J. M., 1975. 'Romans 8:26—Towards a Theology of Glossolalia?', *SJT* 28, 369–377.

— 1988. *The Reasons for Romans.* Edinburgh.

Weiss, B., 1888. *Lehrbuch der Biblischen Theologie des NT.* Berlin.

— [8]1891. *Der Brief an die Römer.* (MeyerK) Göttingen.

Wellhausen, J., 1885. *Prolegomena to the History of Ancient Israel.* Edinburgh.

Wendland, P., [4]1972. *Die Hellenistisch—Römische Kultur in ihren Beziehungen zu Judentum und Christentum.* (HNT 4) Tübingen.

Westermann, C., 1974. *Genesis* I. (BKAT, 1,1) Neukirchen-Vluyn.

Wette de, W. M. L., [4]1847. *Kurze Erklärung des Briefes an die Römer.* (Kurzgefasstes Exegetisches Handbuch zum Neuen Testament II,1) Leipzig.

Wettstein, J. J., 1752. '*Ἡ καινὴ Διαθήκη*', (Novum Testamentum Graecum) Amstelaedami.

Wickham, L. R., 1974. 'The Sons of God and the Daughters of Men: Genesis VI 2 in Early Christian Exegesis', *OTS* XIX,135–147. van der Woude, A. S., ed., Language and Meaning. Papers read at the Joint British-Dutch Old Testament Conference Held at London 1973.

Wiefil, W., 1977. 'The Jewish Community in Ancient Rome and the Origins of Roman Christianity', in Donfried, K. P., ed., *The Romans Debate*, 100–148 (Originally published in Judaica 26 (1970), 65–88.)

Wilcke, H. A., 1967. *Das Problem eines messianischen Zwischenreiches bei Paulus.* (ATANT 51) Zürich—Stuttgart.

Wilckens, U., 1978–1982. *Der Brief an die Römer.* (EKW VI, 1978–1982) Neukirchen.

Wuellner, W., 1977. 'Paul's Rhetoric of Argumentation in Romans: An Alternative to the Donfried—Karris Debate over Romans', in Donfried, K. P., ed., *The Romans Debate.* Originally published in *CBQ* 38 (1976), 330–351.

Zahn, Th., 1865. 'Die seufzende Creatur. Röm 8,18–23 mit Rücksicht auf neuere Auffassungen', *JDT* 10, 511–542.

—[2]1910. *Der Brief des Paulus an die Römer.* (Kommentar zum NT 6) Leipzig.

Zeller, D., 1985. *Der Brief an die Römer.* Regensburg.

Zyro, 1845. 'Neue Erklärung von Röm 8,18–25', *TSK* 18, 403–416.

— 1851. 'Neue Erörterung der Stelle Röm 8,18–25', *TSK* 24, 403–416.

Index of authors

Index of Passages